Nov. 3, 2020 — **Hamm v. Boockvar**, Pennsylvania Commonwealth Court: Dispositive ruling.

Nov. 3, 2020 — **Injunctive Relief of Northampton Cty. Republican Committee**, Pennsylvania Court of Common Pleas, Northampton County: Dismissed.

Nov. 4, 2020 — **Aguilera v. Fontes**, Arizona Superior Court, Maricopa County: Voluntarily dismissed.

Nov. 4, 2020 — **Barnette v. Lawrence**, U.S. District Court for the Eastern District of Pennsylvania: Voluntarily dismissed.

Nov. 4, 2020 — **In re: Enforcement of Election Laws and Securing Ballots Cast or Received after 7:00 pm on November 3, 2020**, Chatham County Superior Court of the Eastern Judicial Circuit of Georgia: Dismissed without prejudice.

Nov. 4, 2020 — **Donald J. Trump for President v. Benson**, Michigan Court of Appeals: Dismissed.

Nov. 4, 2020 — **Stoddard v. City Election Commission of the City of Detroit**, Michigan Third Judicial Circuit Court: Dismissed.

Nov. 4, 2020 — **Donald J. Trump for President, Inc. v. Boockvar and Cty. Bds. Of Elections**, Pennsylvania Commonwealth Court: Dispositive ruling.

Nov. 5, 2020 — **Stokke v. Cegavske**, Nevada District Court: Voluntarily dismissed.

Nov. 5, 2020 — **Donald J. Trump for President v. Montgomery Cty. Bd. of Elections**, Pennsylvania Court of Common Pleas, Montgomery County: Denied and appeal withdrawn.

Nov. 5, 2020 — **Donald J. Trump for President, Inc. v. Philadelphia Cty. Bd. of Elections**, U.S. District Court for the Eastern District of Pennsylvania: Denied without prejudice.

Nov. 7, 2020 — **Donald J. Trump for President, Inc. vs. Hobbs**, Arizona Superior Court, Maricopa County: Dispositive ruling as moot.

Nov. 9, 2020 — **Donald J. Trump v. Bucks Cty. Bd. of Elections**, Pennsylvania Commonwealth Court: Dismissed.

Nov. 9, 2020 — **Cons**t███ ██ i-gan Supreme Court: ██████ moot.

T0046689

Nov. 9, 2020 — **Donal**█ ████ ██, **Inc. v. Boockvar**, U.S. District Court for the Middle District of Pennsylvania: Dismissed.

Nov. 10, 2020 — **In re: Canvass of Absentee and Mail-In Ballots of November 3, 2020, Gen. Election**, Pennsylvania Supreme Court, Pennsylvania Court of Common Pleas, Philadelphia County: Dismissed.

Nov. 10, 2020 — **Pirkle v. Wolf**, U.S. District Court for the Middle District of Pennsylvania: Voluntarily dismissed.

Nov. 11, 2020 — **Brooks v. Mahoney**, U.S. District Court for the Southern District of Georgia (Savannah Division): Voluntarily dismissed.

Nov. 11, 2020 — **Donald J. Trump for President, Inc. v. Benson**, U.S. District Court for the Western District of Michigan: Voluntarily dismissed.

Nov. 11, 2020 — **Bally v. Whitmer**, U.S. District Court for the Western District of Michigan: Voluntarily dismissed.

Nov. 12, 2020 — **Ziccarelli v. Allegeny Cty. Bd. of Elections**, Pennsylvania Supreme Court, Pennsylvania Commonwealth Court, Pennsylvania Court of Common Pleas, Allegheny County: Dismissed after appeal.

Nov. 12, 2020 — **Aguilera v. Fontes**, Arizona Superior Court, Maricopa County: Dismissed with prejudice.

Nov. 12, 2020 — **Langenhorst v. Pecore**, U.S. District Court for the Eastern District of Wisconsin: Voluntarily dismissed.

Nov. 12, 2020 — **Arizona Republican Party v. Fontes**, Arizona Superior Court, Maricopa County: Dismissed.

Nov. 13, 2020 — **Wood v. Raffensperger**, U.S. District Court for the Northern District of Georgia: Dismissed.

(Continued on back page)

FORMER GUY

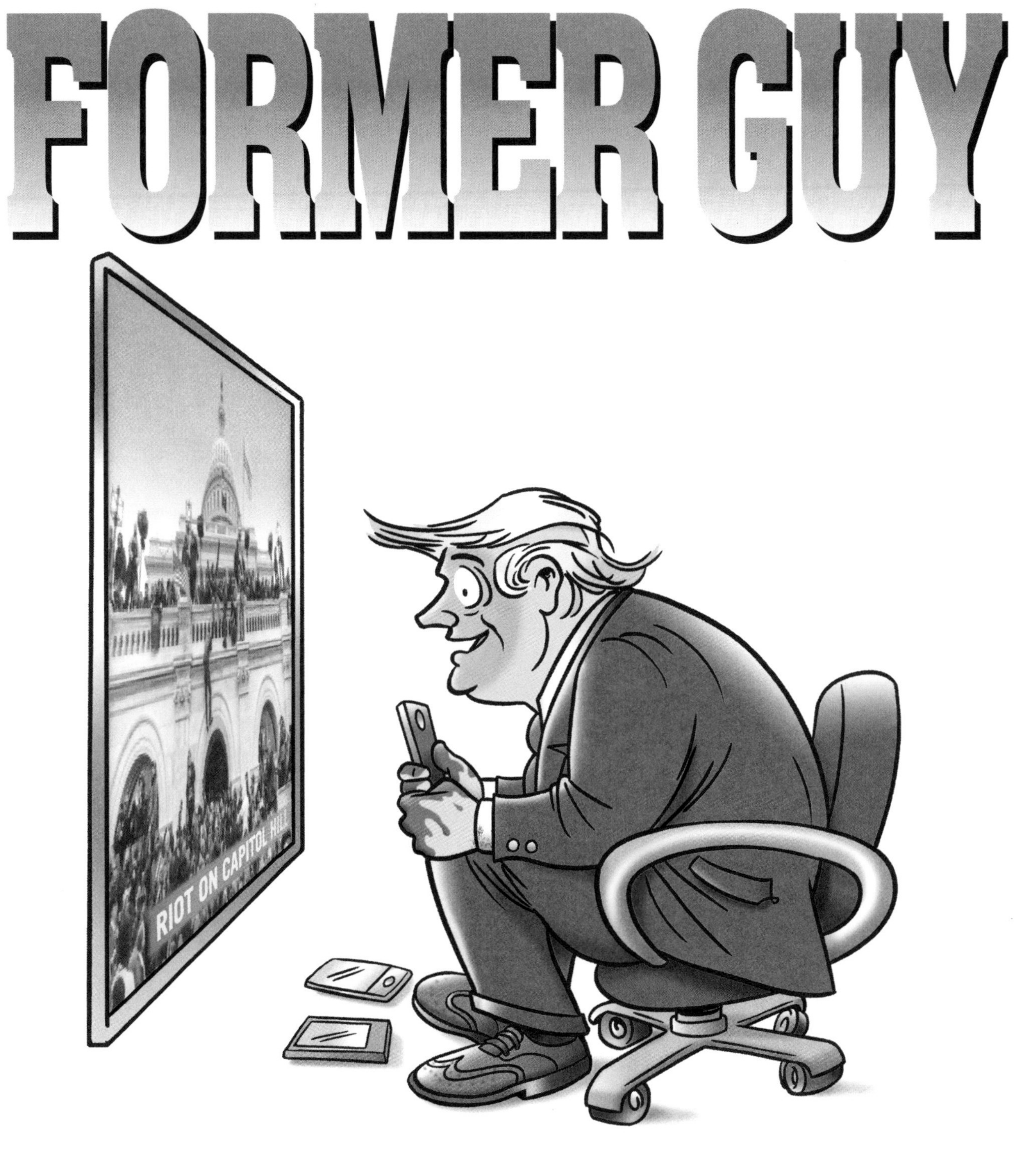
RIOT ON CAPITOL HILL

Recent Collections

Virtual Doonesbury
Planet Doonesbury
Buck Wild Doonesbury
Duke 2000: Whatever It Takes
The Revolt of the English Majors
Peace Out, Dawg!
Got War?
Talk to the Hand
Heckuva Job, Bushie!
Welcome to the Nerd Farm!
Tee Time in Berzerkistan
Red Rascal's War
Squared Away
The Weed Whisperer
YUGE!: 30 Years of Doonesbury on Trump
#SAD!: Doonesbury in the Time of Trump
LEWSER!: More Doonesbury in the Time of Trump

Anthologies

The Doonesbury Chronicles
Doonesbury's Greatest Hits
The People's Doonesbury
Doonesbury Dossier: The Reagan Years
Doonesbury Deluxe: Selected Glances Askance
Recycled Doonesbury: Second Thoughts on a Gilded Age
The Portable Doonesbury
The Bundled Doonesbury
40: A Doonesbury Retrospective

Special Collections

Flashbacks: Twenty-Five Years of Doonesbury
Action Figure!: The Life and Times of Doonesbury's Uncle Duke
Dude: The Big Book of Zonker
The Sandbox: Dispatches from Troops in Iraq and Afghanistan
The War in Quotes
"My Shorts R Bunching. Thoughts?": The Tweets of Roland Hedley
Dbury@50: The Complete Digital Doonesbury

Wounded Warrior Series

The Long Road Home: One Step at a Time
The War Within: One More Step at a Time
Signature Wound: Rocking TBI
Mel's Story: Surviving Military Sexual Assault

FORMER GUY

Doonesbury in the Time of Trumpism

A DOONESBURY BOOK
by G. B. TRUDEAU

Andrews McMeel
PUBLISHING®

DOONESBURY is distributed internationally by Andrews McMeel Syndication.

Andrews McMeel Publishing
a division of Andrews McMeel Universal
1130 Walnut Street, Kansas City, Missouri 64106

www.andrewsmcmeel.com

22 23 24 25 26 RR2 10 9 8 7 6 5 4 3 2 1

ISBN: 978-1-5248-7558-9

Library of Congress Control Number: 2022935333

DOONESBURY may be viewed on the Internet at
www.doonesbury.com and www.GoComics.com.

ATTENTION: SCHOOLS AND BUSINESSES

Andrews McMeel books are available at quantity discounts with bulk purchase for educational, business, or sales promotional use. For information, please e-mail the Andrews McMeel Publishing Special Sales Department: specialsales@amuniversal.com.

PREFACE

"Fox News projects Biden wins PA and NV, has electoral votes to win presidency."
— *November 7, 2020*

Times Square, later that day. I was there. If you squint, you can just make me out to the right of the parade of candy-colored motor trikes tricked out with psychedelic LED grill lights. New York was exploding with joy. Screaming our heads off and hugging each other in the middle of a pandemic probably wasn't the smartest response, but Joe Biden had won. The nightmare was over.

Except it wasn't.

Within days, the defeated president rolled out the gleaming turd he'd been polishing all year—his Big Lie. Firing senior officials who told him the truth (and ignoring the sixty-one judges who confirmed it), Former Guy began to clear the decks for insurrection— even helpfully setting the date and place. The troops were primed because Trump had been prophetic. He'd warned them about The Steal, and it had come to pass, and now it was time for them to rise up and take their country back.

Let's just come right out and say it: It's embarrassing to live in a country with so many willing griftees. We've tried. The liberal impulse is to empathize, and the 2016 election had launched a thousand media sorties to MAGA country to get to the bottom of Trump's appeal. To label his aggrieved supporters "dupes" was once considered patronizing.

No longer. The stakes are too high, the authoritarian threat too real. Trump was once likened to gum disease—an annoying minor condition which, untreated, can actually kill you. Former Guy still infects the political bloodstream, and much smarter politicians are now emulating him.

YUGE!, the first volume of what has become a Trump quartet, was supposed to be a one-off—a cautionary recap of the life of a genuinely awful human being. That Trump became the gift to comedy that has never stopped giving is of small consolation and has only brought joy to my publisher, although she'd never admit it.

I miss the celebratory vibe of Times Square that night, even though one of the candy-colored trikes ran over my foot. I should have picked up on the portent.

Garry Trudeau
April 1, 2022

"I never knew how important being president was."

— Trump

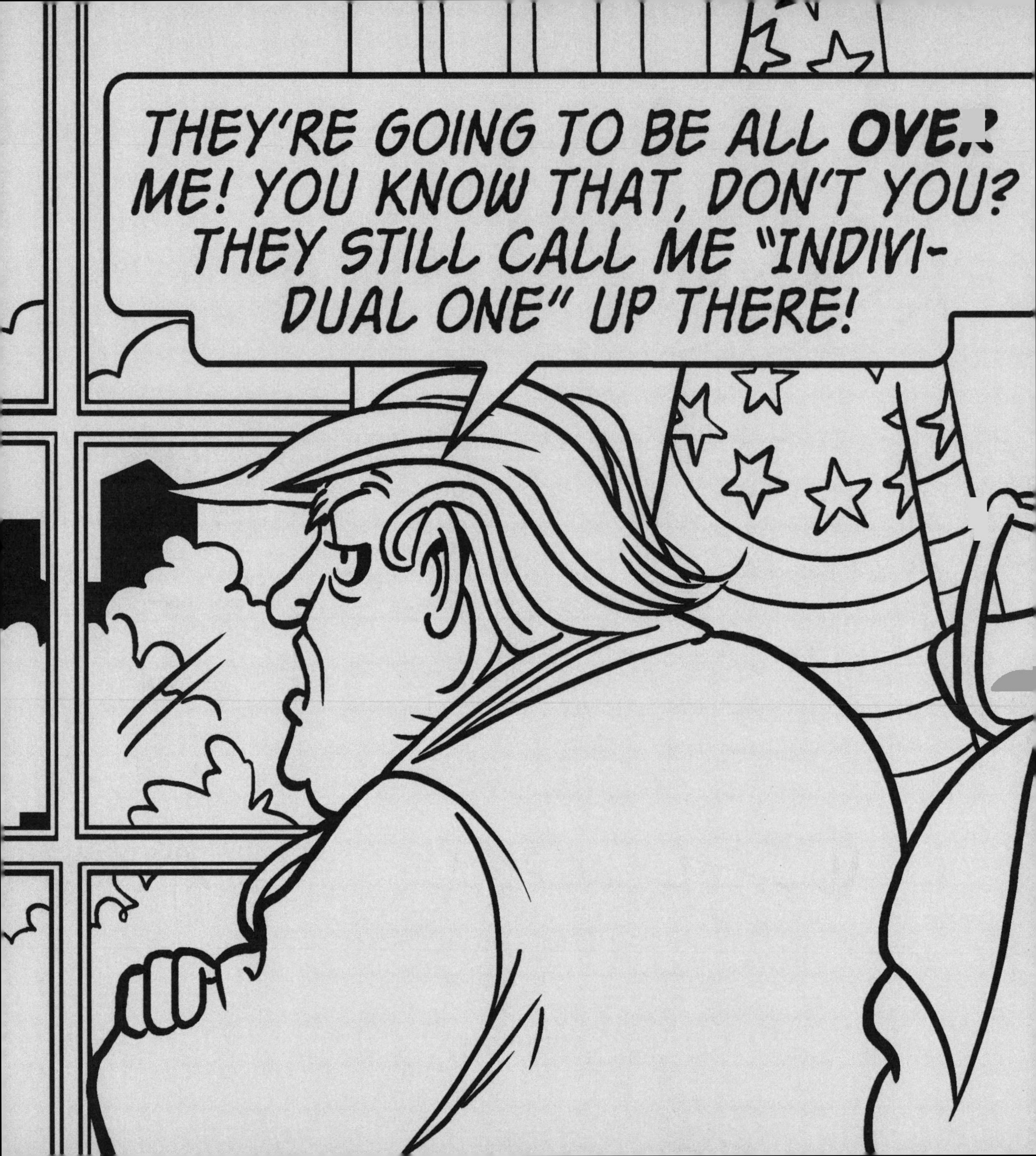
THEY'RE GOING TO BE ALL **OVER** ME! YOU KNOW THAT, DON'T YOU? THEY STILL CALL ME "INDIVI-DUAL ONE" UP THERE!

PART I
Individual One

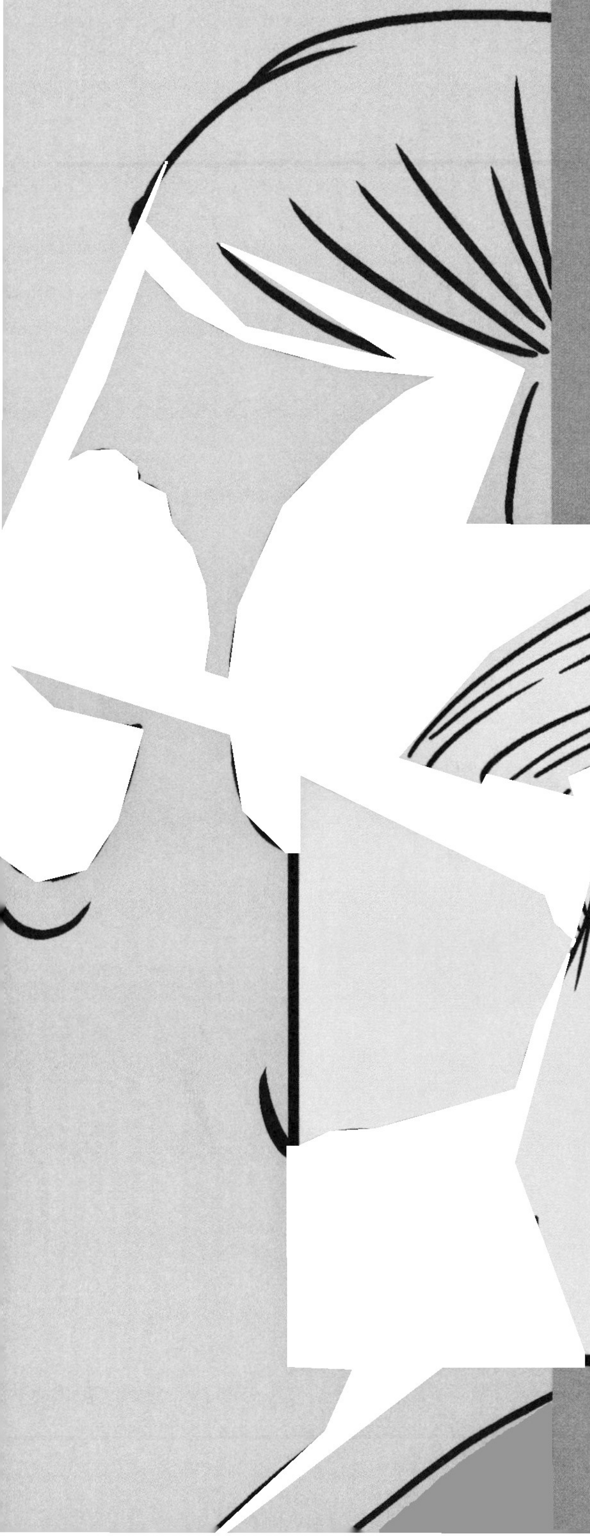

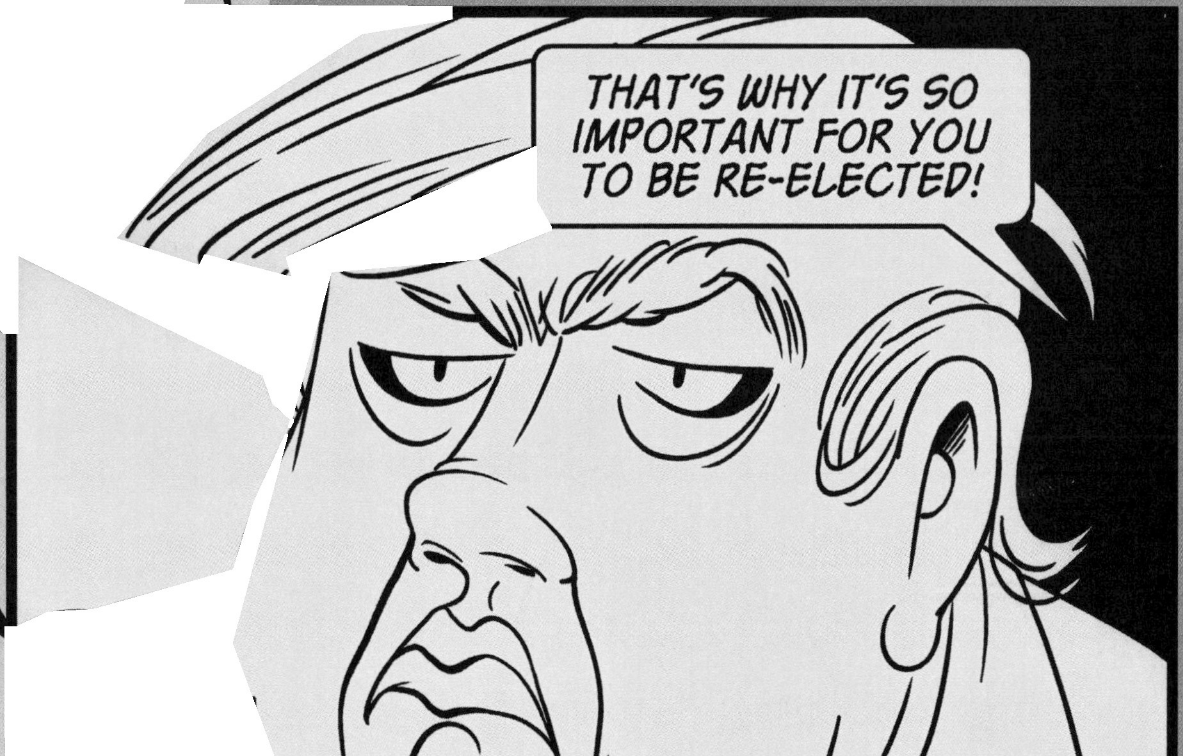
THAT'S WHY IT'S SO IMPORTANT FOR YOU TO BE RE-ELECTED!

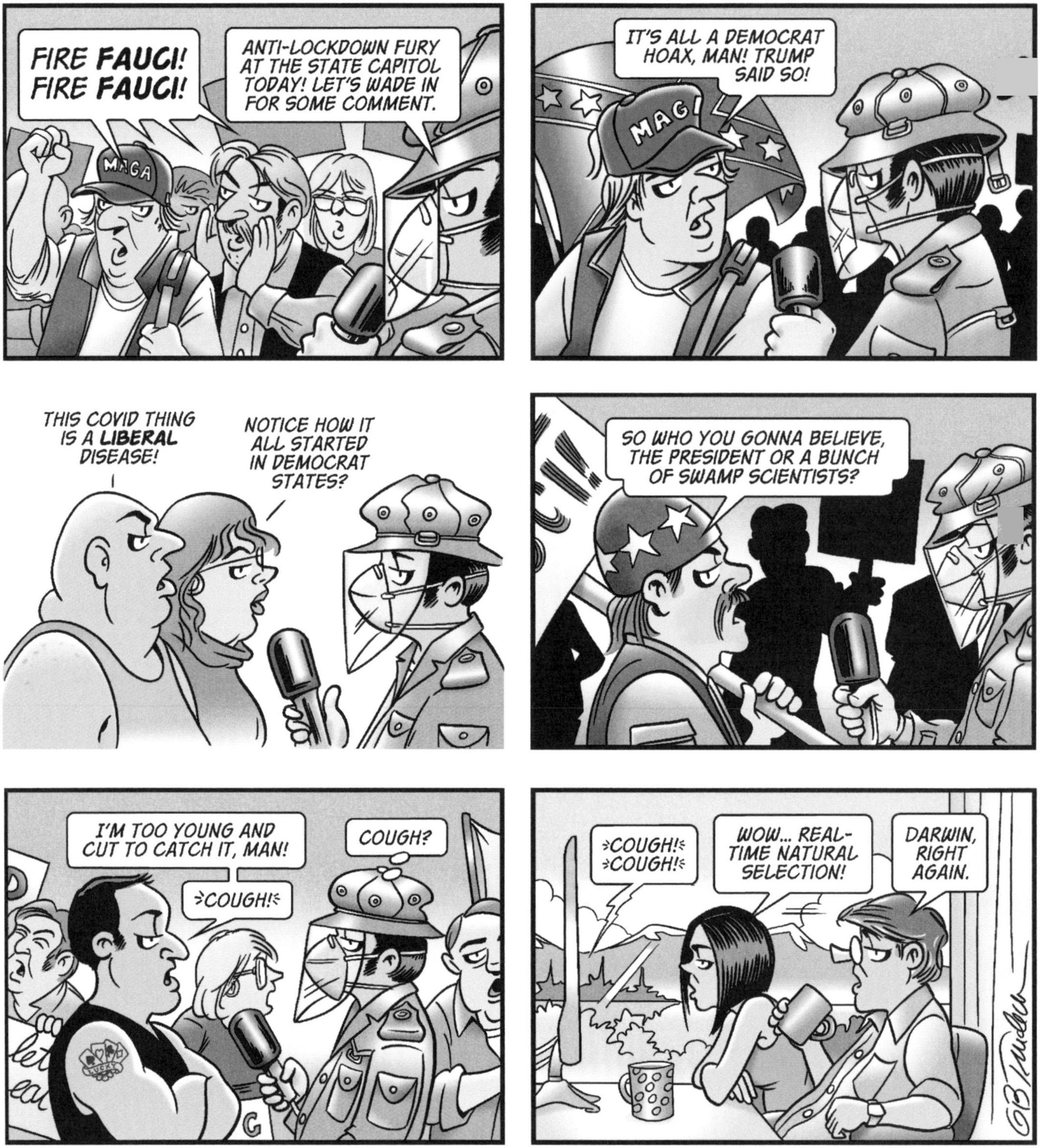
FIRE **FAUCI**! FIRE **FAUCI**!
MAGA
ANTI-LOCKDOWN FURY AT THE STATE CAPITOL TODAY! LET'S WADE IN FOR SOME COMMENT.
IT'S ALL A DEMOCRAT HOAX, MAN! TRUMP SAID SO!
THIS COVID THING IS A **LIBERAL** DISEASE!
NOTICE HOW IT ALL STARTED IN DEMOCRAT STATES?
SO WHO YOU GONNA BELIEVE, THE PRESIDENT OR A BUNCH OF SWAMP SCIENTISTS?
I'M TOO YOUNG AND CUT TO CATCH IT, MAN!
COUGH!
COUGH?
COUGH! COUGH!
WOW... REAL-TIME NATURAL SELECTION!
DARWIN, RIGHT AGAIN.

May 31, 2020

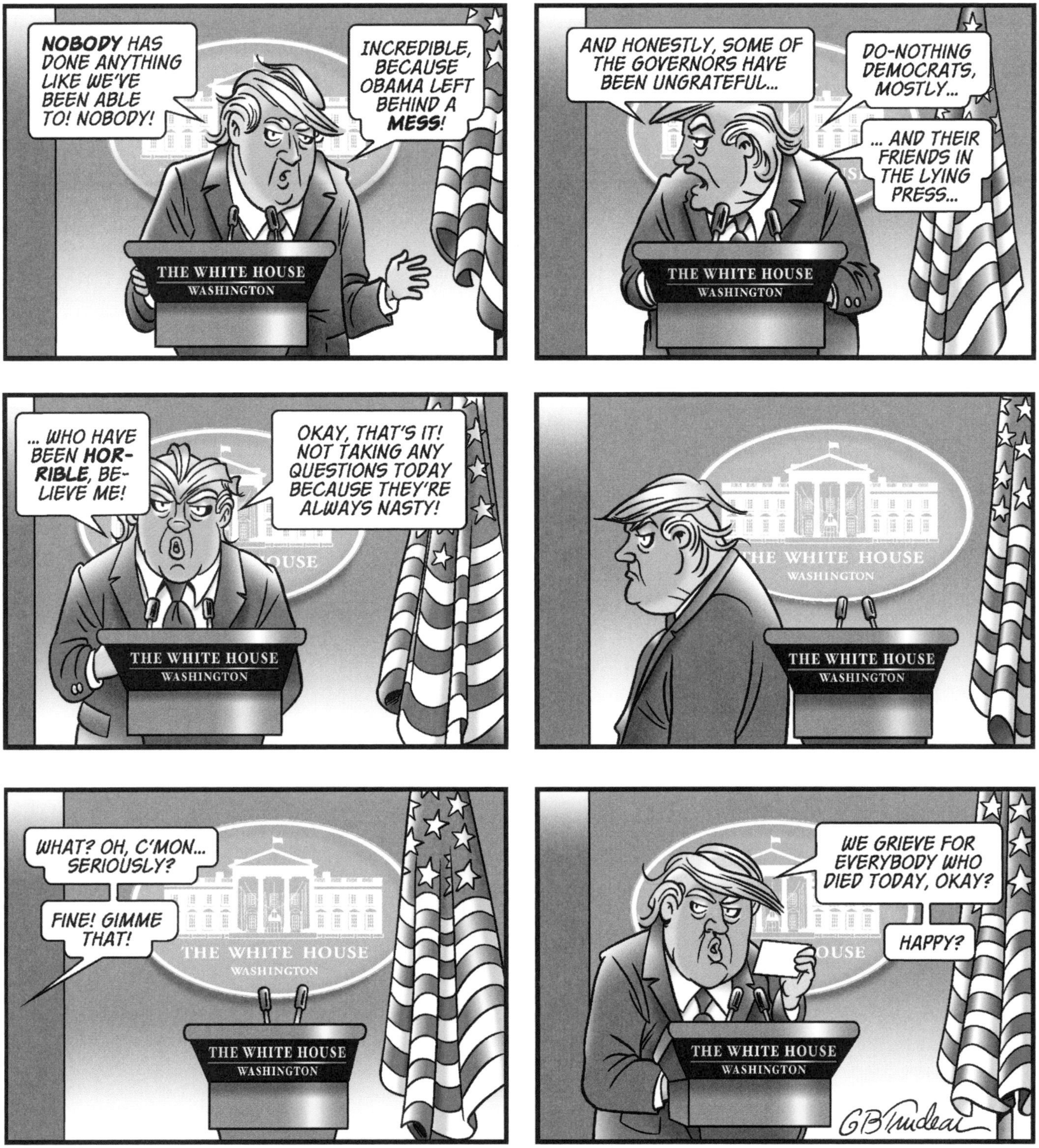
NOBODY HAS DONE ANYTHING LIKE WE'VE BEEN ABLE TO! NOBODY!
INCREDIBLE, BECAUSE OBAMA LEFT BEHIND A MESS!
THE WHITE HOUSE WASHINGTON
AND HONESTLY, SOME OF THE GOVERNORS HAVE BEEN UNGRATEFUL...
DO-NOTHING DEMOCRATS, MOSTLY...
... AND THEIR FRIENDS IN THE LYING PRESS...
THE WHITE HOUSE WASHINGTON
... WHO HAVE BEEN HORRIBLE, BELIEVE ME!
OKAY, THAT'S IT! NOT TAKING ANY QUESTIONS TODAY BECAUSE THEY'RE ALWAYS NASTY!
THE WHITE HOUSE WASHINGTON
THE WHITE HOUSE WASHINGTON
THE WHITE HOUSE WASHINGTON
WHAT? OH, C'MON... SERIOUSLY?
FINE! GIMME THAT!
THE WHITE HOUSE WASHINGTON
THE WHITE HOUSE WASHINGTON
WE GRIEVE FOR EVERYBODY WHO DIED TODAY, OKAY?
HAPPY?
THE WHITE HOUSE WASHINGTON
GBTrudeau

June 14, 2020

HEY, KIDS! TIRED OF BINGEING IN PLACE? GIVE YOUR BRAIN A WORKOUT BY SOLVING OUR *DOONESBURY CROSSWORD*...

... CONSTRUCTED FOR US EXCLUSIVELY BY PUZZLING PRO *ROSS TRUDEAU!*

GOOD LUCK!

GULP!

ACROSS

1. Buttsy's less-toxic pal Mr. ___
4. Second "Doonesbury" character to appear in the strip
8. B.D.'s PTSD counselor
13. Na or Fe: Abbr.
15. "___ it my way"
16. "Heaven forbid!"
17. Whip
18. ; ; ;
20. Layouts
22. One of 62-Down's twin boys
23. Character a.k.a. Toggle
24. Landed
25. Volcano fallout
27. 42-Across's chief of staff
30. Perform a Catholic ceremony
34. "Wise" bird
35. Porridge for Oliver Twist
37. "Hell ___ no fury ..."
39. The "U" in E.U.
41. Boopsie and B.D.'s daughter
42. Late Congresswoman Davenport
43. Ex-WaPo journalist Redfern
44. Hang loosely
46. Gym unit
47. Cloud Mark avoids at protests
50. Stick (to)
52. "___-hoo!"
53. Until
54. Mani-pedi locale
57. "___ Misérables"
59. Big Italian coffee brand
63. Where Chiefs and Royals play
66. Film spool
67. The "A" in Neil A. Armstrong
68. Gumbo veggie
69. Zonker's "uncle"
70. Played (with)
71. Darjeeling and Earl Grey, e.g.
72. Intimate act that Zonker's never had

DOWN

1. ___ Redfern, a.k.a. "Sorkh Razil"
2. French greeting
3. "Doonesbury" is in its 50th
4. More teary-eyed
5. What "i.e." stands for
6. Rosenthal who dropped out of M.I.T. because it was "too easy"
7. Falco of "The Sopranos"
8. Self-centeredness
9. "OMG that comic is 2 funny!"
10. Jimmy Thudpucker, to fans
11. Actress Hathaway
12. Mediocre
14. "Dude!"
19. Potter's material
21. Straighten
26. "That comic is too funny!"
27. Soup du ___
28. Take responsibility for something
29. Elmont's plastic-wrapped wife

GBTrudeau

14

30. JCPenney's competitor
31. ___ mater
32. "___ bleu!"
33. Control the wheel
36. Org. that grades beef quality
38. Overpromote
40. "___, boomer" (2020 meme)
42. Sony or LG product, for short
45. Yellow tropical fruits
48. Journalist Hedley who started on the Saigon sports desk
49. Departs
51. Squirrel away
53. Extremely
54. 32-card trick-taking game
55. ____ Alto, CA
56. Lippincott with a panel on the AIDS Quilt (in real life!)
58. "The fighting young priest" Sloan
60. Ruler of Mt. Olympus
61. J.J.'s husband a.k.a. "Uncle Stupidhead"
62. M.I.T. grad who went into labor at her Ph.D. ceremony
64. Lay eyes on
65. "I Like ___" (old campaign slogan)

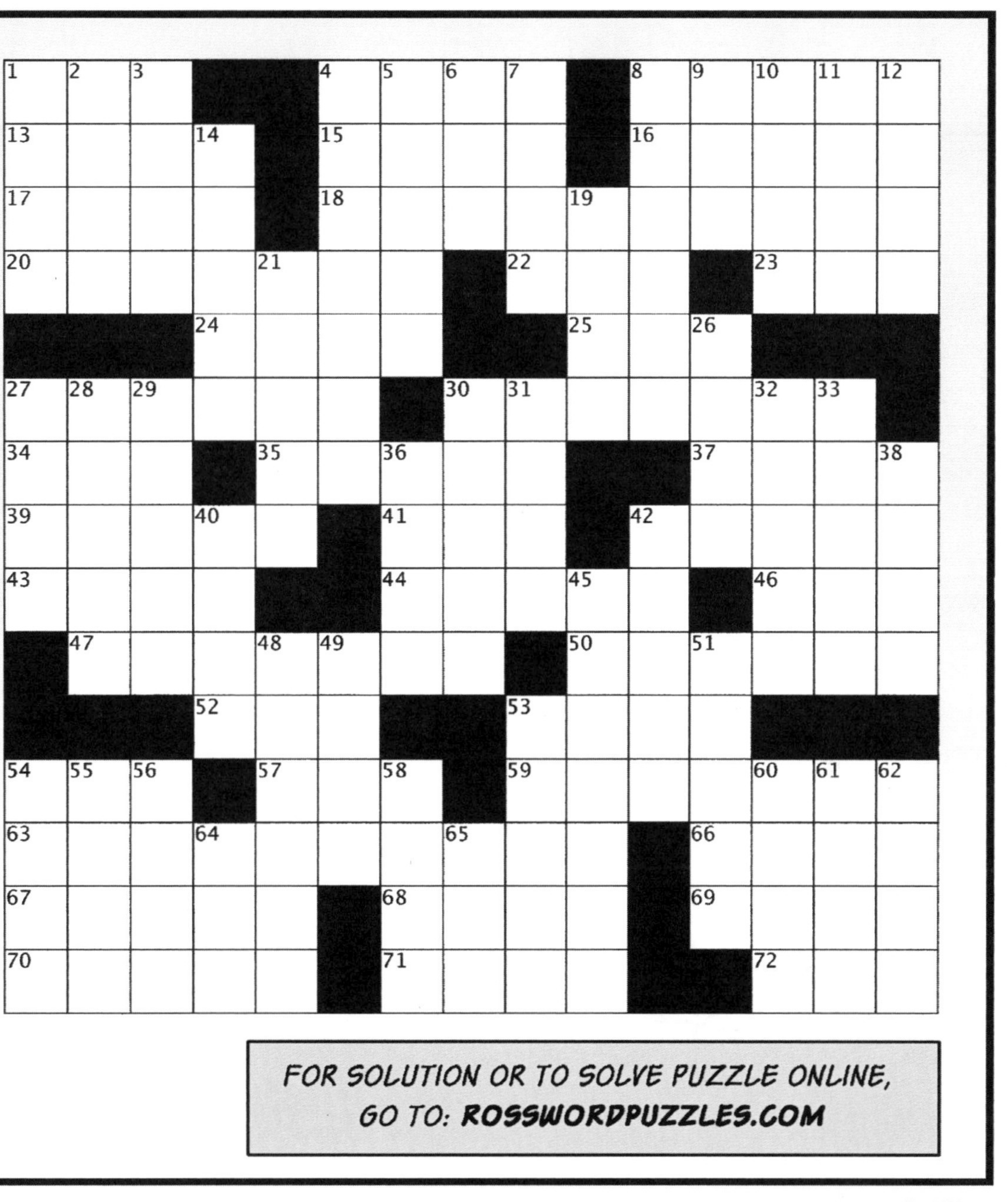

FOR SOLUTION OR TO SOLVE PUZZLE ONLINE, GO TO: ***ROSSWORDPUZZLES.COM***

June 28, 2020

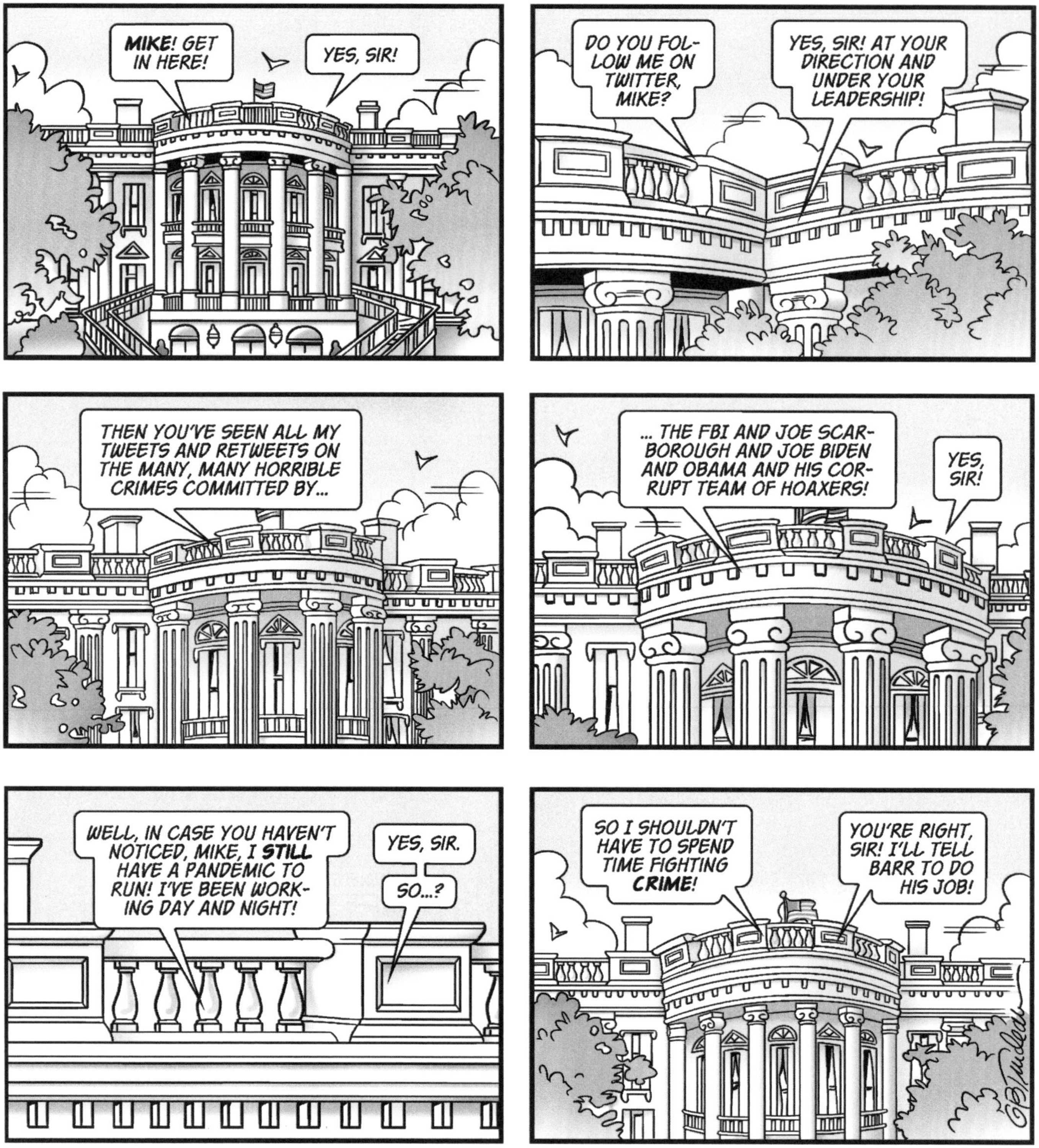
MIKE! GET IN HERE!
YES, SIR!
DO YOU FOL-LOW ME ON TWITTER, MIKE?
YES, SIR! AT YOUR DIRECTION AND UNDER YOUR LEADERSHIP!
THEN YOU'VE SEEN ALL MY TWEETS AND RETWEETS ON THE MANY, MANY HORRIBLE CRIMES COMMITTED BY...
... THE FBI AND JOE SCAR-BOROUGH AND JOE BIDEN AND OBAMA AND HIS COR-RUPT TEAM OF HOAXERS!
YES, SIR!
WELL, IN CASE YOU HAVEN'T NOTICED, MIKE, I STILL HAVE A PANDEMIC TO RUN! I'VE BEEN WORK-ING DAY AND NIGHT!
YES, SIR.
SO...?
SO I SHOULDN'T HAVE TO SPEND TIME FIGHTING CRIME!
YOU'RE RIGHT, SIR! I'LL TELL BARR TO DO HIS JOB!
GBTrudeau

June 21, 2020

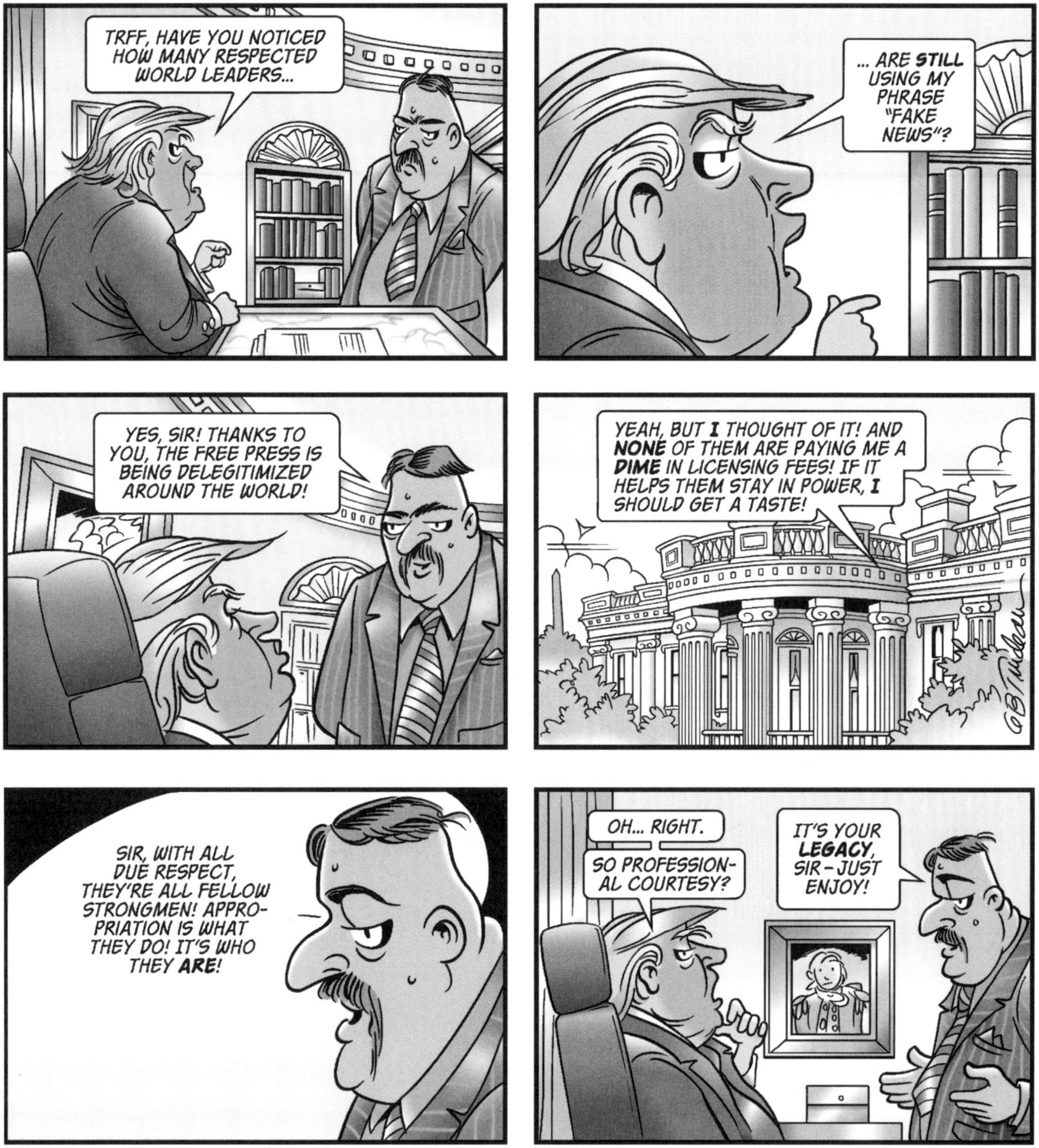
TRFF, HAVE YOU NOTICED HOW MANY RESPECTED WORLD LEADERS...
... ARE **STILL** USING MY PHRASE "FAKE NEWS"?
YES, SIR! THANKS TO YOU, THE FREE PRESS IS BEING DELEGITIMIZED AROUND THE WORLD!
YEAH, BUT **I** THOUGHT OF IT! AND **NONE** OF THEM ARE PAYING ME A **DIME** IN LICENSING FEES! IF IT HELPS THEM STAY IN POWER, **I** SHOULD GET A TASTE!
SIR, WITH ALL DUE RESPECT, THEY'RE ALL FELLOW STRONGMEN! APPROPRIATION IS WHAT THEY DO! IT'S WHO THEY **ARE**!
OH... RIGHT.
SO PROFESSIONAL COURTESY?
IT'S YOUR **LEGACY**, SIR – JUST ENJOY!

July 5, 2020

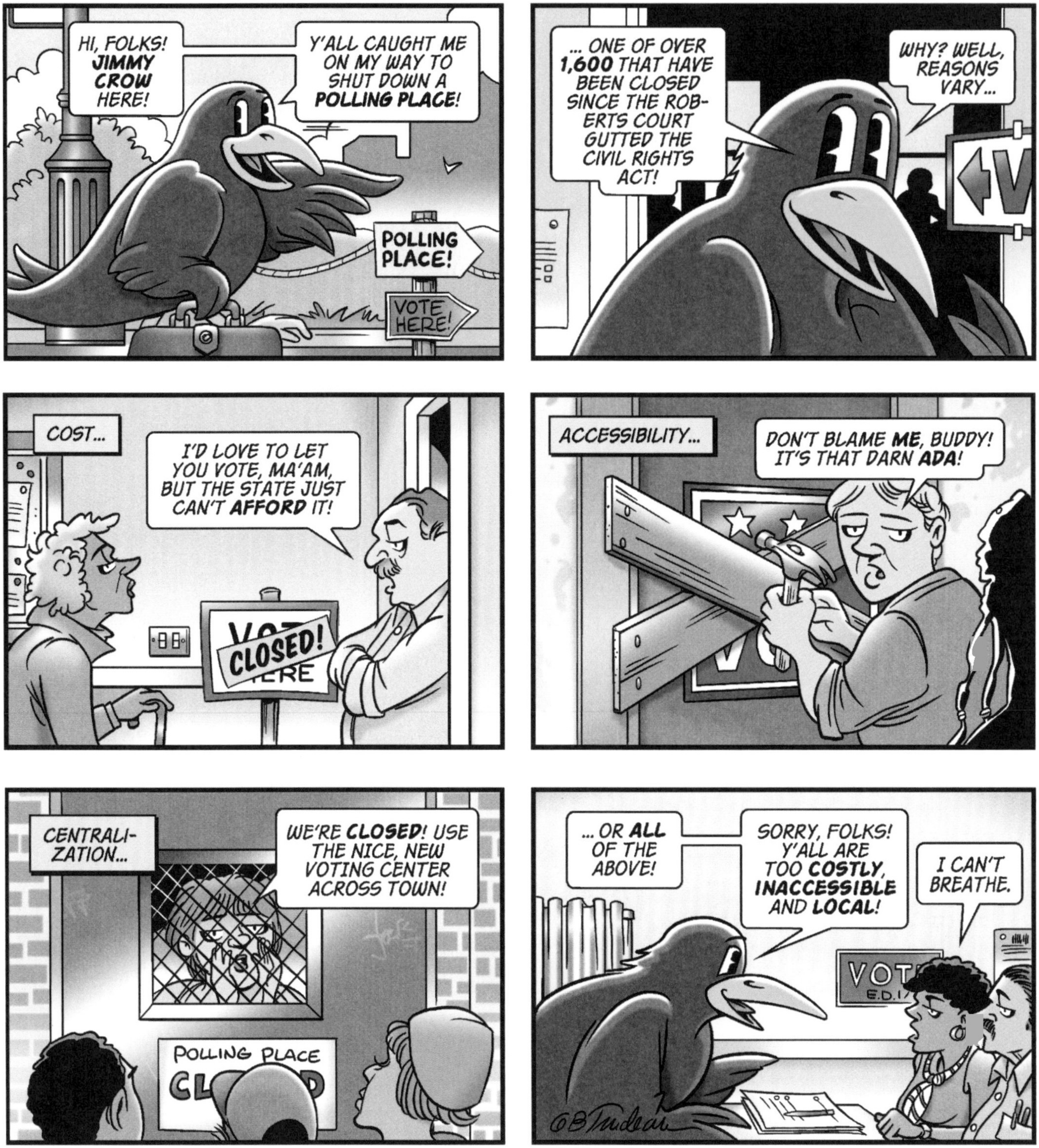
HI, FOLKS! JIMMY CROW HERE!
Y'ALL CAUGHT ME ON MY WAY TO SHUT DOWN A POLLING PLACE!
POLLING PLACE!
VOTE HERE!
... ONE OF OVER 1,600 THAT HAVE BEEN CLOSED SINCE THE ROB-ERTS COURT GUTTED THE CIVIL RIGHTS ACT!
WHY? WELL, REASONS VARY...
COST...
I'D LOVE TO LET YOU VOTE, MA'AM, BUT THE STATE JUST CAN'T AFFORD IT!
CLOSED!
ACCESSIBILITY...
DON'T BLAME ME, BUDDY! IT'S THAT DARN ADA!
CENTRALI-ZATION...
WE'RE CLOSED! USE THE NICE, NEW VOTING CENTER ACROSS TOWN!
POLLING PLACE
...OR ALL OF THE ABOVE!
SORRY, FOLKS! Y'ALL ARE TOO COSTLY, INACCESSIBLE AND LOCAL!
I CAN'T BREATHE.
©B Trudeau

July 12, 2020

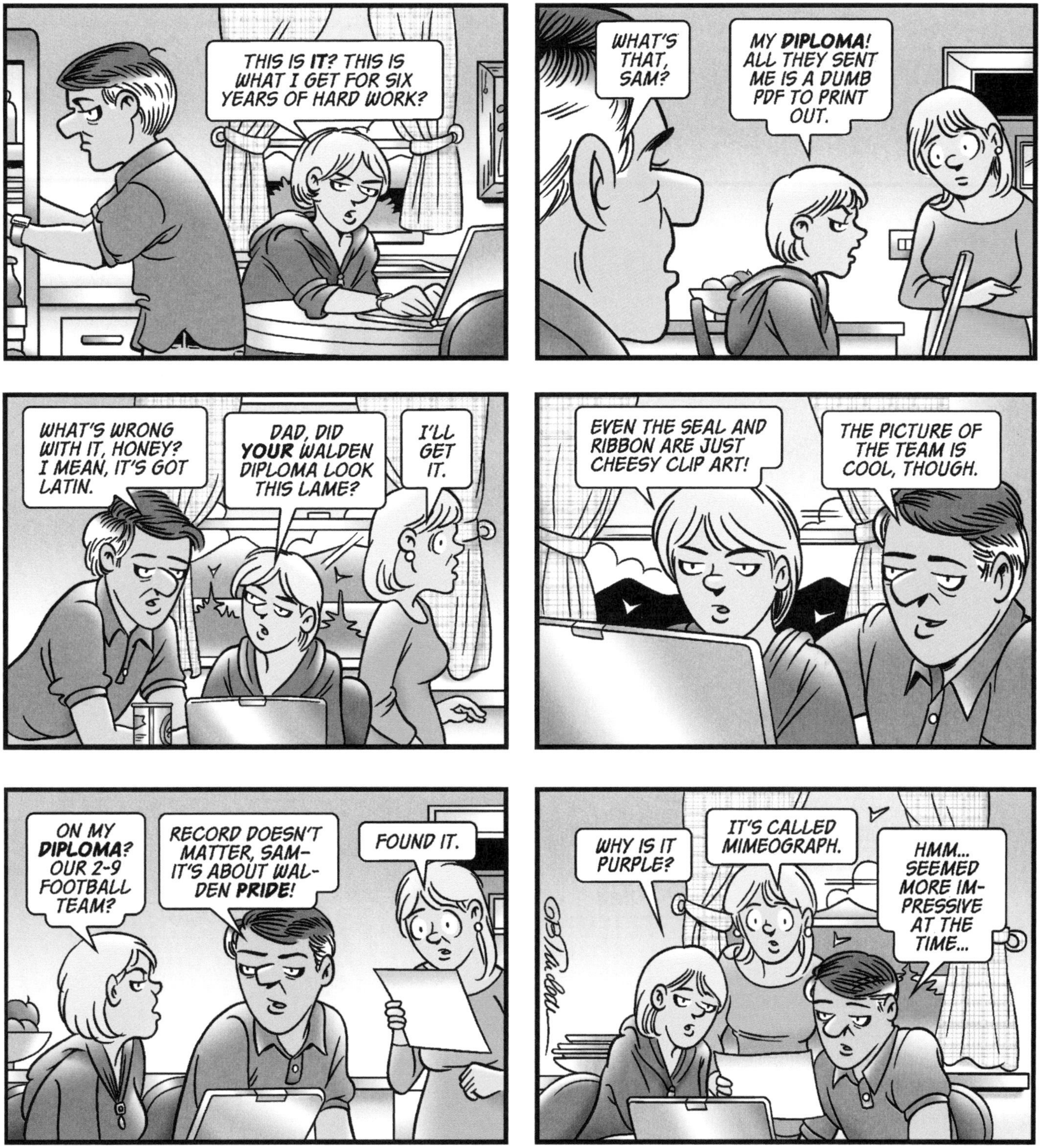
THIS IS **IT**? THIS IS WHAT I GET FOR SIX YEARS OF HARD WORK?
WHAT'S THAT, SAM?
MY **DIPLOMA**! ALL THEY SENT ME IS A DUMB PDF TO PRINT OUT.
WHAT'S WRONG WITH IT, HONEY? I MEAN, IT'S GOT LATIN.
DAD, DID **YOUR** WALDEN DIPLOMA LOOK THIS LAME?
I'LL GET IT.
EVEN THE SEAL AND RIBBON ARE JUST CHEESY CLIP ART!
THE PICTURE OF THE TEAM IS COOL, THOUGH.
ON MY **DIPLOMA**? OUR 2-9 FOOTBALL TEAM?
RECORD DOESN'T MATTER, SAM– IT'S ABOUT WAL-DEN **PRIDE**!
FOUND IT.
WHY IS IT PURPLE?
IT'S CALLED MIMEOGRAPH.
HMM... SEEMED MORE IM-PRESSIVE AT THE TIME...

July 19, 2020

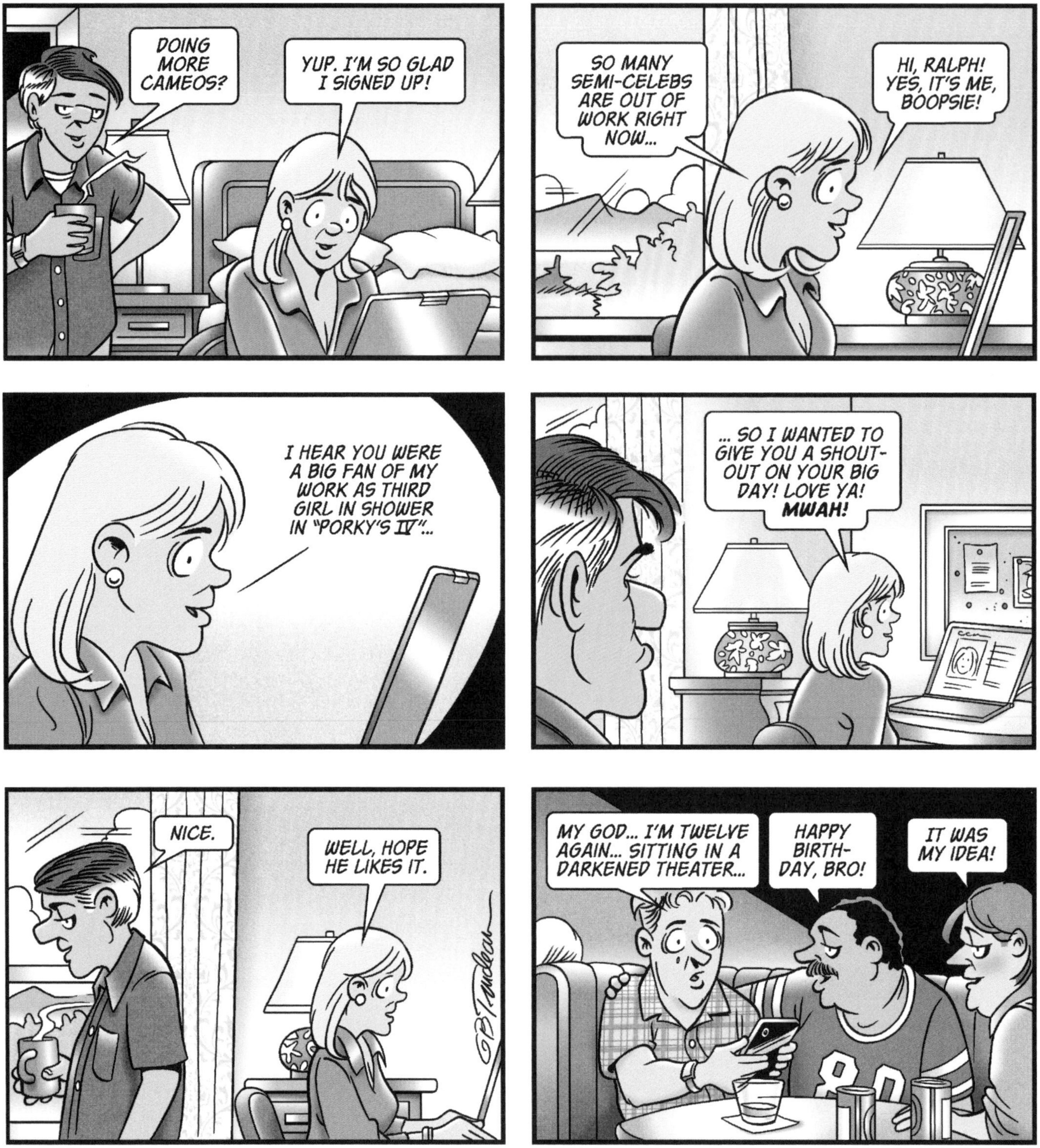
DOING MORE CAMEOS?
YUP. I'M SO GLAD I SIGNED UP!
SO MANY SEMI-CELEBS ARE OUT OF WORK RIGHT NOW...
HI, RALPH! YES, IT'S ME, BOOPSIE!
I HEAR YOU WERE A BIG FAN OF MY WORK AS THIRD GIRL IN SHOWER IN "PORKY'S IV"...
... SO I WANTED TO GIVE YOU A SHOUT-OUT ON YOUR BIG DAY! LOVE YA! **MWAH!**
NICE.
WELL, HOPE HE LIKES IT.
MY GOD... I'M TWELVE AGAIN... SITTING IN A DARKENED THEATER...
HAPPY BIRTH-DAY, BRO!
IT WAS MY IDEA!

July 26, 2020

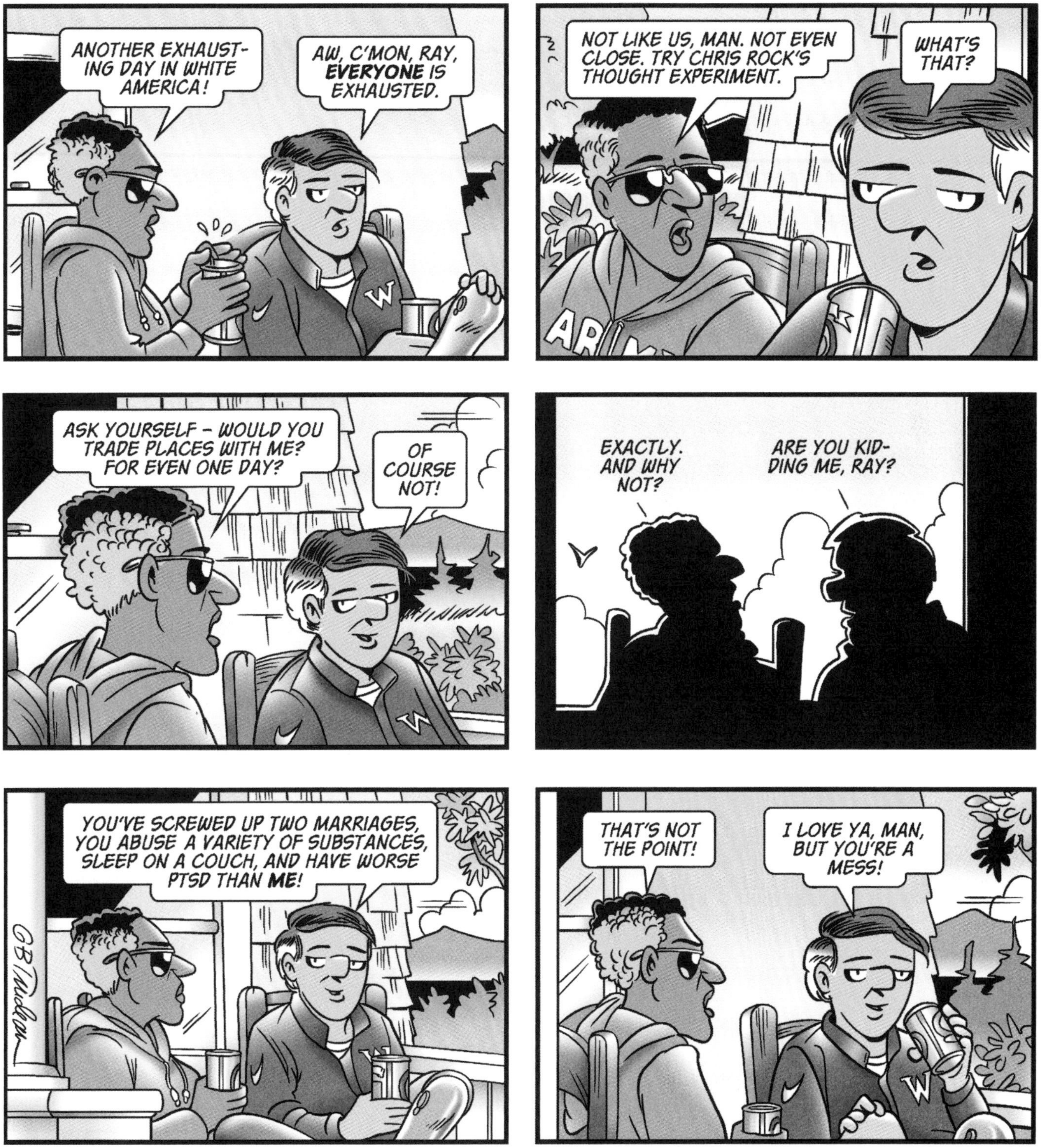
ANOTHER EXHAUST-ING DAY IN WHITE AMERICA!
AW, C'MON, RAY, **EVERYONE** IS EXHAUSTED.
NOT LIKE US, MAN. NOT EVEN CLOSE. TRY CHRIS ROCK'S THOUGHT EXPERIMENT.
WHAT'S THAT?
ASK YOURSELF – WOULD YOU TRADE PLACES WITH ME? FOR EVEN ONE DAY?
OF COURSE NOT!
EXACTLY. AND WHY NOT?
ARE YOU KID-DING ME, RAY?
YOU'VE SCREWED UP TWO MARRIAGES, YOU ABUSE A VARIETY OF SUBSTANCES, SLEEP ON A COUCH, AND HAVE WORSE PTSD THAN **ME**!
THAT'S NOT THE POINT!
I LOVE YA, MAN, BUT YOU'RE A MESS!
GBTrudeau

August 2, 2020

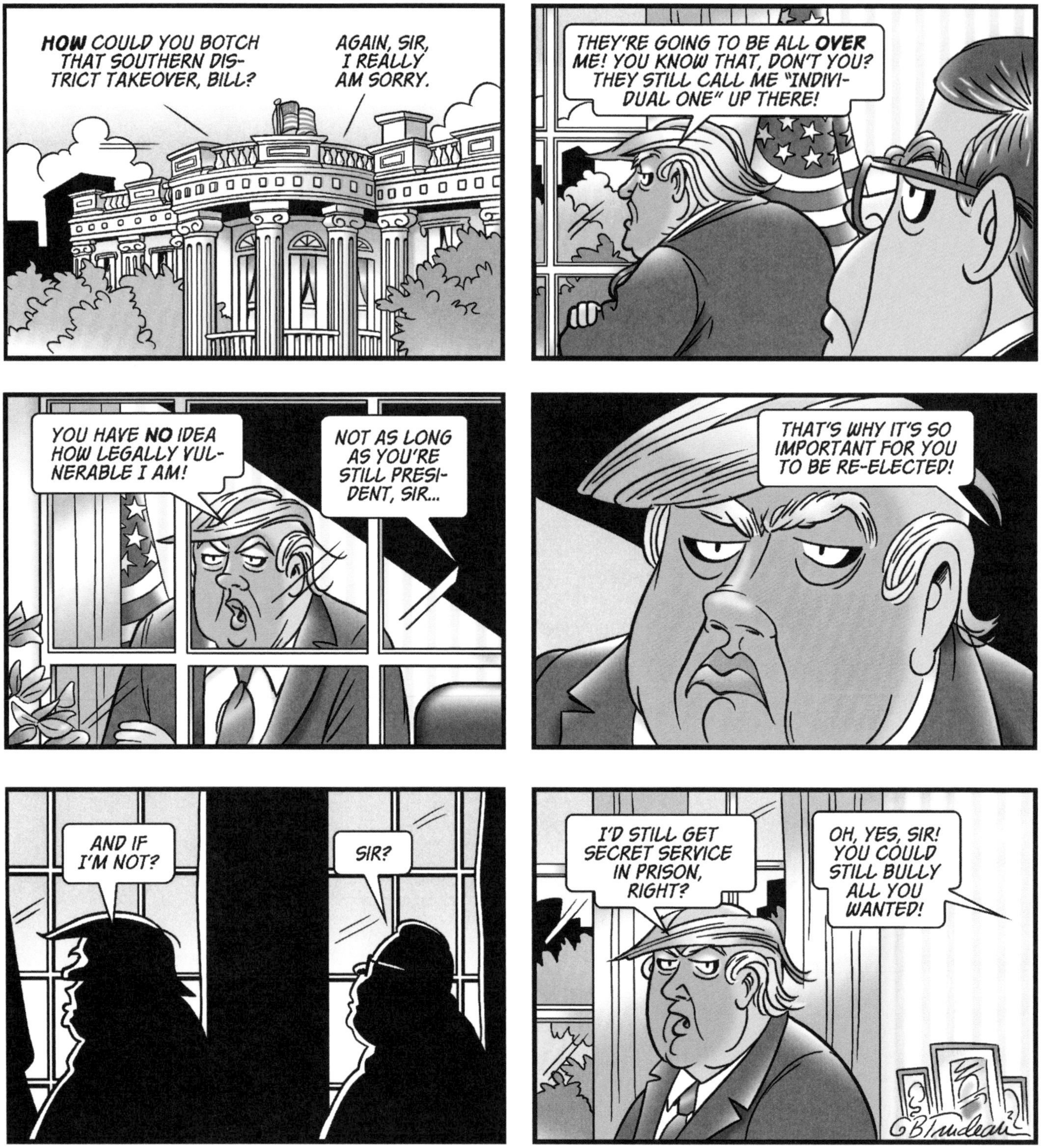
HOW COULD YOU BOTCH THAT SOUTHERN DISTRICT TAKEOVER, BILL?
AGAIN, SIR, I REALLY AM SORRY.
THEY'RE GOING TO BE ALL OVER ME! YOU KNOW THAT, DON'T YOU? THEY STILL CALL ME "INDIVIDUAL ONE" UP THERE!
YOU HAVE NO IDEA HOW LEGALLY VULNERABLE I AM!
NOT AS LONG AS YOU'RE STILL PRESIDENT, SIR...
THAT'S WHY IT'S SO IMPORTANT FOR YOU TO BE RE-ELECTED!
AND IF I'M NOT?
SIR?
I'D STILL GET SECRET SERVICE IN PRISON, RIGHT?
OH, YES, SIR! YOU COULD STILL BULLY ALL YOU WANTED!
GBTrudeau
August 9, 2020

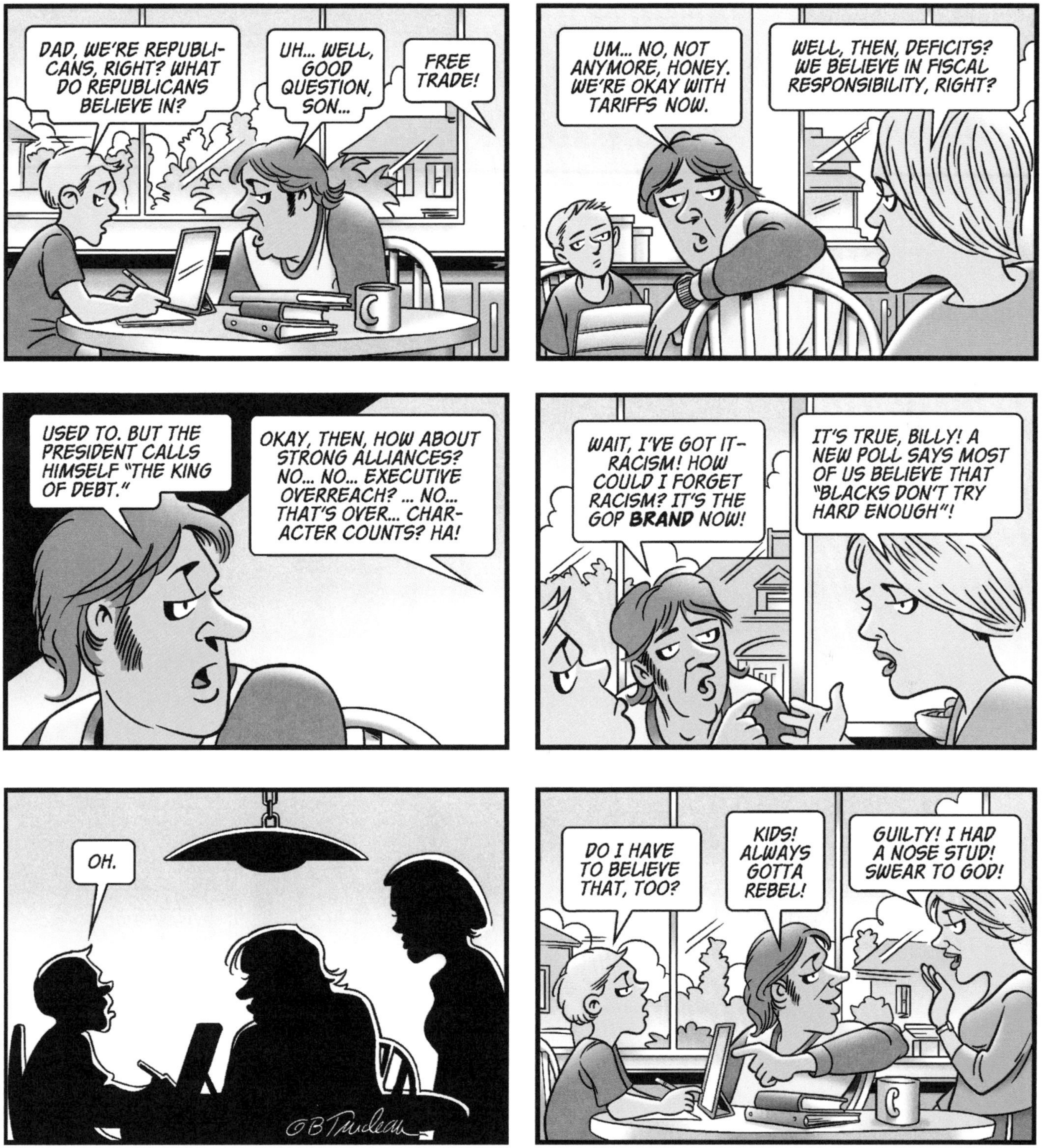
DAD, WE'RE REPUBLICANS, RIGHT? WHAT DO REPUBLICANS BELIEVE IN?
UH... WELL, GOOD QUESTION, SON...
FREE TRADE!
UM... NO, NOT ANYMORE, HONEY. WE'RE OKAY WITH TARIFFS NOW.
WELL, THEN, DEFICITS? WE BELIEVE IN FISCAL RESPONSIBILITY, RIGHT?
USED TO. BUT THE PRESIDENT CALLS HIMSELF "THE KING OF DEBT."
OKAY, THEN, HOW ABOUT STRONG ALLIANCES? NO... NO... EXECUTIVE OVERREACH? ... NO... THAT'S OVER... CHARACTER COUNTS? HA!
WAIT, I'VE GOT IT—RACISM! HOW COULD I FORGET RACISM? IT'S THE GOP **BRAND** NOW!
IT'S TRUE, BILLY! A NEW POLL SAYS MOST OF US BELIEVE THAT "BLACKS DON'T TRY HARD ENOUGH"!
OH.
©B Trudeau
DO I HAVE TO BELIEVE THAT, TOO?
KIDS! ALWAYS GOTTA REBEL!
GUILTY! I HAD A NOSE STUD! SWEAR TO GOD!

August 16, 2020

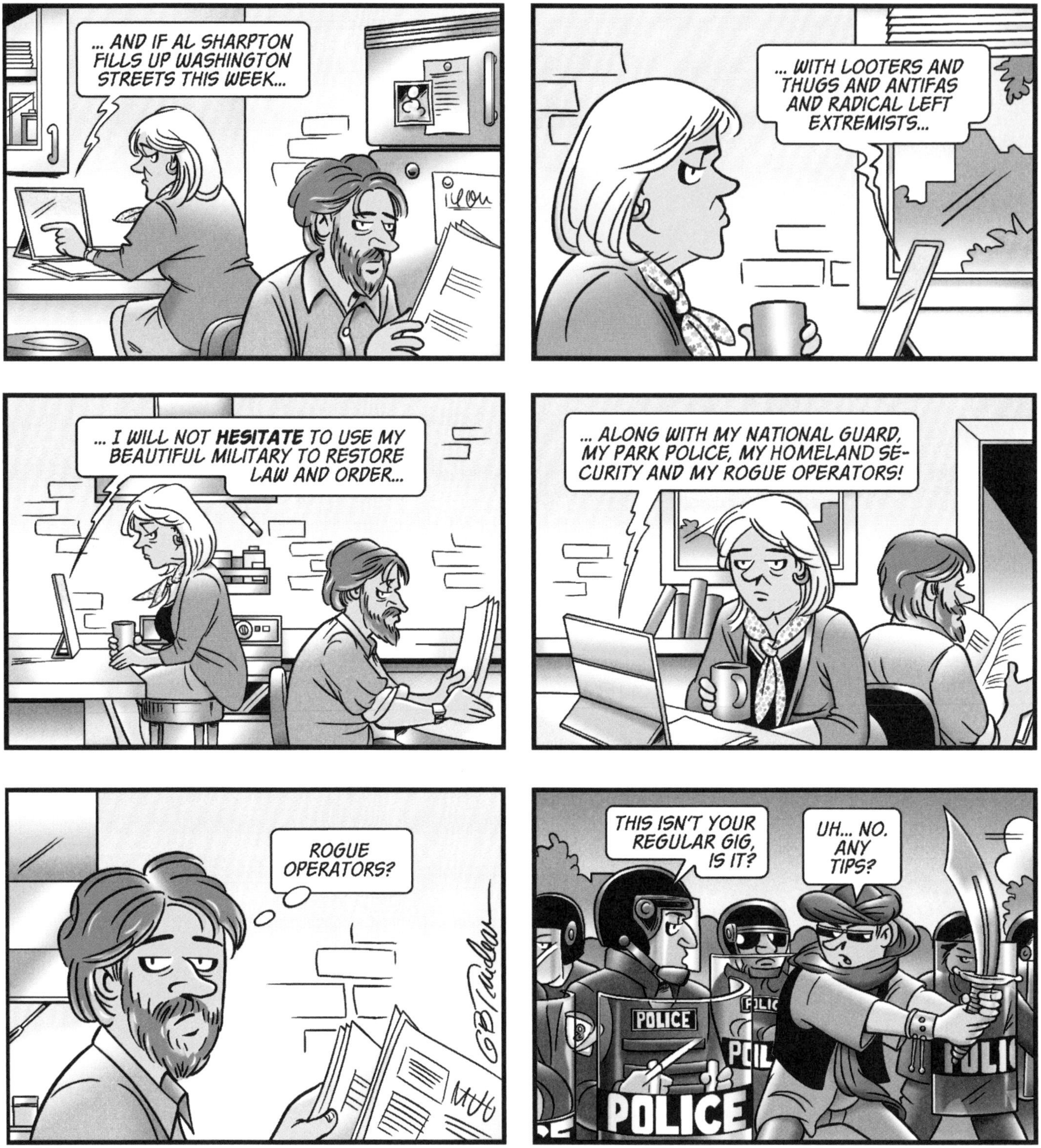
... AND IF AL SHARPTON FILLS UP WASHINGTON STREETS THIS WEEK...
... WITH LOOTERS AND THUGS AND ANTIFAS AND RADICAL LEFT EXTREMISTS...
... I WILL NOT HESITATE TO USE MY BEAUTIFUL MILITARY TO RESTORE LAW AND ORDER...
... ALONG WITH MY NATIONAL GUARD, MY PARK POLICE, MY HOMELAND SE-CURITY AND MY ROGUE OPERATORS!
ROGUE OPERATORS?
GBTrudeau
THIS ISN'T YOUR REGULAR GIG, IS IT?
UH... NO. ANY TIPS?
POLICE
POLICE

August 23, 2020

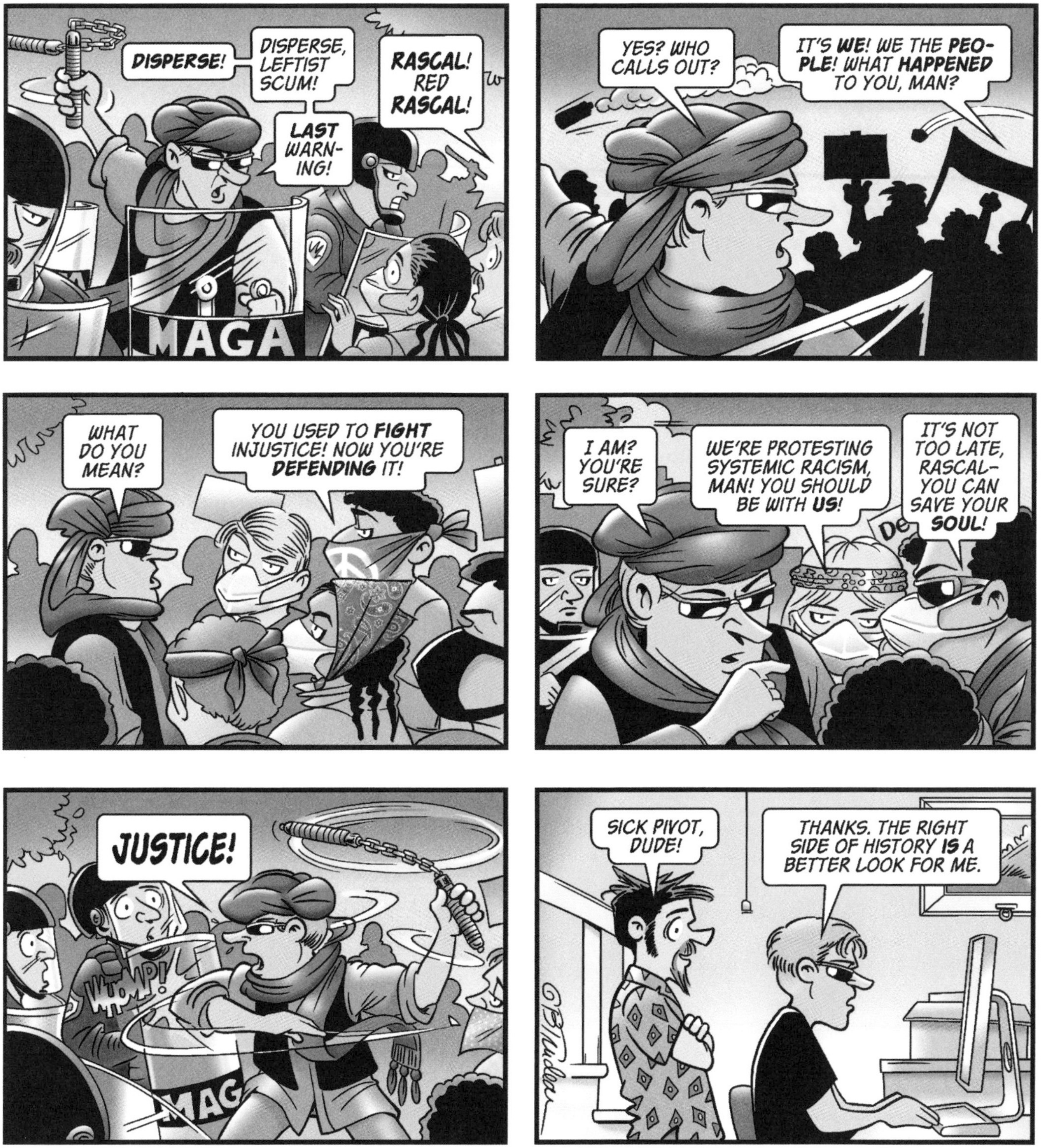
DISPERSE!
DISPERSE, LEFTIST SCUM!
LAST WARNING!
RASCAL! RED RASCAL!
MAGA
YES? WHO CALLS OUT?
IT'S WE! WE THE PEOPLE! WHAT HAPPENED TO YOU, MAN?
WHAT DO YOU MEAN?
YOU USED TO FIGHT INJUSTICE! NOW YOU'RE DEFENDING IT!
I AM? YOU'RE SURE?
WE'RE PROTESTING SYSTEMIC RACISM, MAN! YOU SHOULD BE WITH US!
IT'S NOT TOO LATE, RASCAL-YOU CAN SAVE YOUR SOUL!
JUSTICE!
WHOMP!
MAG
©B Trudeau
SICK PIVOT, DUDE!
THANKS. THE RIGHT SIDE OF HISTORY IS A BETTER LOOK FOR ME.

August 30, 2020

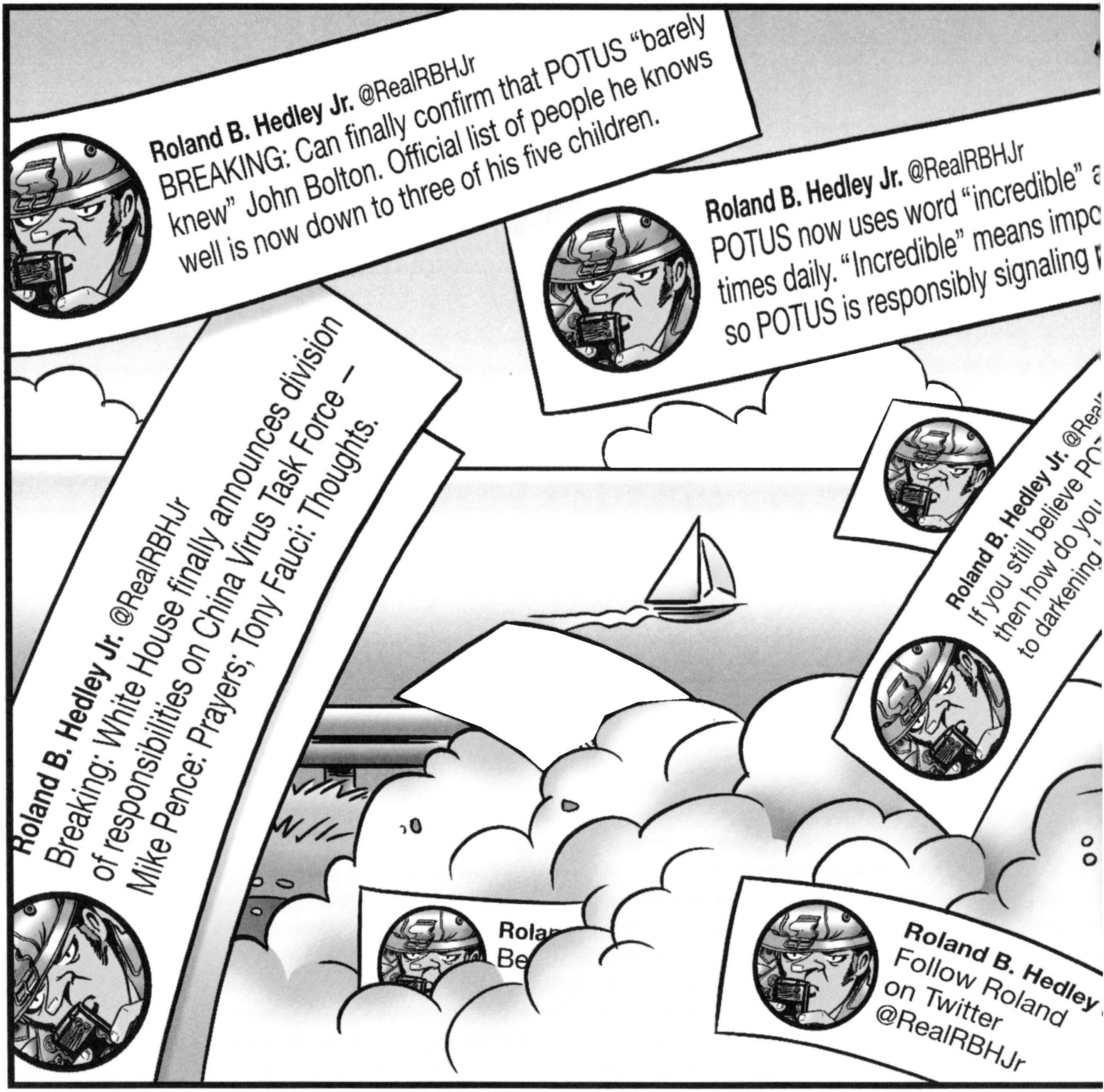

Roland B. Hedley Jr. @RealRBHJr
BREAKING: Can finally confirm that POTUS "barely knew" John Bolton. Official list of people he knows well is now down to three of his five children.
Roland B. Hedley Jr. @RealRBHJr
POTUS now uses word "incredible" a
times daily. "Incredible" means impo
so POTUS is responsibly signaling
Roland B. Hedley Jr. @RealRBHJr
Breaking: White House finally announces division of responsibilities on China Virus Task Force – Mike Pence: Prayers; Tony Fauci: Thoughts.
Roland B. Hedley Jr.
If you still believe PO
then how do you
to darkening
Rola
Be
Roland B. Hedley
Follow Roland on Twitter @RealRBHJr

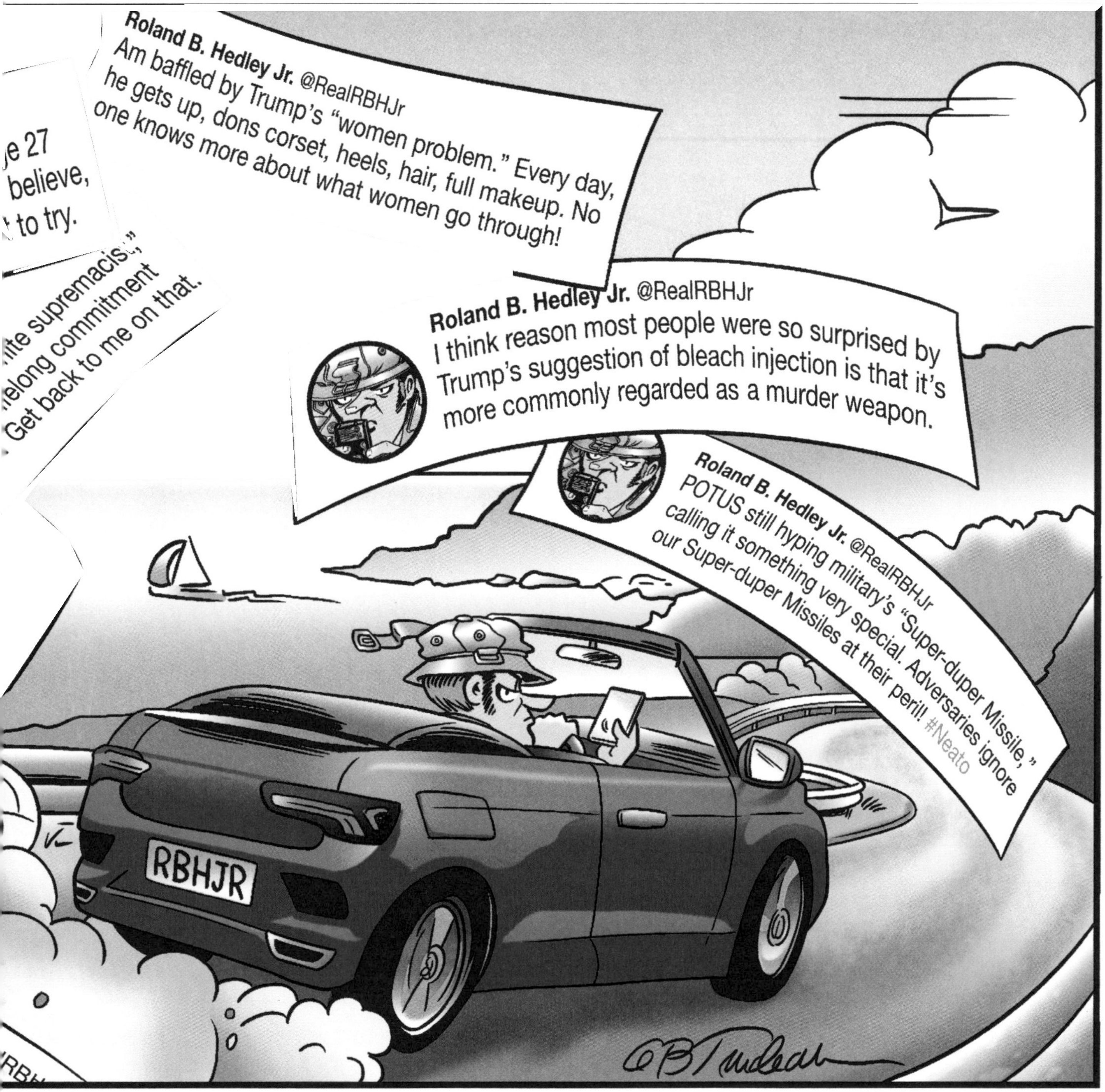
e 27
believe,
to try.
Roland B. Hedley Jr. @RealRBHJr
Am baffled by Trump's "women problem." Every day, he gets up, dons corset, heels, hair, full makeup. No one knows more about what women go through!
ite supremacist,"
elong commitment
Get back to me on that.
Roland B. Hedley Jr. @RealRBHJr
I think reason most people were so surprised by Trump's suggestion of bleach injection is that it's more commonly regarded as a murder weapon.
Roland B. Hedley Jr. @RealRBHJr
POTUS still hyping military's "Super-duper Missile," calling it something very special. Adversaries ignore our Super-duper Missiles at their peril! #Neato
RBHJR
RBH

September 13, 2020

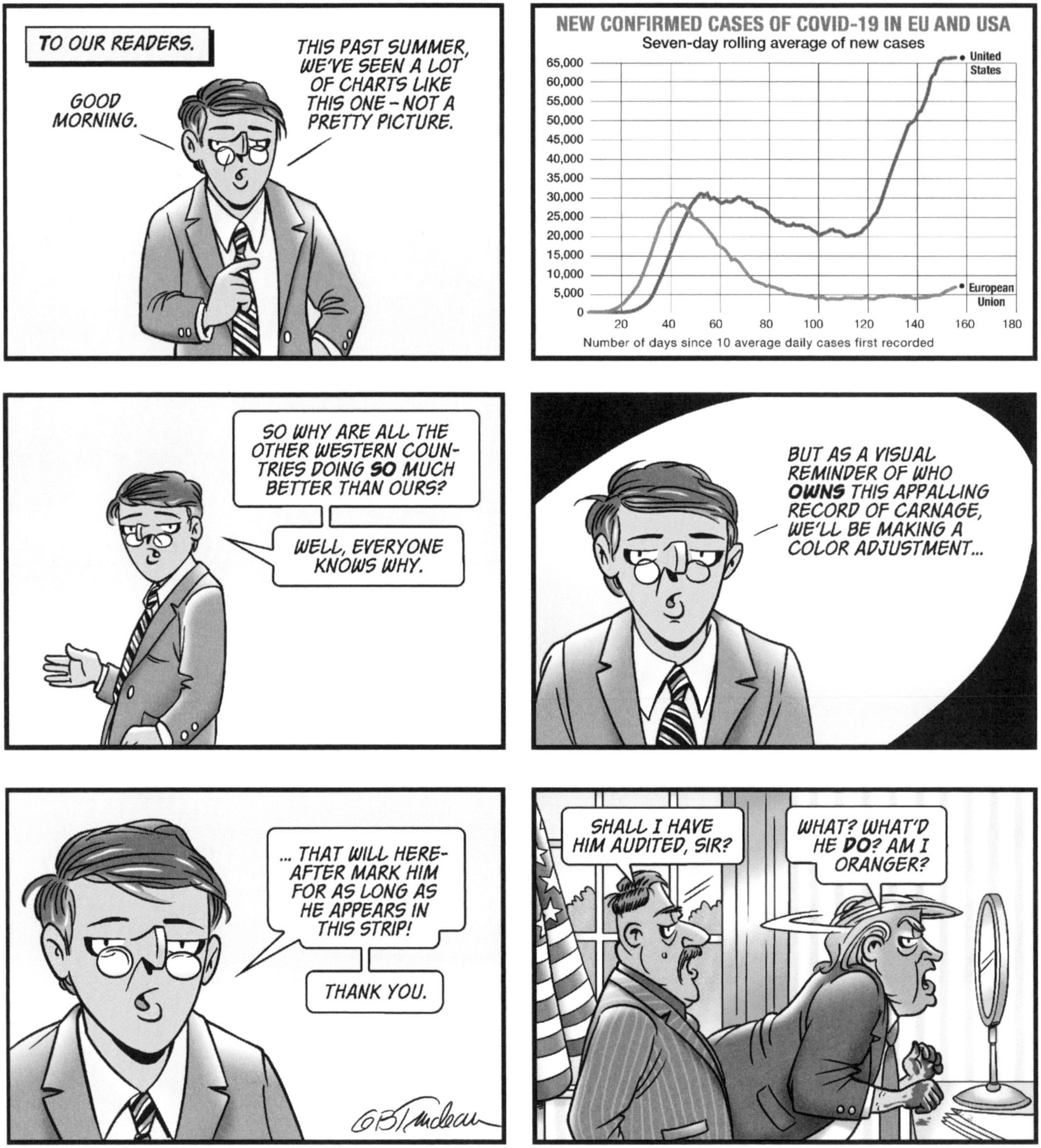
TO OUR READERS.
GOOD MORNING.
THIS PAST SUMMER, WE'VE SEEN A LOT OF CHARTS LIKE THIS ONE – NOT A PRETTY PICTURE.
NEW CONFIRMED CASES OF COVID-19 IN EU AND USA
Seven-day rolling average of new cases
65,000
60,000
55,000
50,000
45,000
40,000
35,000
30,000
25,000
20,000
15,000
10,000
5,000
0
20
40
60
80
100
120
140
160
180
United States
European Union
Number of days since 10 average daily cases first recorded
SO WHY ARE ALL THE OTHER WESTERN COUNTRIES DOING SO MUCH BETTER THAN OURS?
WELL, EVERYONE KNOWS WHY.
BUT AS A VISUAL REMINDER OF WHO OWNS THIS APPALLING RECORD OF CARNAGE, WE'LL BE MAKING A COLOR ADJUSTMENT...
... THAT WILL HEREAFTER MARK HIM FOR AS LONG AS HE APPEARS IN THIS STRIP!
THANK YOU.
SHALL I HAVE HIM AUDITED, SIR?
WHAT? WHAT'D HE DO? AM I ORANGER?

September 6, 2020

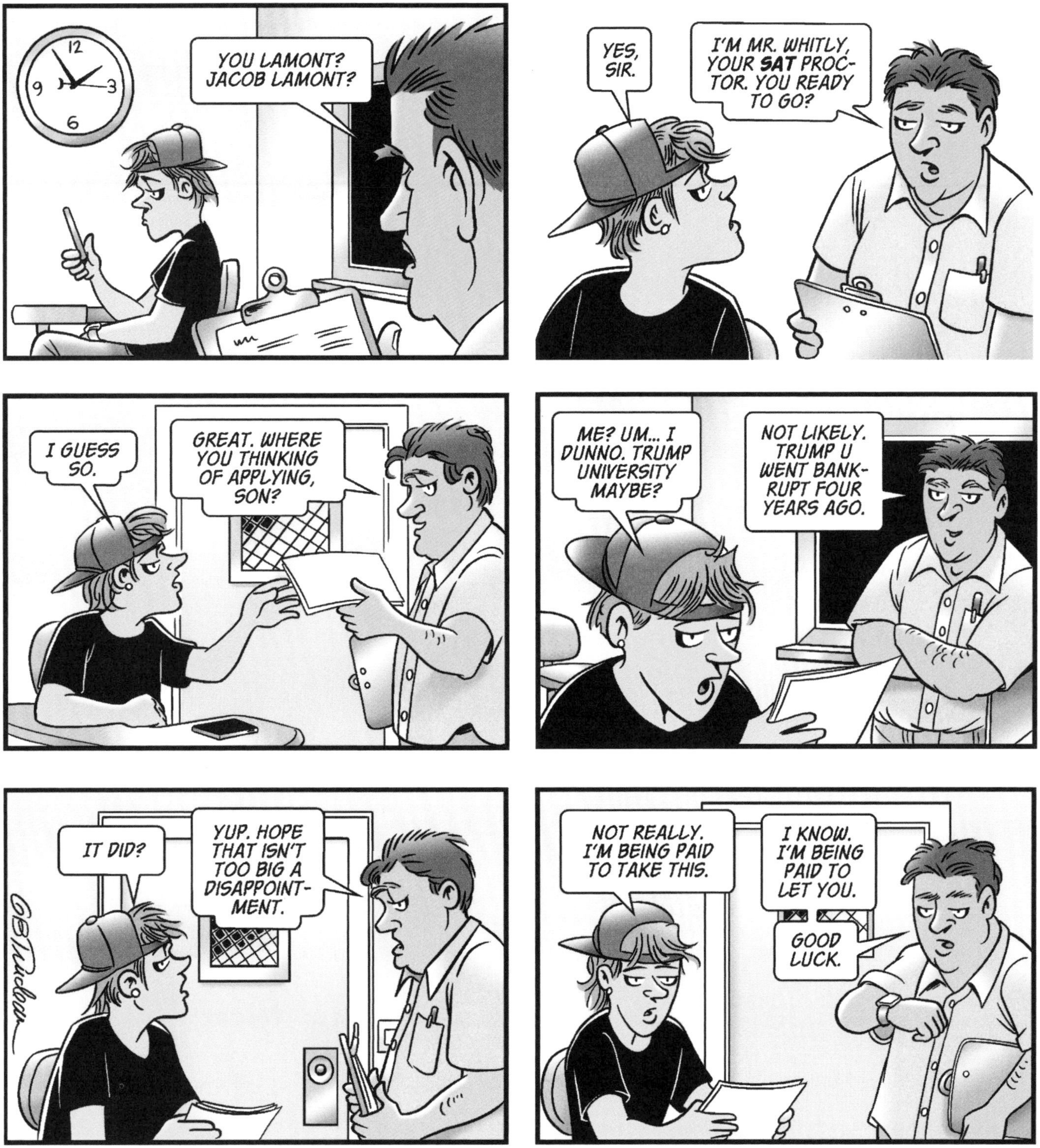

YOU LAMONT? JACOB LAMONT?
YES, SIR.
I'M MR. WHITLY, YOUR **SAT** PROCTOR. YOU READY TO GO?
I GUESS SO.
GREAT. WHERE YOU THINKING OF APPLYING, SON?
ME? UM... I DUNNO. TRUMP UNIVERSITY MAYBE?
NOT LIKELY. TRUMP U WENT BANKRUPT FOUR YEARS AGO.
IT DID?
YUP. HOPE THAT ISN'T TOO BIG A DISAPPOINTMENT.
GBTrudeau
NOT REALLY. I'M BEING PAID TO TAKE THIS.
I KNOW. I'M BEING PAID TO LET YOU.
GOOD LUCK.

September 20, 2020

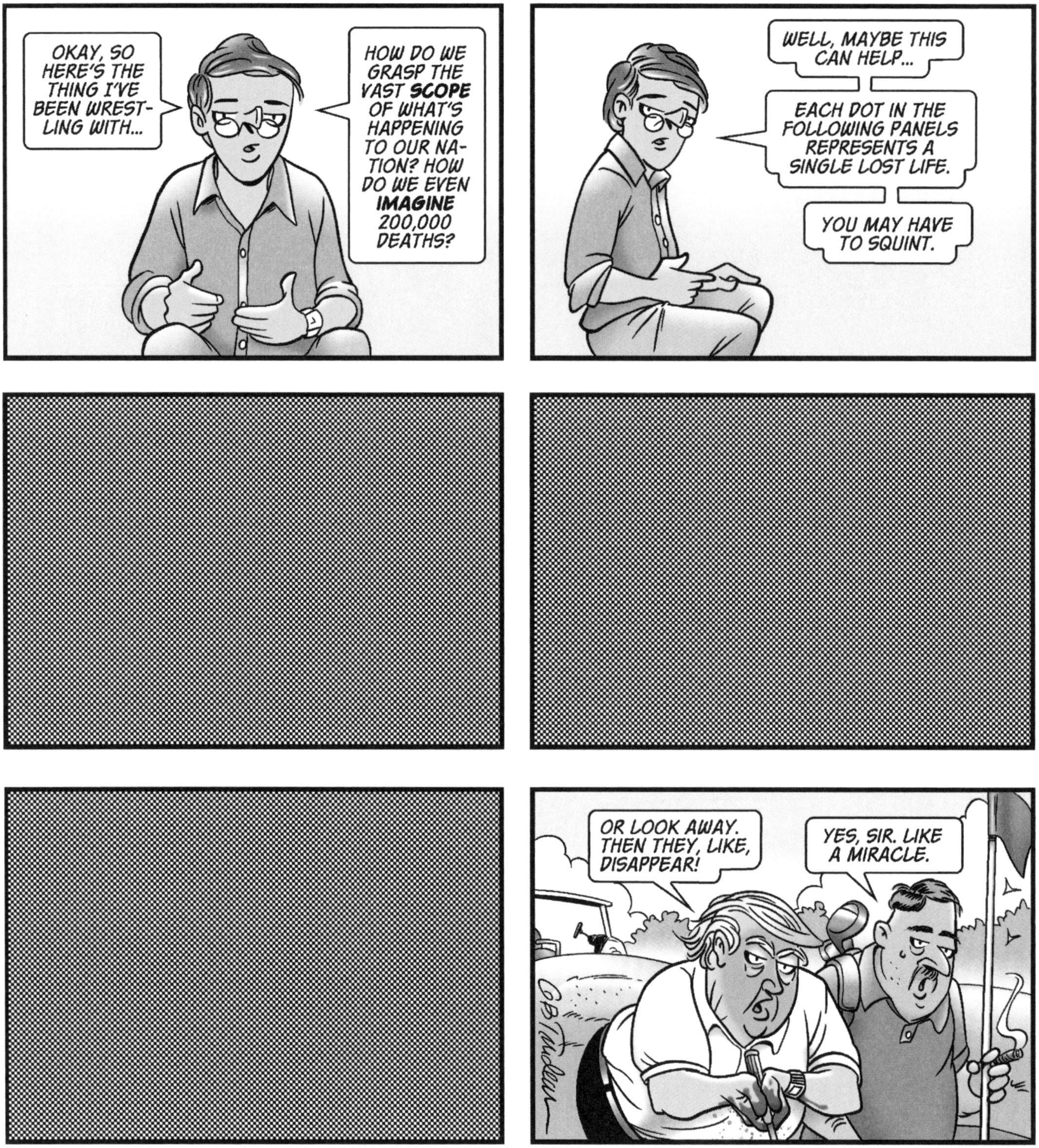
OKAY, SO HERE'S THE THING I'VE BEEN WRESTLING WITH...
HOW DO WE GRASP THE VAST **SCOPE** OF WHAT'S HAPPENING TO OUR NATION? HOW DO WE EVEN **IMAGINE** 200,000 DEATHS?
WELL, MAYBE THIS CAN HELP...
EACH DOT IN THE FOLLOWING PANELS REPRESENTS A SINGLE LOST LIFE.
YOU MAY HAVE TO SQUINT.
OR LOOK AWAY. THEN THEY, LIKE, DISAPPEAR!
YES, SIR. LIKE A MIRACLE.

September 27, 2020

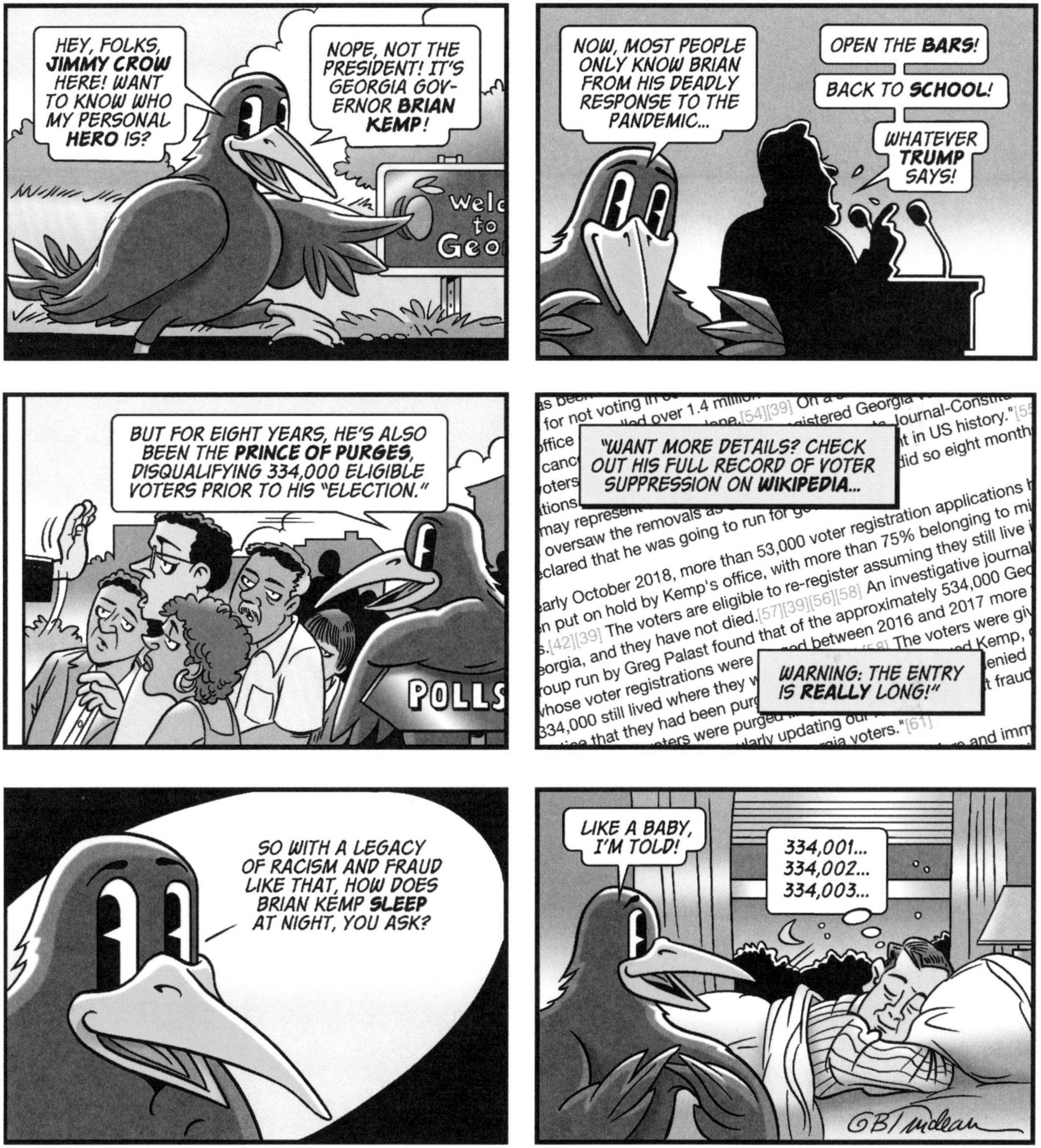

HEY, FOLKS, **JIMMY CROW** HERE! WANT TO KNOW WHO MY PERSONAL **HERO** IS?
NOPE, NOT THE PRESIDENT! IT'S GEORGIA GOV-ERNOR **BRIAN KEMP**!
Welc to Geo
NOW, MOST PEOPLE ONLY KNOW BRIAN FROM HIS DEADLY RESPONSE TO THE PANDEMIC...
OPEN THE **BARS**!
BACK TO **SCHOOL**!
WHATEVER **TRUMP** SAYS!
BUT FOR EIGHT YEARS, HE'S ALSO BEEN THE **PRINCE OF PURGES**, DISQUALIFYING 334,000 ELIGIBLE VOTERS PRIOR TO HIS "ELECTION."
POLLS
"WANT MORE DETAILS? CHECK OUT HIS FULL RECORD OF VOTER SUPPRESSION ON **WIKIPEDIA**...
WARNING: THE ENTRY IS **REALLY** LONG!"
SO WITH A LEGACY OF RACISM AND FRAUD LIKE THAT, HOW DOES BRIAN KEMP **SLEEP** AT NIGHT, YOU ASK?
LIKE A BABY, I'M TOLD!
334,001... 334,002... 334,003...

October 4, 2020

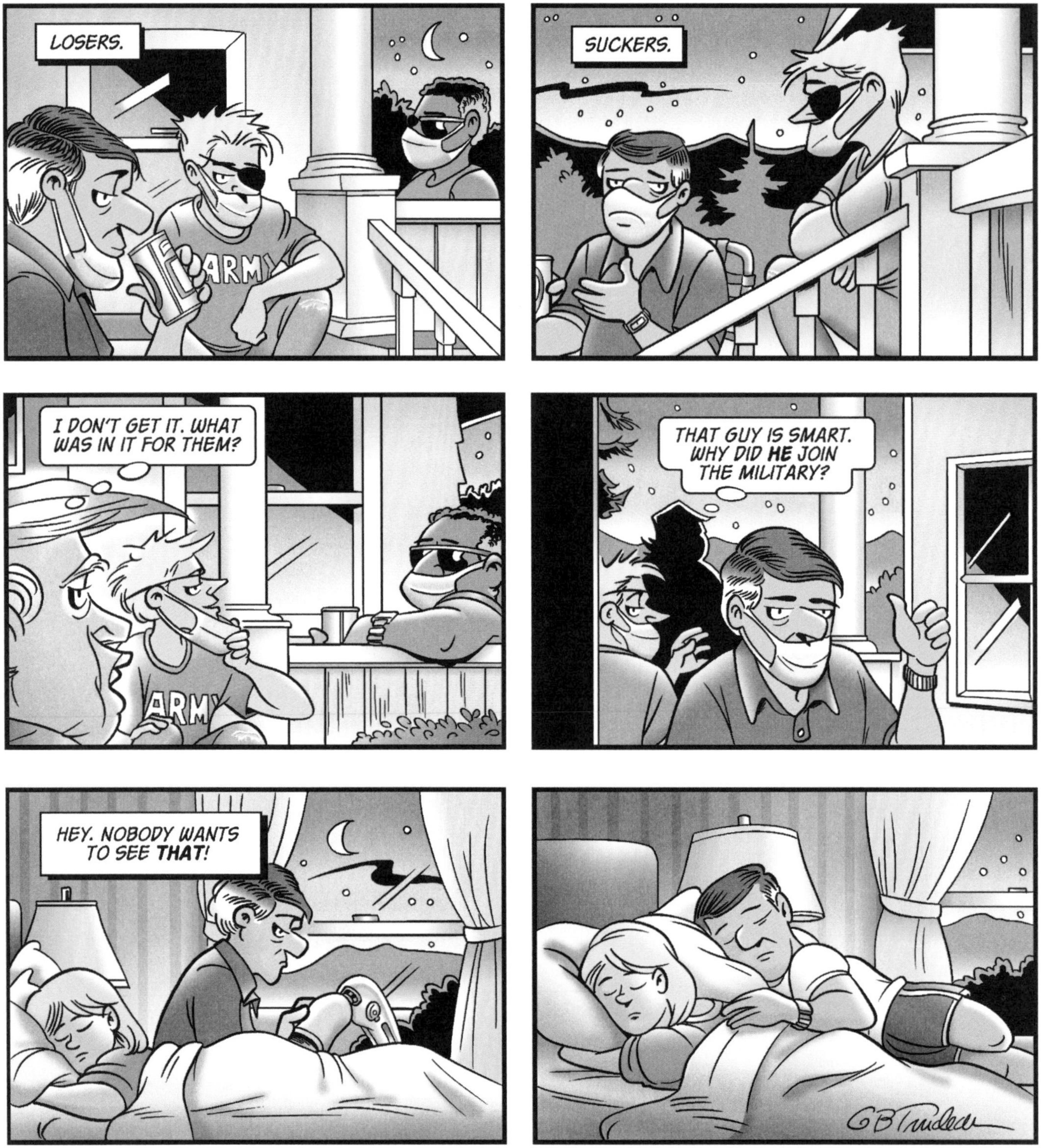
LOSERS.
SUCKERS.
I DON'T GET IT. WHAT WAS IN IT FOR THEM?
THAT GUY IS SMART. WHY DID HE JOIN THE MILITARY?
HEY. NOBODY WANTS TO SEE THAT!
GB Trudeau

October 11, 2020

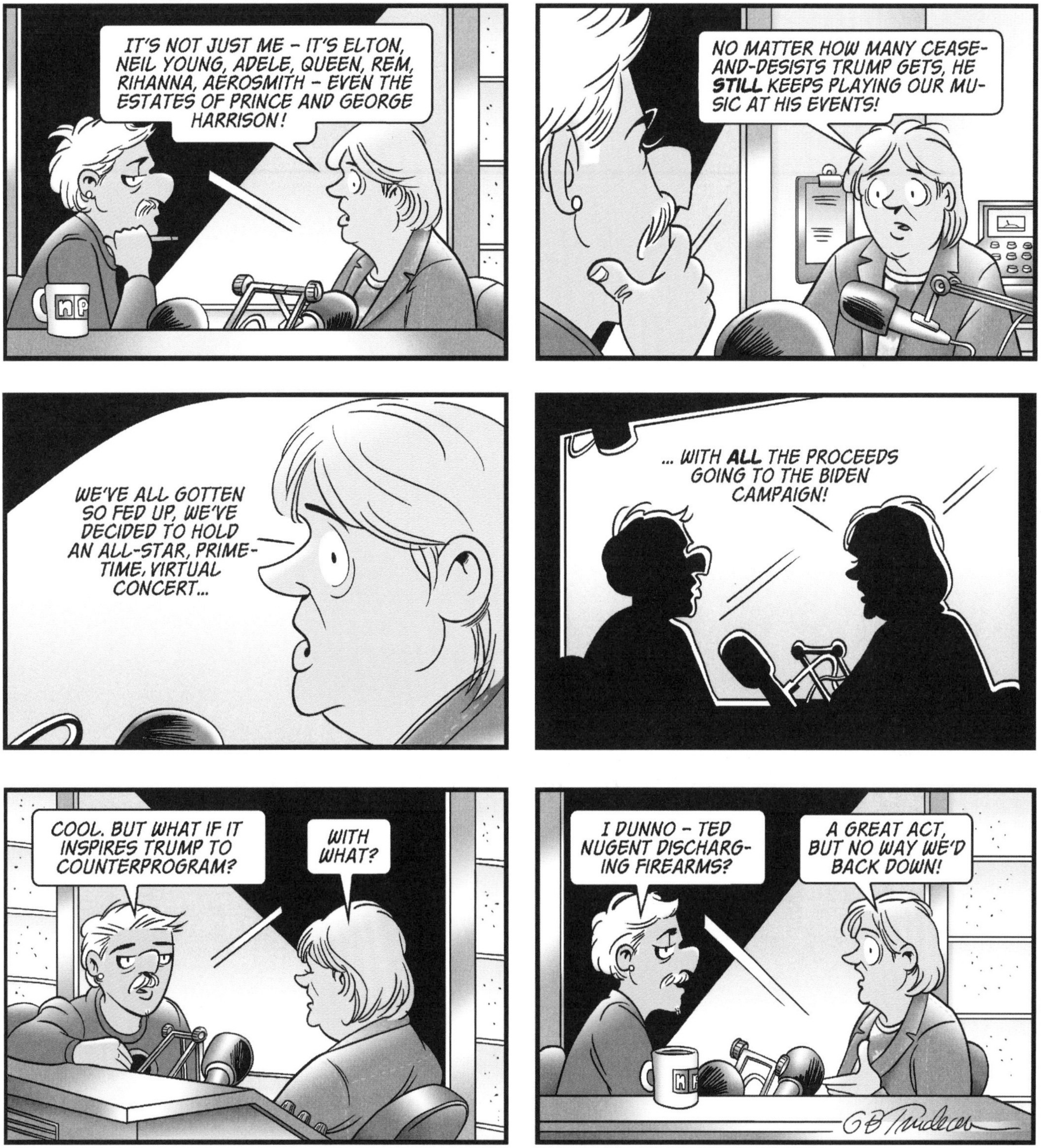
IT'S NOT JUST ME – IT'S ELTON, NEIL YOUNG, ADELE, QUEEN, REM, RIHANNA, AEROSMITH – EVEN THE ESTATES OF PRINCE AND GEORGE HARRISON!
NO MATTER HOW MANY CEASE-AND-DESISTS TRUMP GETS, HE **STILL** KEEPS PLAYING OUR MUSIC AT HIS EVENTS!
WE'VE ALL GOTTEN SO FED UP, WE'VE DECIDED TO HOLD AN ALL-STAR, PRIME-TIME, VIRTUAL CONCERT...
... WITH **ALL** THE PROCEEDS GOING TO THE BIDEN CAMPAIGN!
COOL. BUT WHAT IF IT INSPIRES TRUMP TO COUNTERPROGRAM?
WITH WHAT?
I DUNNO – TED NUGENT DISCHARGING FIREARMS?
A GREAT ACT, BUT NO WAY WE'D BACK DOWN!
GB Trudeau

October 18, 2020

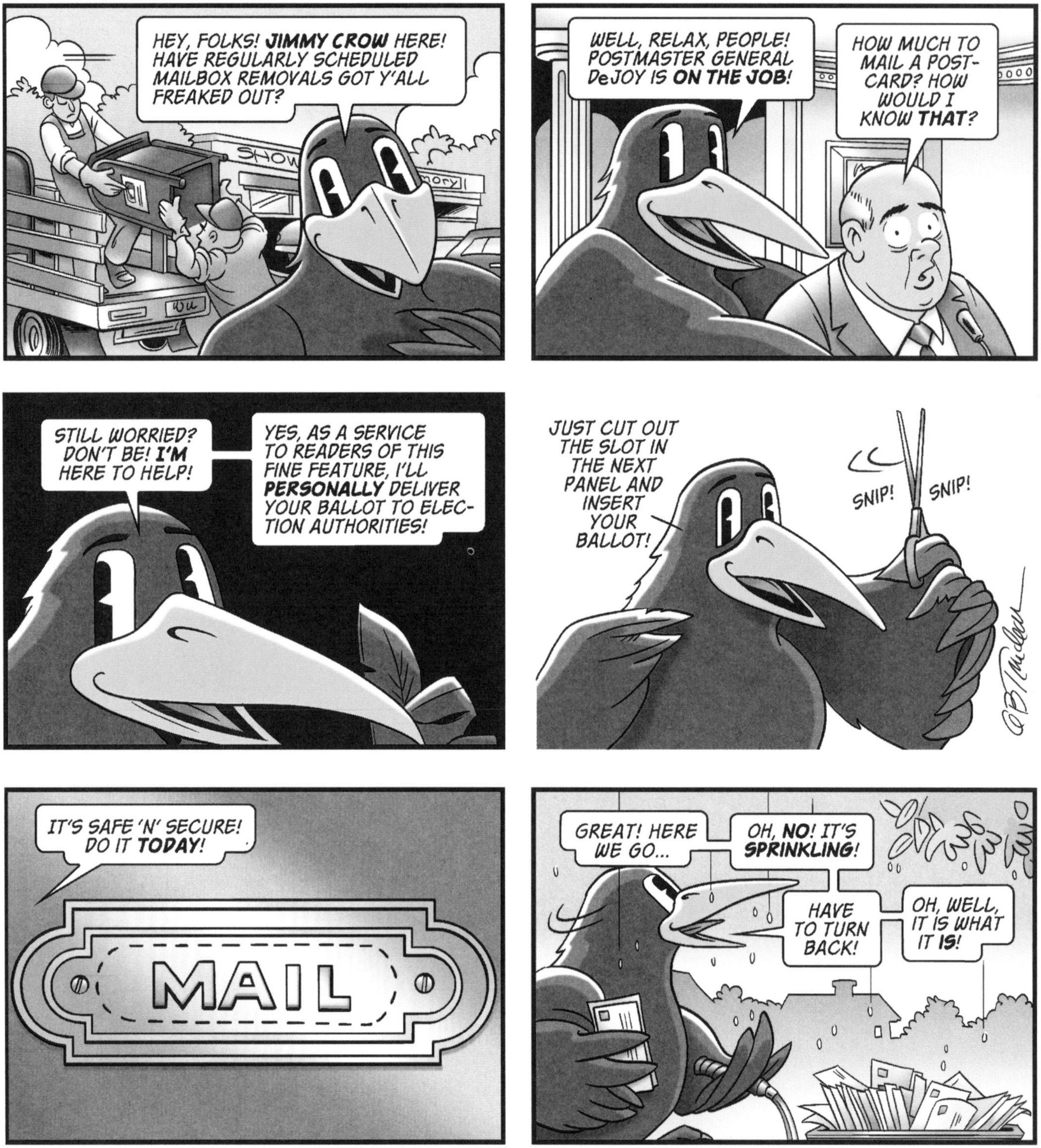
HEY, FOLKS! JIMMY CROW HERE! HAVE REGULARLY SCHEDULED MAILBOX REMOVALS GOT Y'ALL FREAKED OUT?
WELL, RELAX, PEOPLE! POSTMASTER GENERAL DeJOY IS ON THE JOB!
HOW MUCH TO MAIL A POST-CARD? HOW WOULD I KNOW THAT?
STILL WORRIED? DON'T BE! I'M HERE TO HELP!
YES, AS A SERVICE TO READERS OF THIS FINE FEATURE, I'LL PERSONALLY DELIVER YOUR BALLOT TO ELECTION AUTHORITIES!
JUST CUT OUT THE SLOT IN THE NEXT PANEL AND INSERT YOUR BALLOT!
SNIP! SNIP!
IT'S SAFE 'N' SECURE! DO IT TODAY!
MAIL
GREAT! HERE WE GO...
OH, NO! IT'S SPRINKLING!
HAVE TO TURN BACK!
OH, WELL, IT IS WHAT IT IS!

October 25, 2020

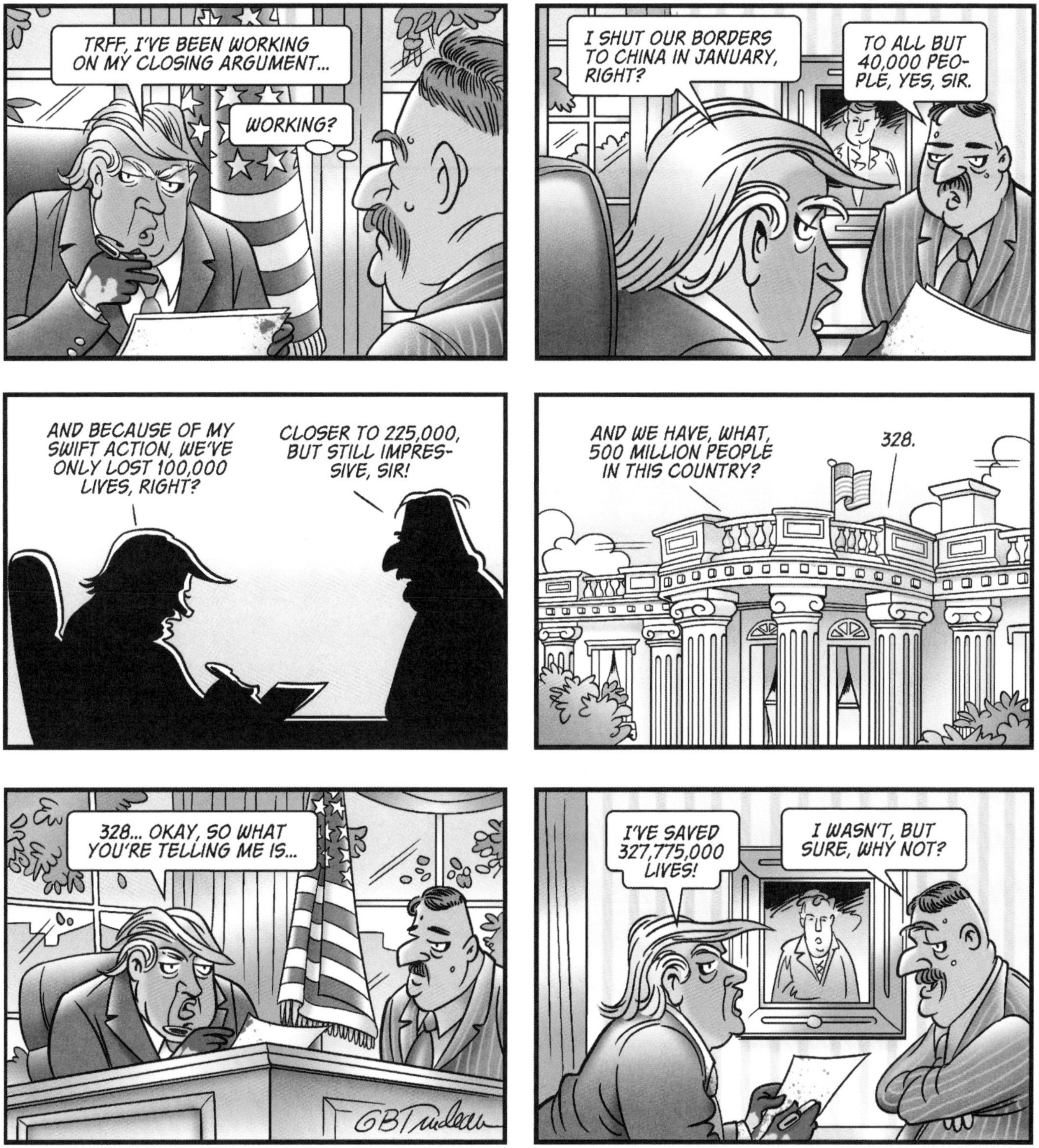

TRFF, I'VE BEEN WORKING ON MY CLOSING ARGUMENT...
WORKING?
I SHUT OUR BORDERS TO CHINA IN JANUARY, RIGHT?
TO ALL BUT 40,000 PEOPLE, YES, SIR.
AND BECAUSE OF MY SWIFT ACTION, WE'VE ONLY LOST 100,000 LIVES, RIGHT?
CLOSER TO 225,000, BUT STILL IMPRESSIVE, SIR!
AND WE HAVE, WHAT, 500 MILLION PEOPLE IN THIS COUNTRY?
328.
328... OKAY, SO WHAT YOU'RE TELLING ME IS...
I'VE SAVED 327,775,000 LIVES!
I WASN'T, BUT SURE, WHY NOT?
GBTrudeau

November 1, 2020

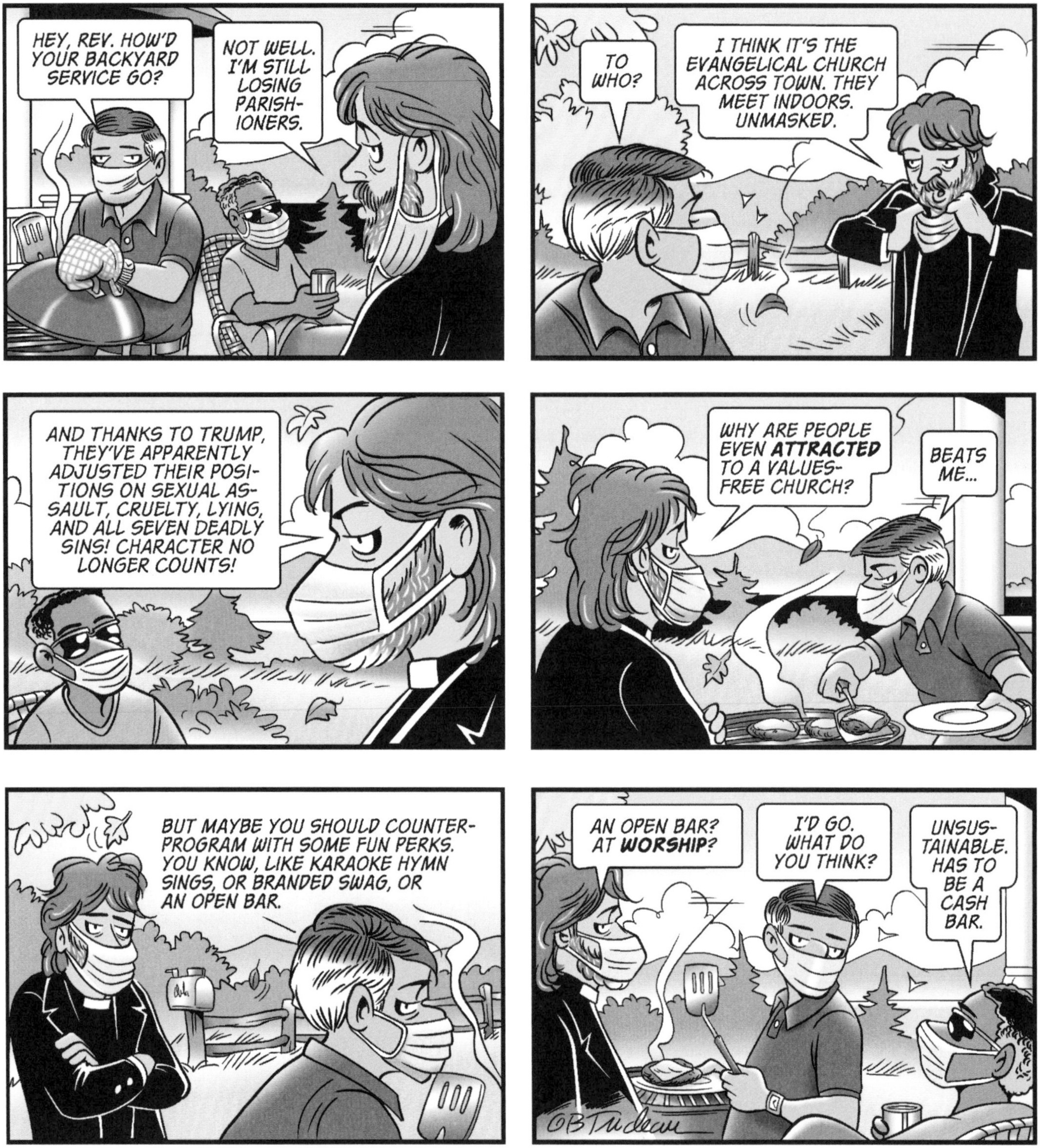
HEY, REV. HOW'D YOUR BACKYARD SERVICE GO?
NOT WELL. I'M STILL LOSING PARISH-IONERS.
TO WHO?
I THINK IT'S THE EVANGELICAL CHURCH ACROSS TOWN. THEY MEET INDOORS. UNMASKED.
AND THANKS TO TRUMP, THEY'VE APPARENTLY ADJUSTED THEIR POSI-TIONS ON SEXUAL AS-SAULT, CRUELTY, LYING, AND ALL SEVEN DEADLY SINS! CHARACTER NO LONGER COUNTS!
WHY ARE PEOPLE EVEN ATTRACTED TO A VALUES-FREE CHURCH?
BEATS ME...
BUT MAYBE YOU SHOULD COUNTER-PROGRAM WITH SOME FUN PERKS. YOU KNOW, LIKE KARAOKE HYMN SINGS, OR BRANDED SWAG, OR AN OPEN BAR.
AN OPEN BAR? AT WORSHIP?
I'D GO. WHAT DO YOU THINK?
UNSUS-TAINABLE. HAS TO BE A CASH BAR.
©B Trudeau

November 8, 2020

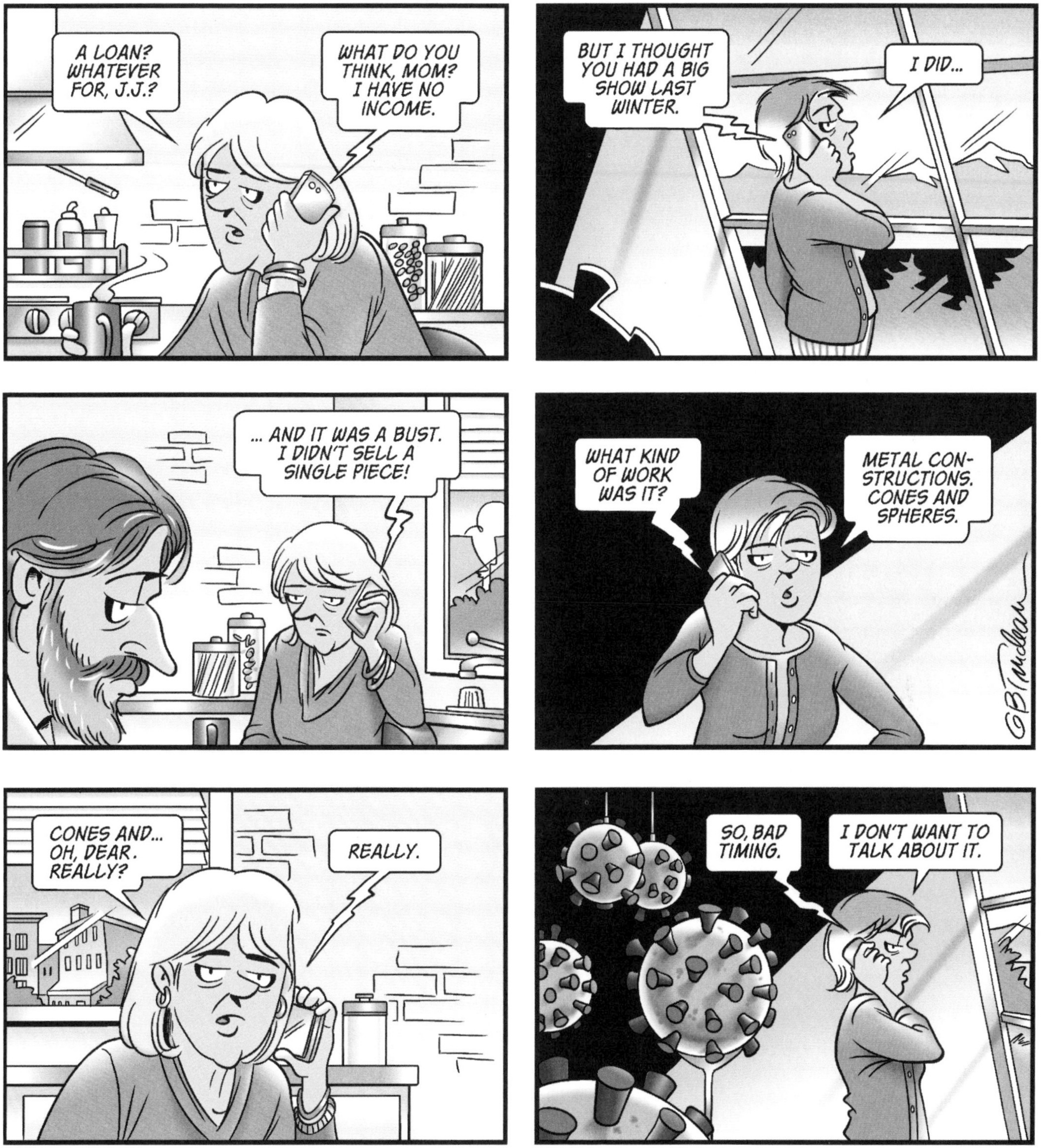
A LOAN? WHATEVER FOR, J.J.?
WHAT DO YOU THINK, MOM? I HAVE NO INCOME.
BUT I THOUGHT YOU HAD A BIG SHOW LAST WINTER.
I DID...
... AND IT WAS A BUST. I DIDN'T SELL A SINGLE PIECE!
WHAT KIND OF WORK WAS IT?
METAL CONSTRUCTIONS. CONES AND SPHERES.
CONES AND... OH, DEAR. REALLY?
REALLY.
SO, BAD TIMING.
I DON'T WANT TO TALK ABOUT IT.

November 15, 2020

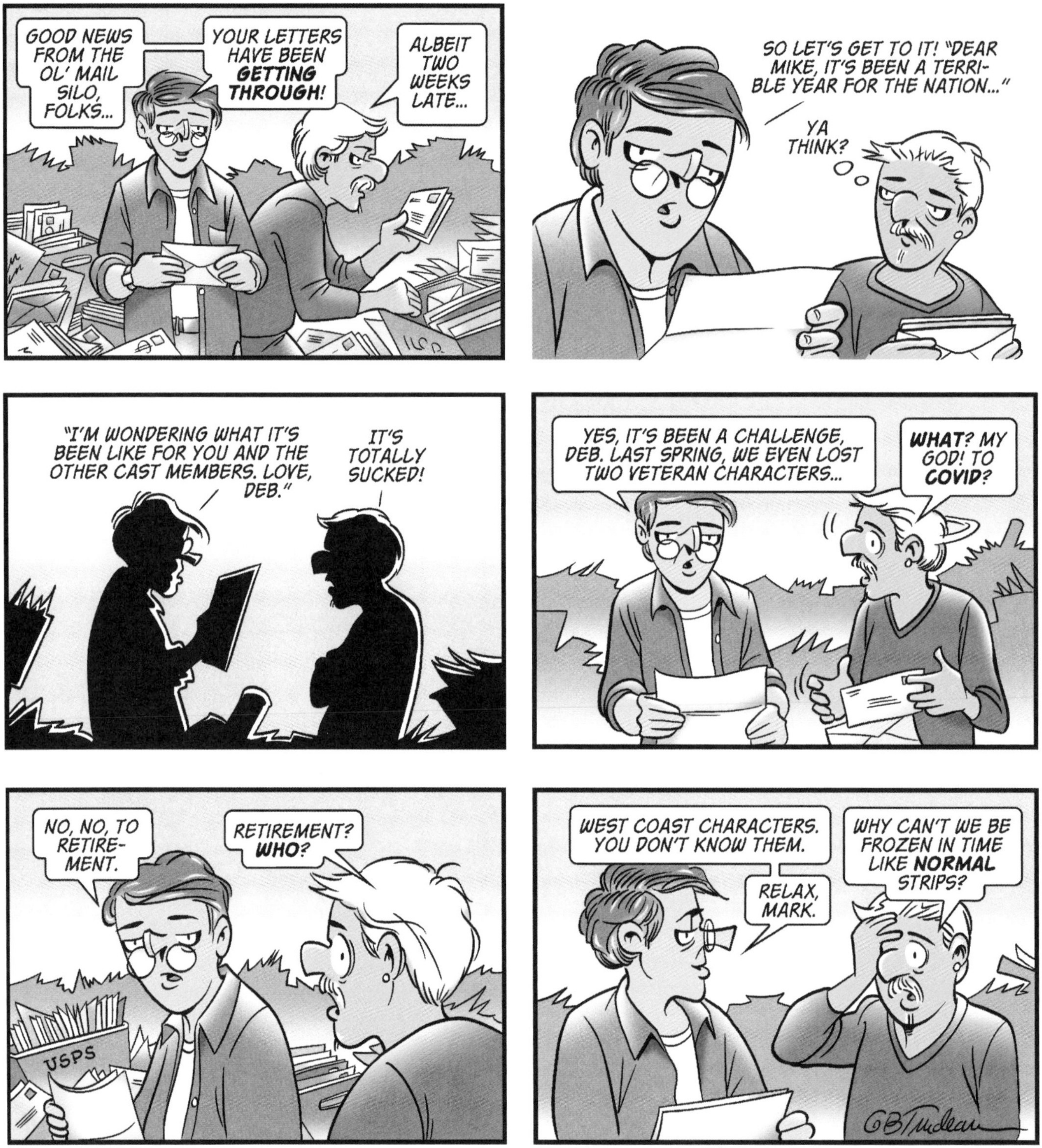
GOOD NEWS FROM THE OL' MAIL SILO, FOLKS...
YOUR LETTERS HAVE BEEN **GETTING THROUGH**!
ALBEIT TWO WEEKS LATE...
SO LET'S GET TO IT! "DEAR MIKE, IT'S BEEN A TERRIBLE YEAR FOR THE NATION..."
YA THINK?
"I'M WONDERING WHAT IT'S BEEN LIKE FOR YOU AND THE OTHER CAST MEMBERS. LOVE, DEB."
IT'S TOTALLY SUCKED!
YES, IT'S BEEN A CHALLENGE, DEB. LAST SPRING, WE EVEN LOST TWO VETERAN CHARACTERS...
WHAT? MY GOD! TO **COVID**?
NO, NO, TO RETIREMENT.
RETIREMENT? **WHO**?
USPS
WEST COAST CHARACTERS. YOU DON'T KNOW THEM.
RELAX, MARK.
WHY CAN'T WE BE FROZEN IN TIME LIKE **NORMAL** STRIPS?
GBTrudeau

November 22, 2020

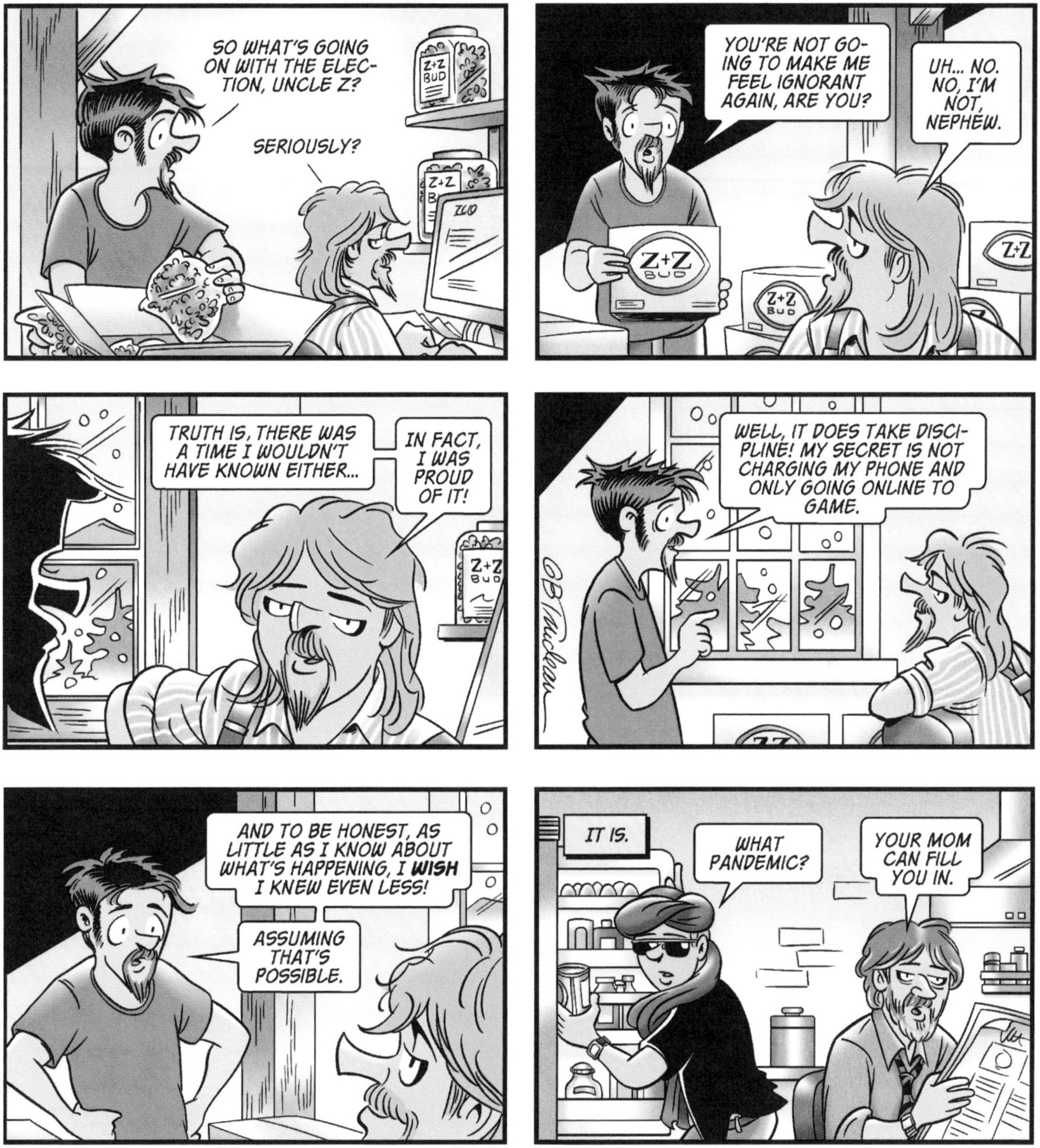
SO WHAT'S GOING ON WITH THE ELECTION, UNCLE Z?
SERIOUSLY?
Z+Z BUD
YOU'RE NOT GOING TO MAKE ME FEEL IGNORANT AGAIN, ARE YOU?
UH... NO. NO, I'M NOT, NEPHEW.
TRUTH IS, THERE WAS A TIME I WOULDN'T HAVE KNOWN EITHER...
IN FACT, I WAS PROUD OF IT!
WELL, IT DOES TAKE DISCIPLINE! MY SECRET IS NOT CHARGING MY PHONE AND ONLY GOING ONLINE TO GAME.
AND TO BE HONEST, AS LITTLE AS I KNOW ABOUT WHAT'S HAPPENING, I **WISH** I KNEW EVEN LESS!
ASSUMING THAT'S POSSIBLE.
IT IS.
WHAT PANDEMIC?
YOUR MOM CAN FILL YOU IN.

November 29, 2020

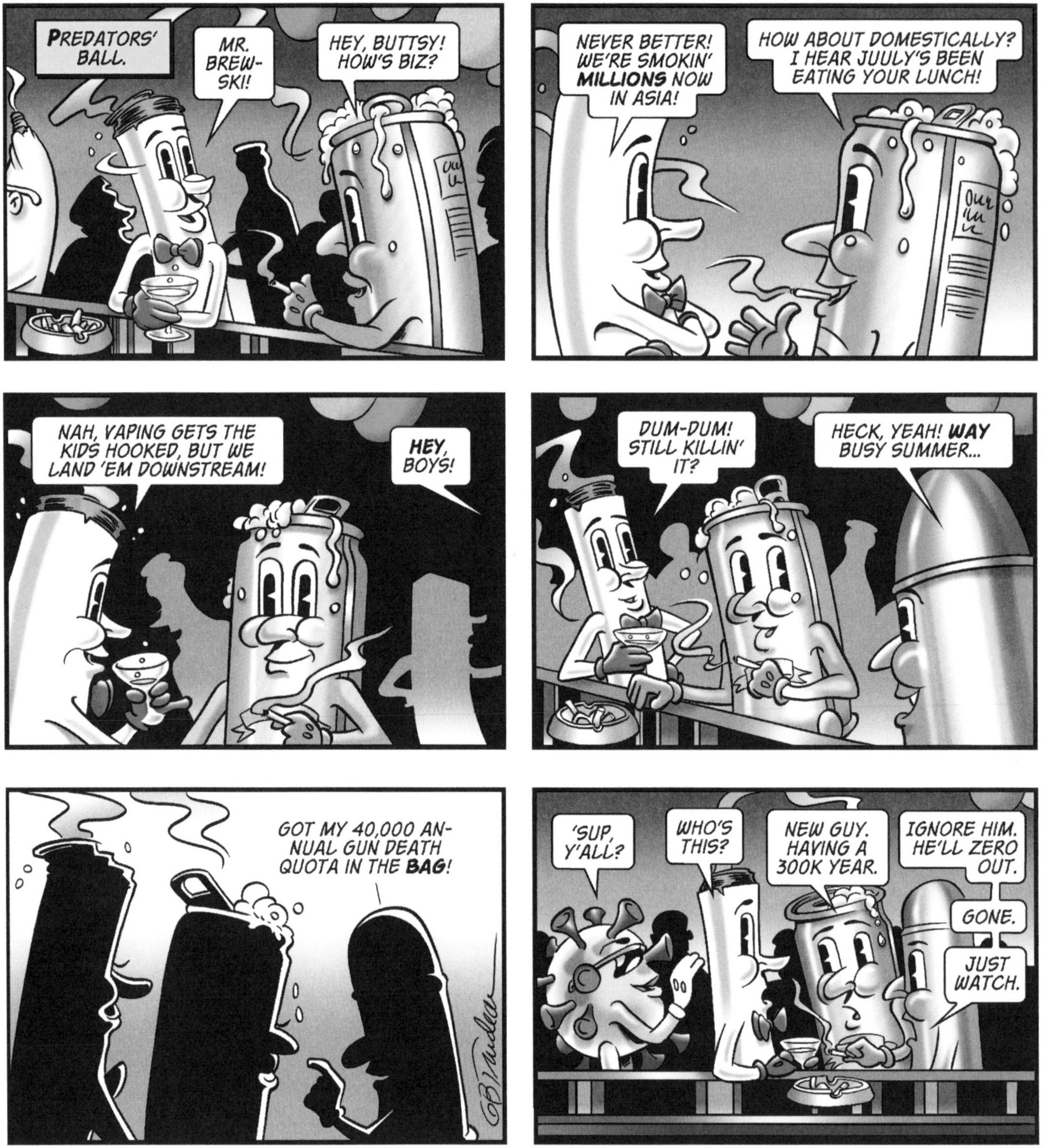
PREDATORS' BALL.
MR. BREW-SKI!
HEY, BUTTSY! HOW'S BIZ?
NEVER BETTER! WE'RE SMOKIN' MILLIONS NOW IN ASIA!
HOW ABOUT DOMESTICALLY? I HEAR JUULY'S BEEN EATING YOUR LUNCH!
NAH, VAPING GETS THE KIDS HOOKED, BUT WE LAND 'EM DOWNSTREAM!
HEY, BOYS!
DUM-DUM! STILL KILLIN' IT?
HECK, YEAH! WAY BUSY SUMMER...
GOT MY 40,000 ANNUAL GUN DEATH QUOTA IN THE BAG!
'SUP, Y'ALL?
WHO'S THIS?
NEW GUY. HAVING A 300K YEAR.
IGNORE HIM. HE'LL ZERO OUT.
GONE.
JUST WATCH.

December 6, 2020

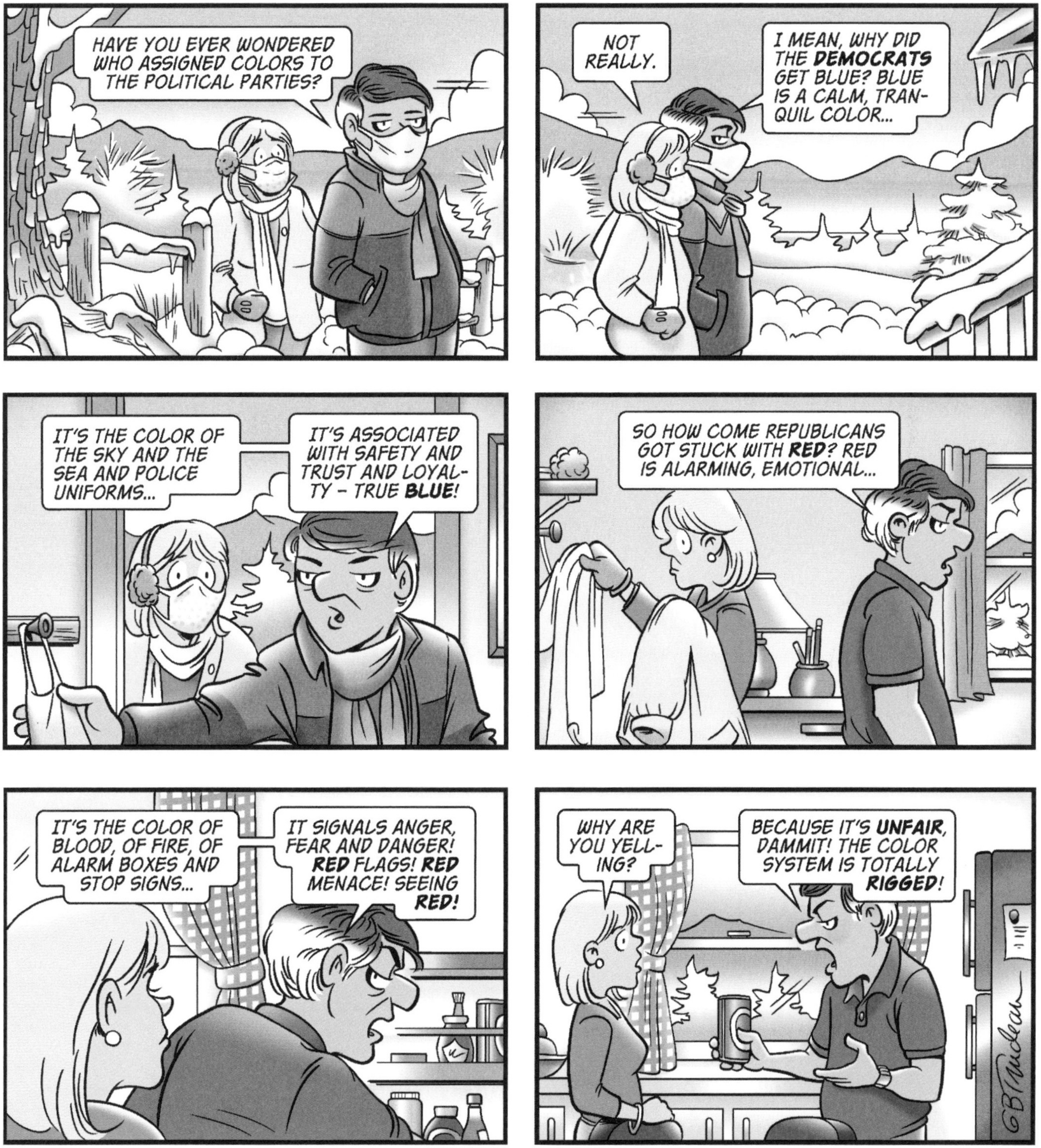
HAVE YOU EVER WONDERED WHO ASSIGNED COLORS TO THE POLITICAL PARTIES?
NOT REALLY.
I MEAN, WHY DID THE **DEMOCRATS** GET BLUE? BLUE IS A CALM, TRANQUIL COLOR...
IT'S THE COLOR OF THE SKY AND THE SEA AND POLICE UNIFORMS...
IT'S ASSOCIATED WITH SAFETY AND TRUST AND LOYALTY - TRUE **BLUE**!
SO HOW COME REPUBLICANS GOT STUCK WITH **RED**? RED IS ALARMING, EMOTIONAL...
IT'S THE COLOR OF BLOOD, OF FIRE, OF ALARM BOXES AND STOP SIGNS...
IT SIGNALS ANGER, FEAR AND DANGER! **RED** FLAGS! **RED** MENACE! SEEING **RED**!
WHY ARE YOU YELLING?
BECAUSE IT'S **UNFAIR**, DAMMIT! THE COLOR SYSTEM IS TOTALLY **RIGGED**!
GBTrudeau

December 13, 2020

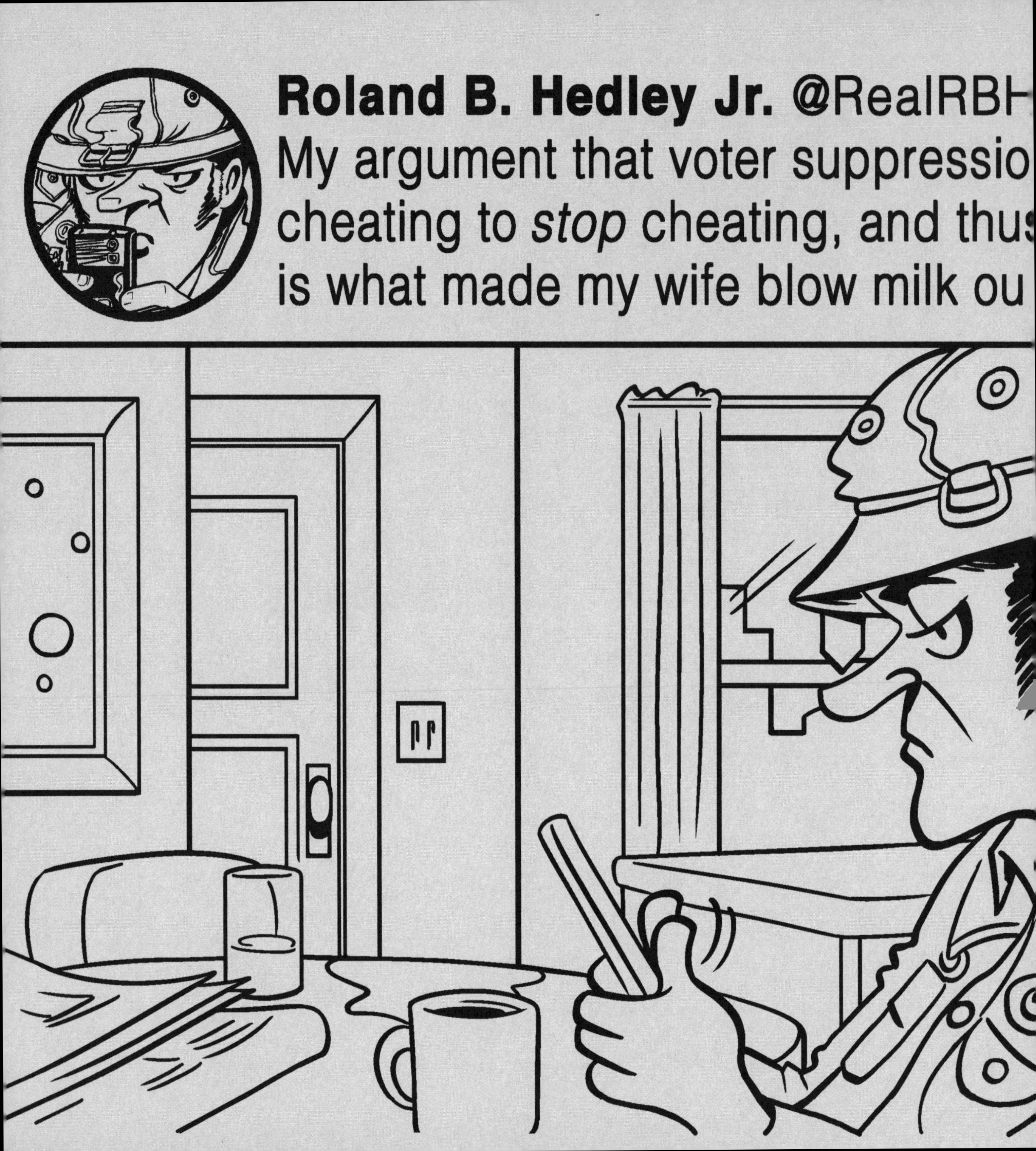
Roland B. Hedley Jr. @RealRBH
My argument that voter suppressio
cheating to *stop* cheating, and thus
is what made my wife blow milk ou

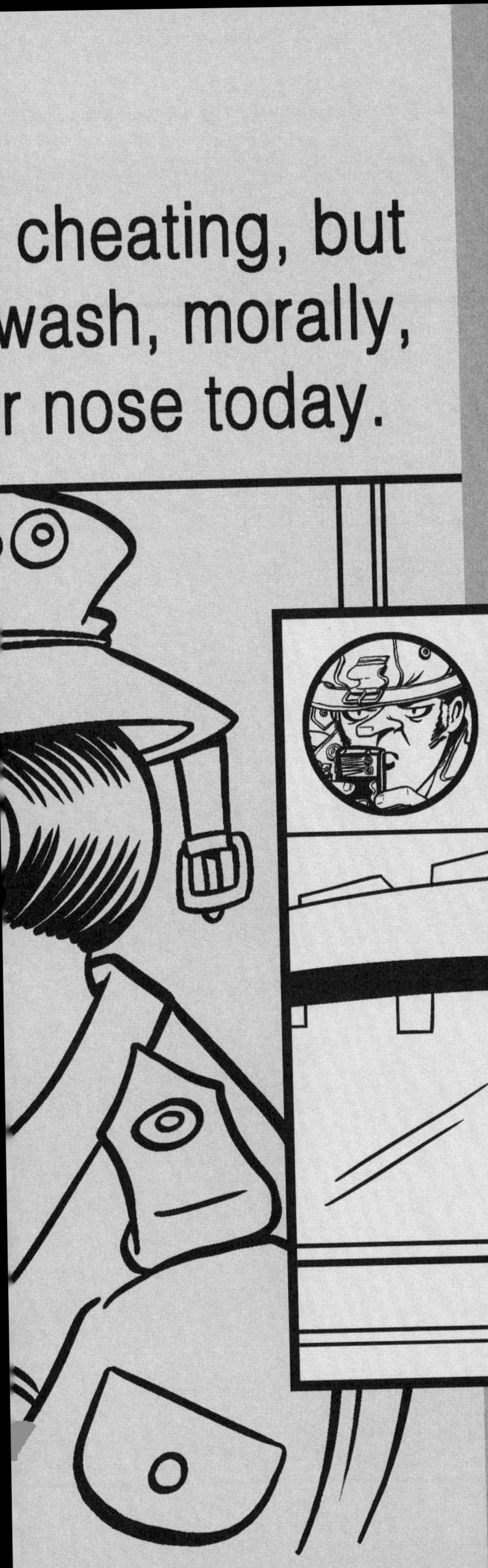
cheating, but
wash, morally,
r nose today.

PART 2
The Big Lie

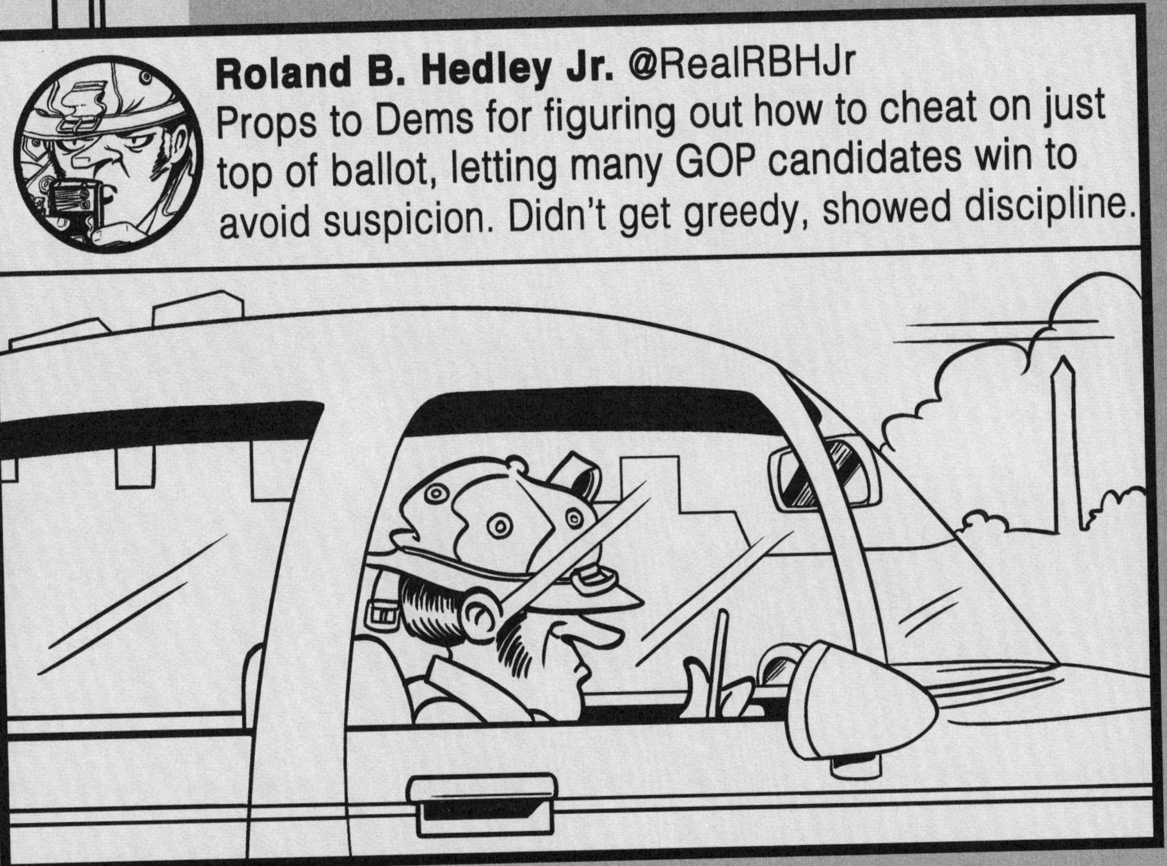
Roland B. Hedley Jr. @RealRBHJr
Props to Dems for figuring out how to cheat on just top of ballot, letting many GOP candidates win to avoid suspicion. Didn't get greedy, showed discipline.

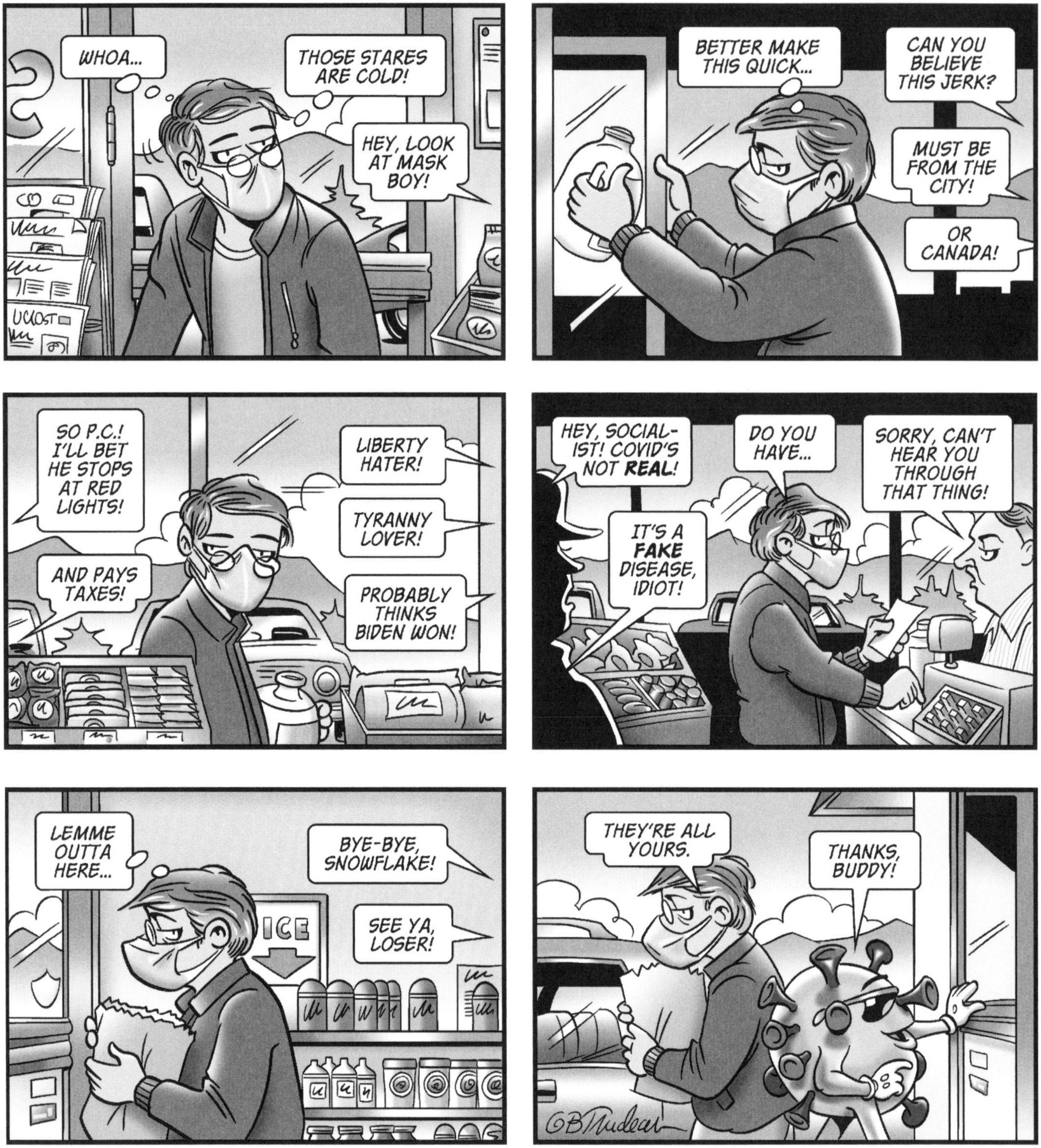
WHOA...
THOSE STARES ARE COLD!
HEY, LOOK AT MASK BOY!
BETTER MAKE THIS QUICK...
CAN YOU BELIEVE THIS JERK?
MUST BE FROM THE CITY!
OR CANADA!
SO P.C.! I'LL BET HE STOPS AT RED LIGHTS!
AND PAYS TAXES!
LIBERTY HATER!
TYRANNY LOVER!
PROBABLY THINKS BIDEN WON!
HEY, SOCIAL-IST! COVID'S NOT **REAL**!
IT'S A **FAKE** DISEASE, IDIOT!
DO YOU HAVE...
SORRY, CAN'T HEAR YOU THROUGH THAT THING!
LEMME OUTTA HERE...
BYE-BYE, SNOWFLAKE!
SEE YA, LOSER!
ICE
THEY'RE ALL YOURS.
THANKS, BUDDY!
GBTrudeau

December 20, 2020

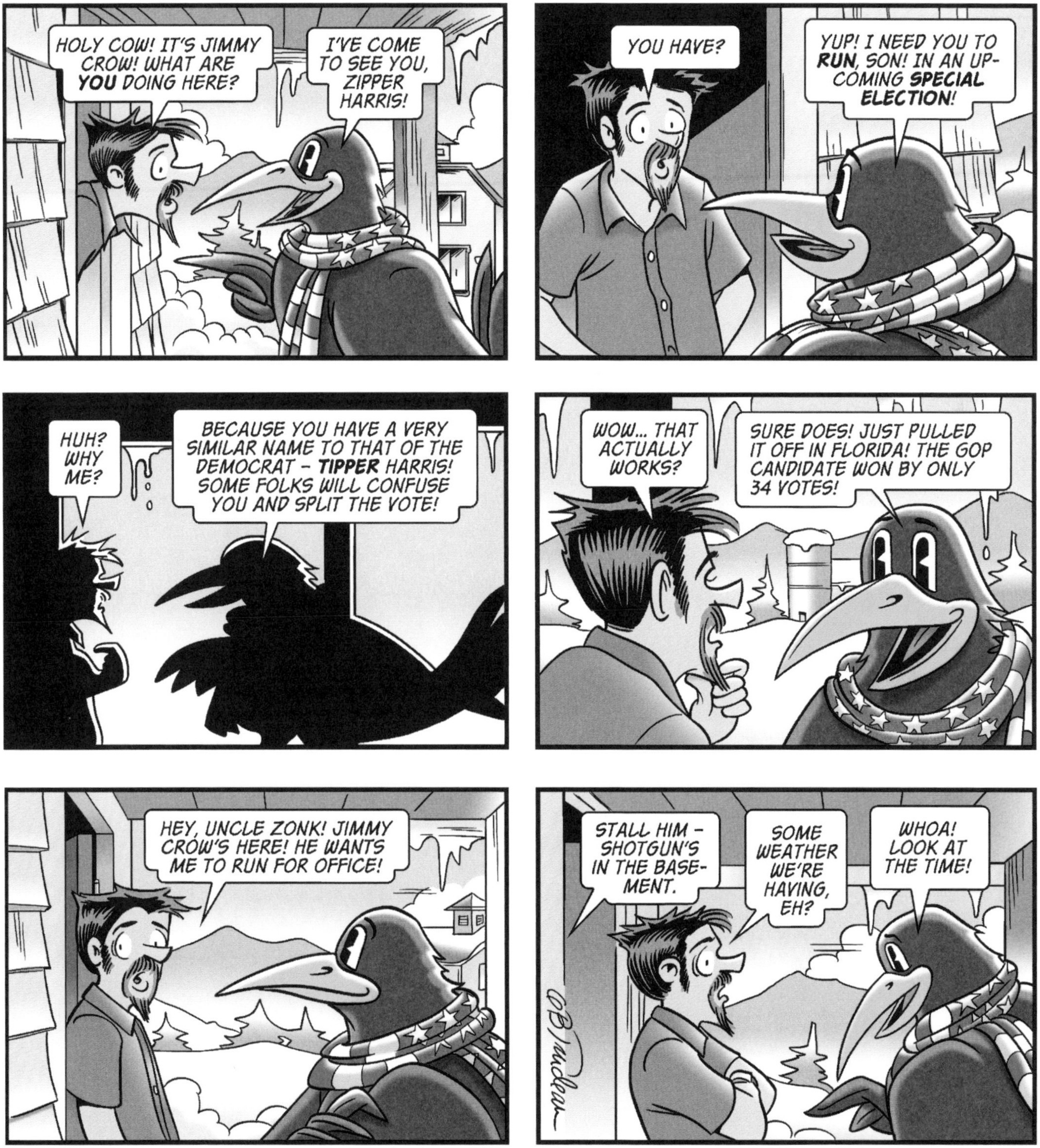
HOLY COW! IT'S JIMMY CROW! WHAT ARE YOU DOING HERE?
I'VE COME TO SEE YOU, ZIPPER HARRIS!
YOU HAVE?
YUP! I NEED YOU TO RUN, SON! IN AN UP-COMING SPECIAL ELECTION!
HUH? WHY ME?
BECAUSE YOU HAVE A VERY SIMILAR NAME TO THAT OF THE DEMOCRAT - TIPPER HARRIS! SOME FOLKS WILL CONFUSE YOU AND SPLIT THE VOTE!
WOW... THAT ACTUALLY WORKS?
SURE DOES! JUST PULLED IT OFF IN FLORIDA! THE GOP CANDIDATE WON BY ONLY 34 VOTES!
HEY, UNCLE ZONK! JIMMY CROW'S HERE! HE WANTS ME TO RUN FOR OFFICE!
STALL HIM - SHOTGUN'S IN THE BASE-MENT.
SOME WEATHER WE'RE HAVING, EH?
WHOA! LOOK AT THE TIME!

December 27, 2020

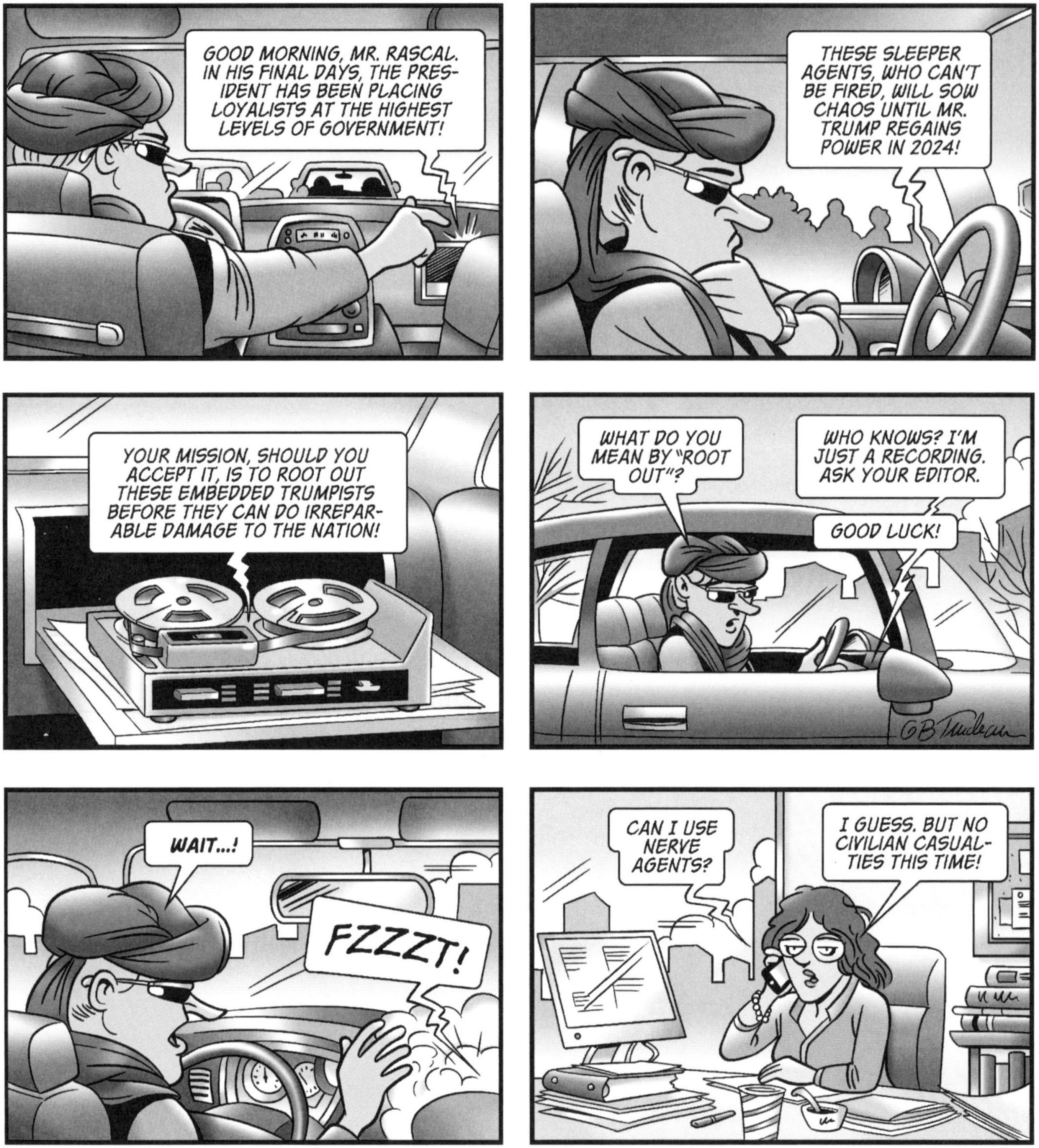
GOOD MORNING, MR. RASCAL. IN HIS FINAL DAYS, THE PRES-IDENT HAS BEEN PLACING LOYALISTS AT THE HIGHEST LEVELS OF GOVERNMENT!
THESE SLEEPER AGENTS, WHO CAN'T BE FIRED, WILL SOW CHAOS UNTIL MR. TRUMP REGAINS POWER IN 2024!
YOUR MISSION, SHOULD YOU ACCEPT IT, IS TO ROOT OUT THESE EMBEDDED TRUMPISTS BEFORE THEY CAN DO IRREPAR-ABLE DAMAGE TO THE NATION!
WHAT DO YOU MEAN BY "ROOT OUT"?
WHO KNOWS? I'M JUST A RECORDING. ASK YOUR EDITOR.
GOOD LUCK!
WAIT...!
FZZZZT!
CAN I USE NERVE AGENTS?
I GUESS. BUT NO CIVILIAN CASUAL-TIES THIS TIME!

January 3, 2021

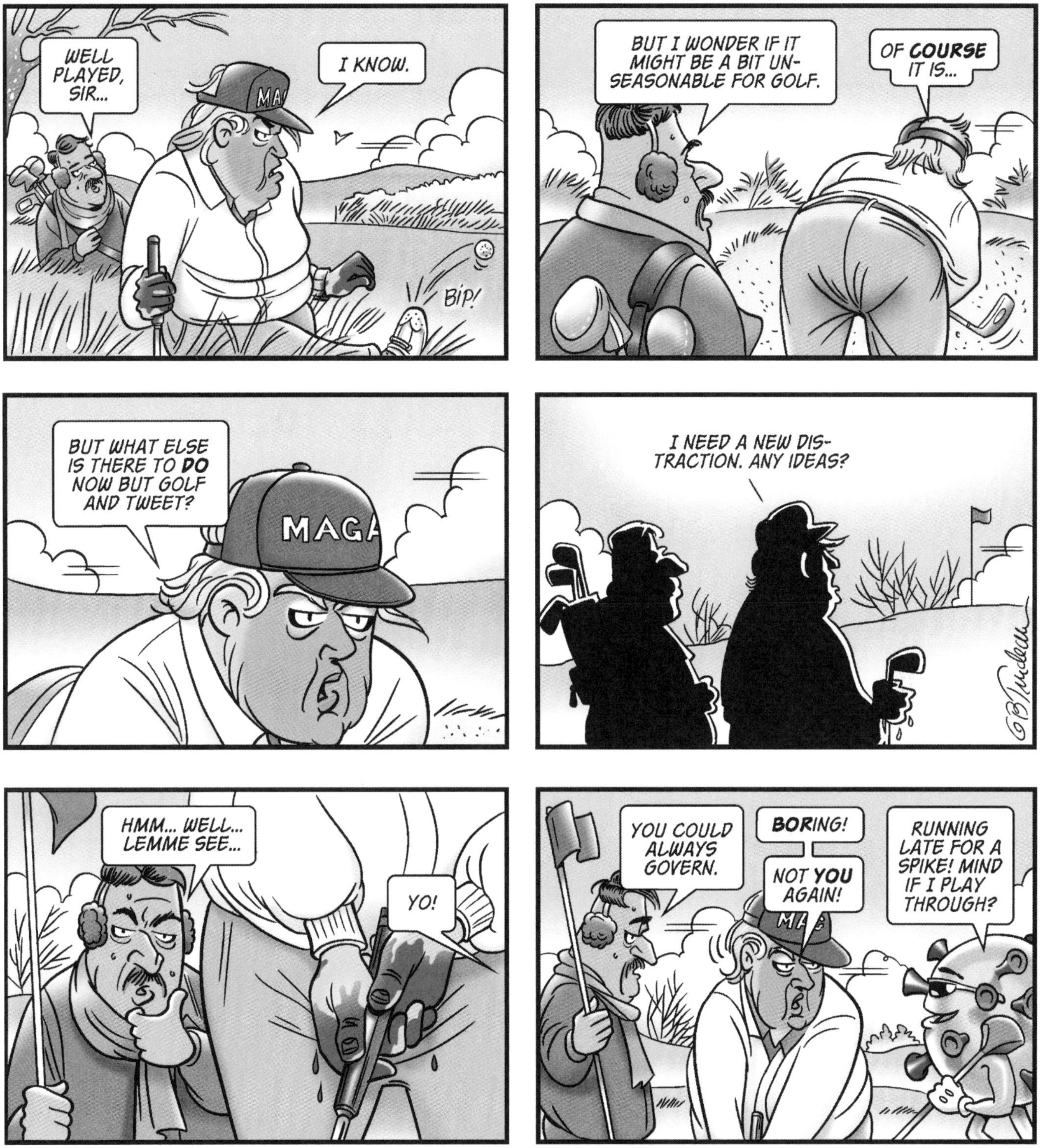
WELL PLAYED, SIR...
I KNOW.
BIP!
BUT I WONDER IF IT MIGHT BE A BIT UN-SEASONABLE FOR GOLF.
OF COURSE IT IS...
BUT WHAT ELSE IS THERE TO DO NOW BUT GOLF AND TWEET?
MAGA
I NEED A NEW DIS-TRACTION. ANY IDEAS?
HMM... WELL... LEMME SEE...
YO!
YOU COULD ALWAYS GOVERN.
BORING!
NOT YOU AGAIN!
RUNNING LATE FOR A SPIKE! MIND IF I PLAY THROUGH?

January 10, 2021

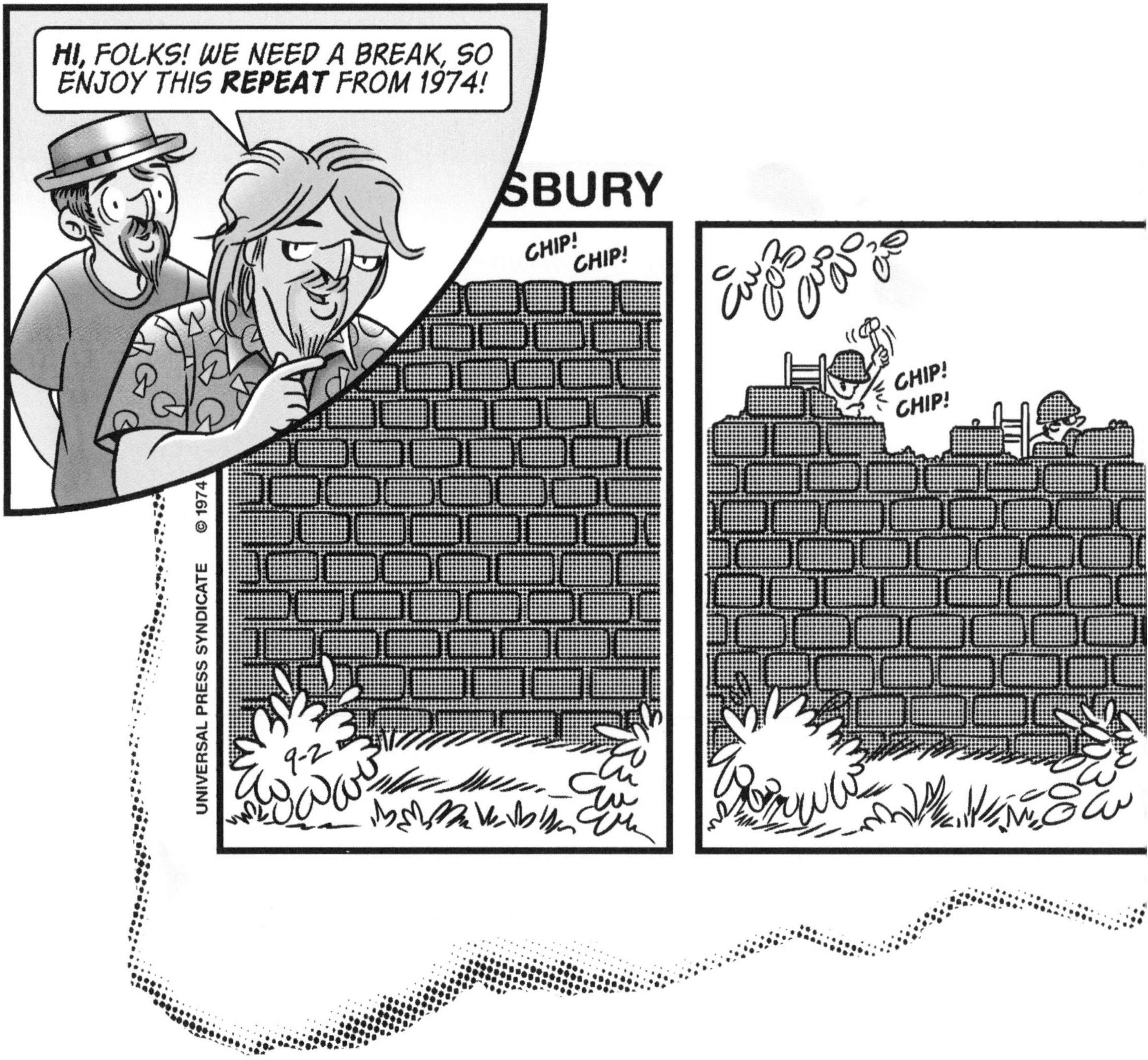
HI, FOLKS! WE NEED A BREAK, SO ENJOY THIS REPEAT FROM 1974!
SBURY
CHIP! CHIP!
CHIP! CHIP!
UNIVERSAL PRESS SYNDICATE © 1974
9-2

by Garry Trudeau

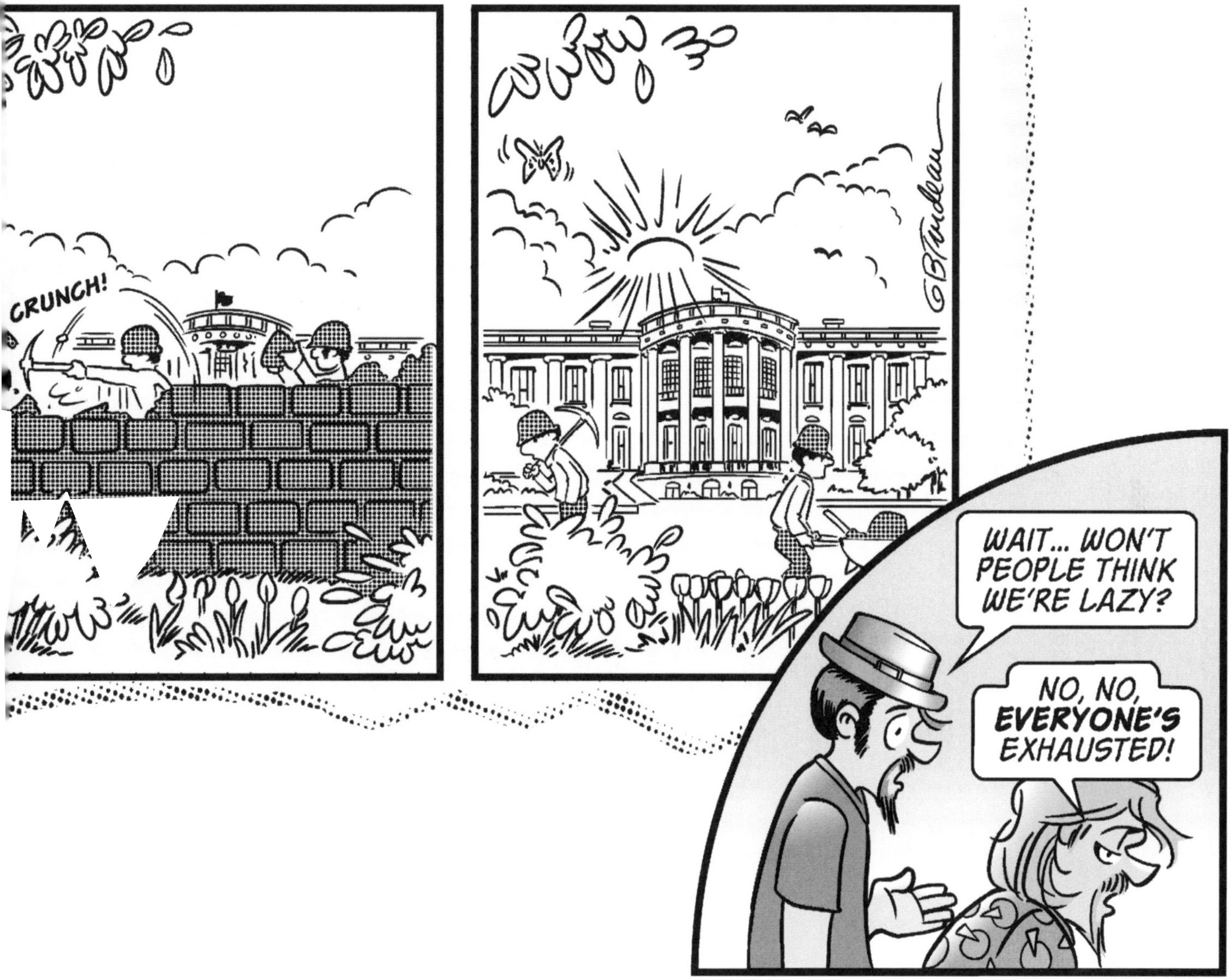

CRUNCH!
GBTrudeau
WAIT... WON'T PEOPLE THINK WE'RE LAZY?
NO, NO, **EVERYONE'S** EXHAUSTED!

January 24, 2021

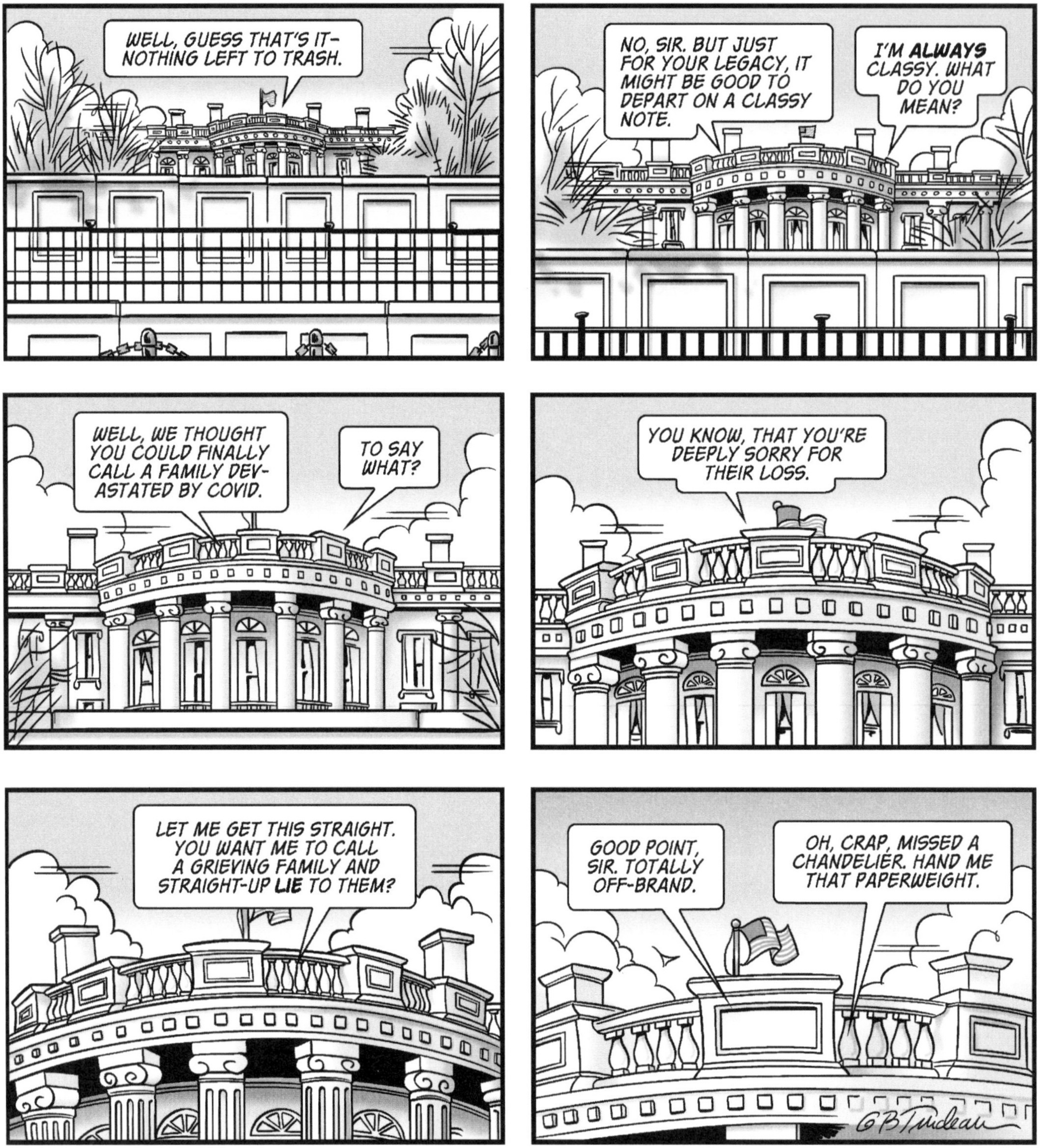
WELL, GUESS THAT'S IT– NOTHING LEFT TO TRASH.
NO, SIR. BUT JUST FOR YOUR LEGACY, IT MIGHT BE GOOD TO DEPART ON A CLASSY NOTE.
I'M **ALWAYS** CLASSY. WHAT DO YOU MEAN?
WELL, WE THOUGHT YOU COULD FINALLY CALL A FAMILY DEV-ASTATED BY COVID.
TO SAY WHAT?
YOU KNOW, THAT YOU'RE DEEPLY SORRY FOR THEIR LOSS.
LET ME GET THIS STRAIGHT. YOU WANT ME TO CALL A GRIEVING FAMILY AND STRAIGHT-UP **LIE** TO THEM?
GOOD POINT, SIR. TOTALLY OFF-BRAND.
OH, CRAP, MISSED A CHANDELIER. HAND ME THAT PAPERWEIGHT.
GBTrudeau

January 17, 2021

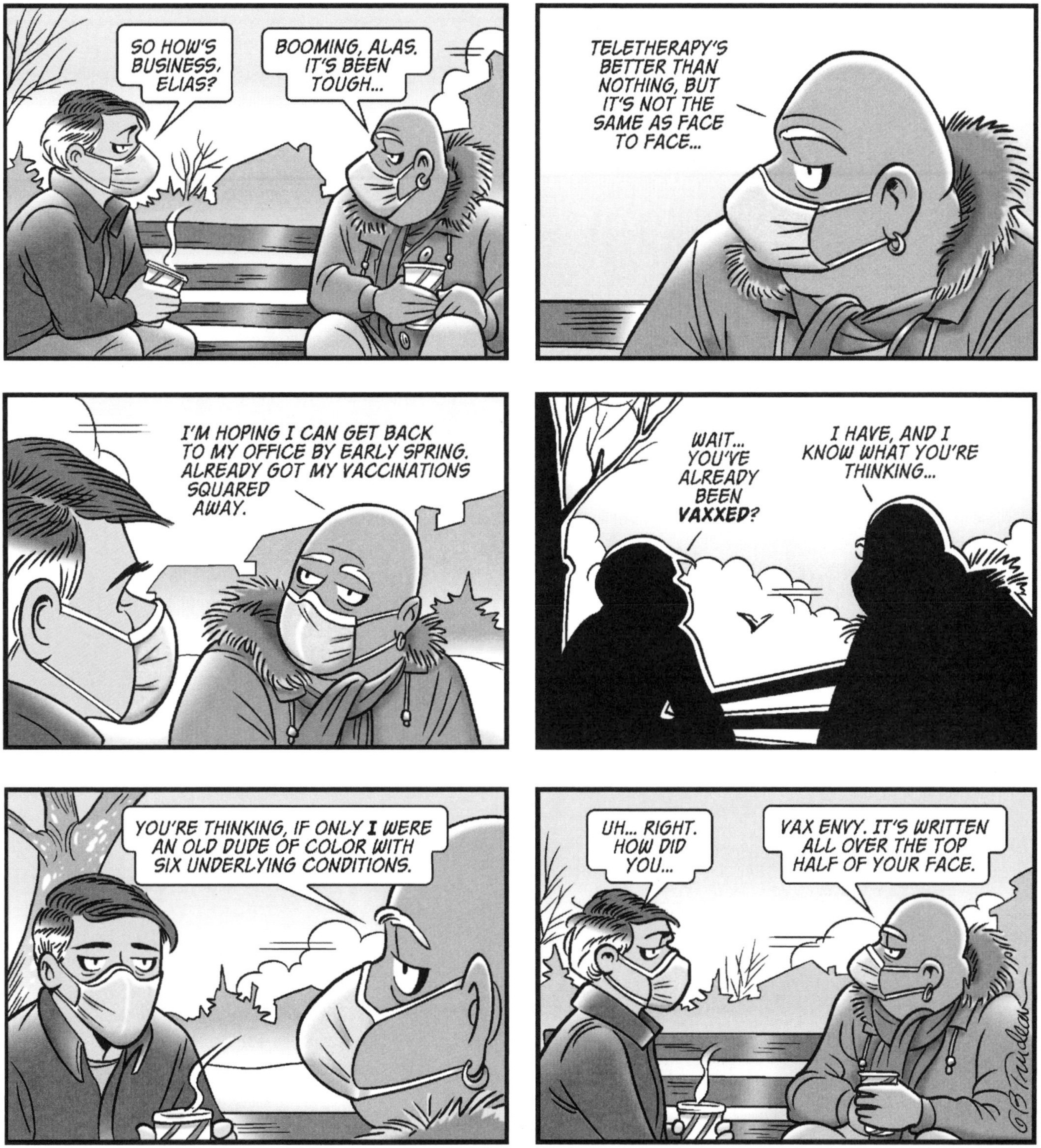
SO HOW'S BUSINESS, ELIAS?
BOOMING, ALAS. IT'S BEEN TOUGH...
TELETHERAPY'S BETTER THAN NOTHING, BUT IT'S NOT THE SAME AS FACE TO FACE...
I'M HOPING I CAN GET BACK TO MY OFFICE BY EARLY SPRING. ALREADY GOT MY VACCINATIONS SQUARED AWAY.
WAIT... YOU'VE ALREADY BEEN **VAXXED**?
I HAVE, AND I KNOW WHAT YOU'RE THINKING...
YOU'RE THINKING, IF ONLY **I** WERE AN OLD DUDE OF COLOR WITH SIX UNDERLYING CONDITIONS.
UH... RIGHT. HOW DID YOU...
VAX ENVY. IT'S WRITTEN ALL OVER THE TOP HALF OF YOUR FACE.
©B Trudeau

January 31, 2021

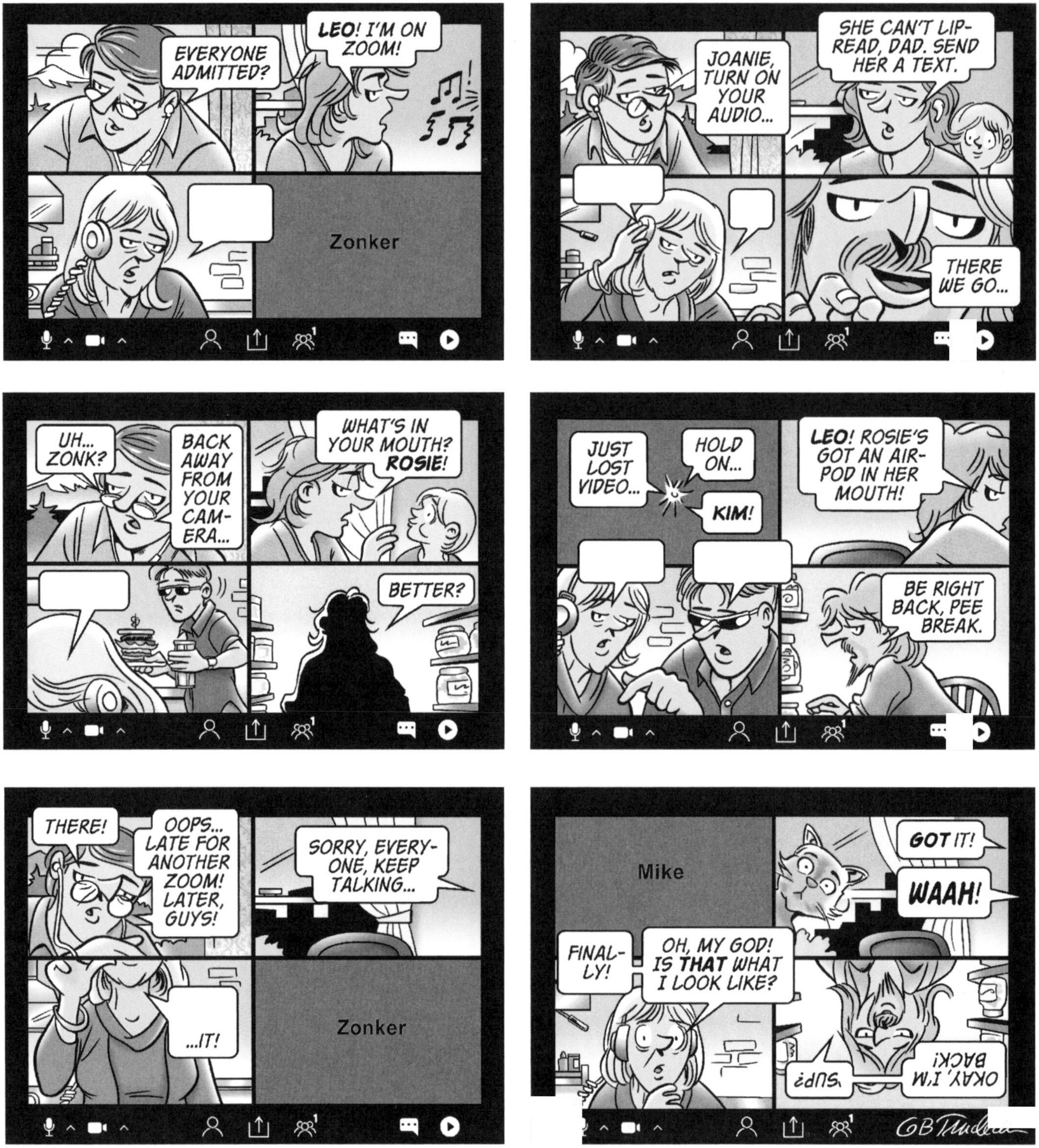
EVERYONE ADMITTED?
LEO! I'M ON ZOOM!
Zonker
JOANIE, TURN ON YOUR AUDIO...
SHE CAN'T LIP-READ, DAD. SEND HER A TEXT.
THERE WE GO...
UH... ZONK?
BACK AWAY FROM YOUR CAM-ERA...
WHAT'S IN YOUR MOUTH? ROSIE!
BETTER?
JUST LOST VIDEO...
HOLD ON...
KIM!
LEO! ROSIE'S GOT AN AIR-POD IN HER MOUTH!
BE RIGHT BACK, PEE BREAK.
THERE!
OOPS... LATE FOR ANOTHER ZOOM! LATER, GUYS!
SORRY, EVERY-ONE, KEEP TALKING...
...IT!
Zonker
Mike
GOT IT!
WAAH!
FINAL-LY!
OH, MY GOD! IS THAT WHAT I LOOK LIKE?
OKAY, I'M BACK!
'SUP?

February 7, 2021

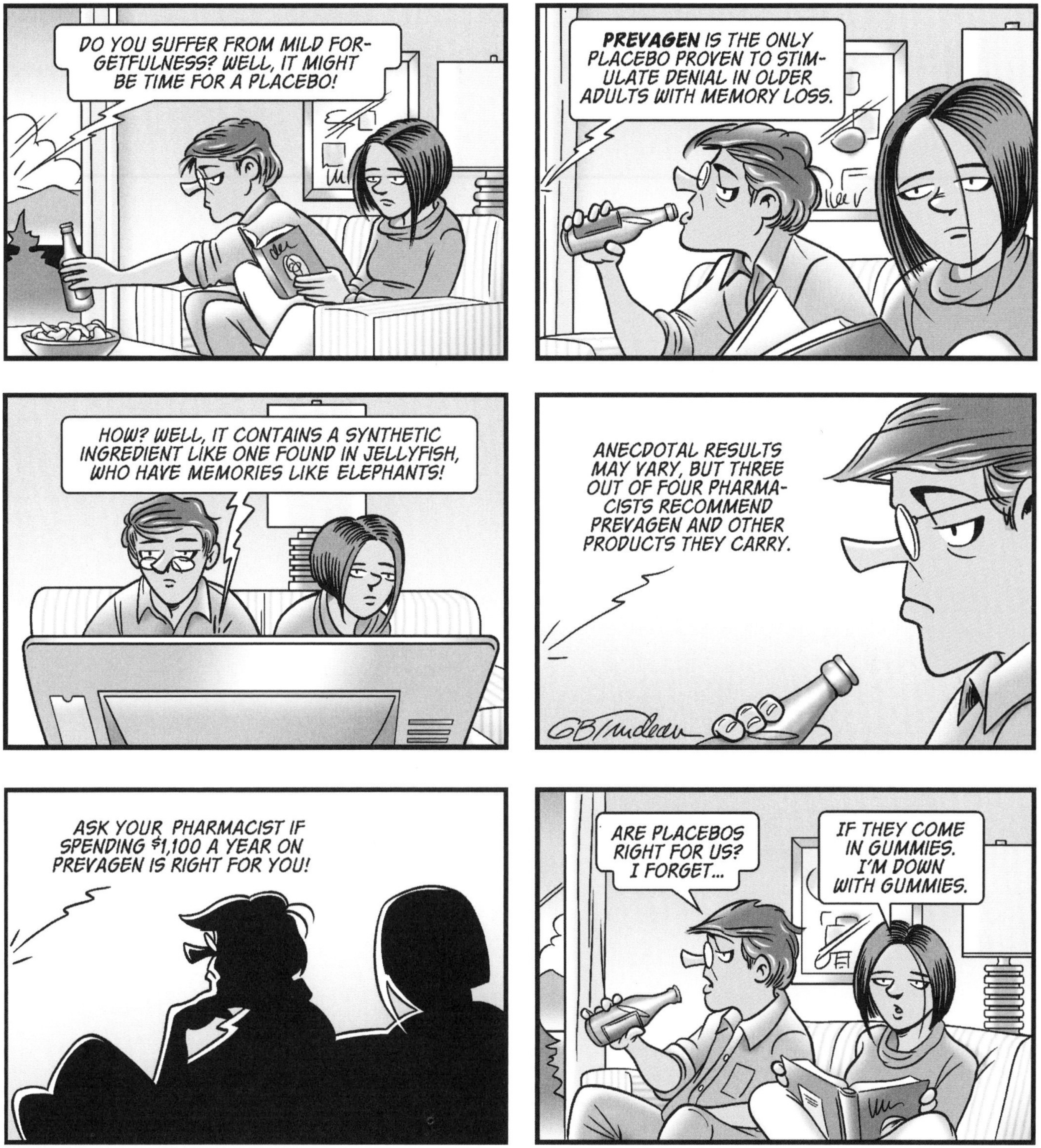
DO YOU SUFFER FROM MILD FORGETFULNESS? WELL, IT MIGHT BE TIME FOR A PLACEBO!
PREVAGEN IS THE ONLY PLACEBO PROVEN TO STIMULATE DENIAL IN OLDER ADULTS WITH MEMORY LOSS.
HOW? WELL, IT CONTAINS A SYNTHETIC INGREDIENT LIKE ONE FOUND IN JELLYFISH, WHO HAVE MEMORIES LIKE ELEPHANTS!
ANECDOTAL RESULTS MAY VARY, BUT THREE OUT OF FOUR PHARMACISTS RECOMMEND PREVAGEN AND OTHER PRODUCTS THEY CARRY.
GBTrudeau
ASK YOUR PHARMACIST IF SPENDING $1,100 A YEAR ON PREVAGEN IS RIGHT FOR YOU!
ARE PLACEBOS RIGHT FOR US? I FORGET...
IF THEY COME IN GUMMIES. I'M DOWN WITH GUMMIES.

February 14, 2021

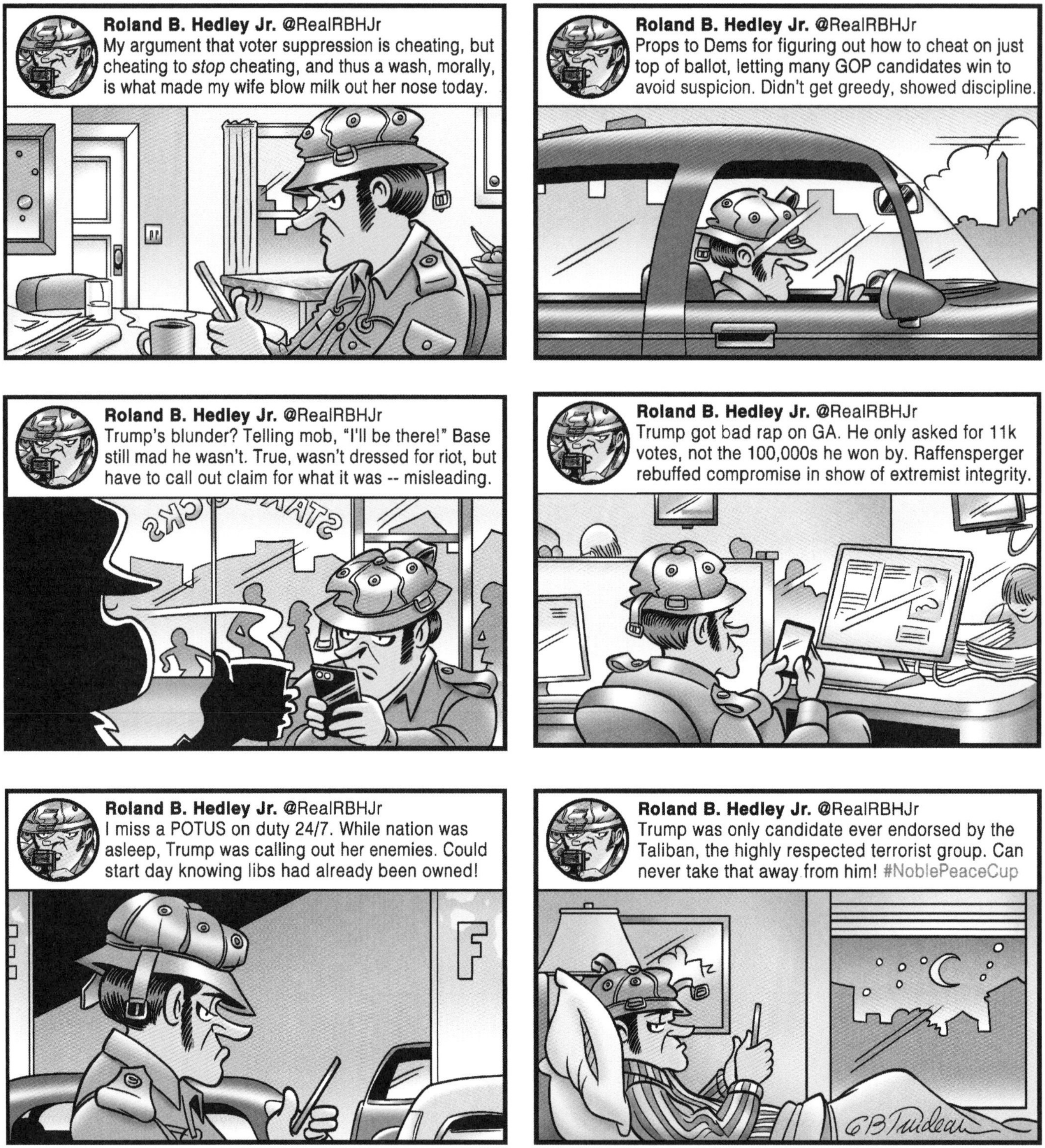
Roland B. Hedley Jr. @RealRBHJr
My argument that voter suppression is cheating, but cheating to *stop* cheating, and thus a wash, morally, is what made my wife blow milk out her nose today.
Roland B. Hedley Jr. @RealRBHJr
Props to Dems for figuring out how to cheat on just top of ballot, letting many GOP candidates win to avoid suspicion. Didn't get greedy, showed discipline.
Roland B. Hedley Jr. @RealRBHJr
Trump's blunder? Telling mob, "I'll be there!" Base still mad he wasn't. True, wasn't dressed for riot, but have to call out claim for what it was -- misleading.
Roland B. Hedley Jr. @RealRBHJr
Trump got bad rap on GA. He only asked for 11k votes, not the 100,000s he won by. Raffensperger rebuffed compromise in show of extremist integrity.
Roland B. Hedley Jr. @RealRBHJr
I miss a POTUS on duty 24/7. While nation was asleep, Trump was calling out her enemies. Could start day knowing libs had already been owned!
Roland B. Hedley Jr. @RealRBHJr
Trump was only candidate ever endorsed by the Taliban, the highly respected terrorist group. Can never take that away from him! #NoblePeaceCup

February 21, 2021

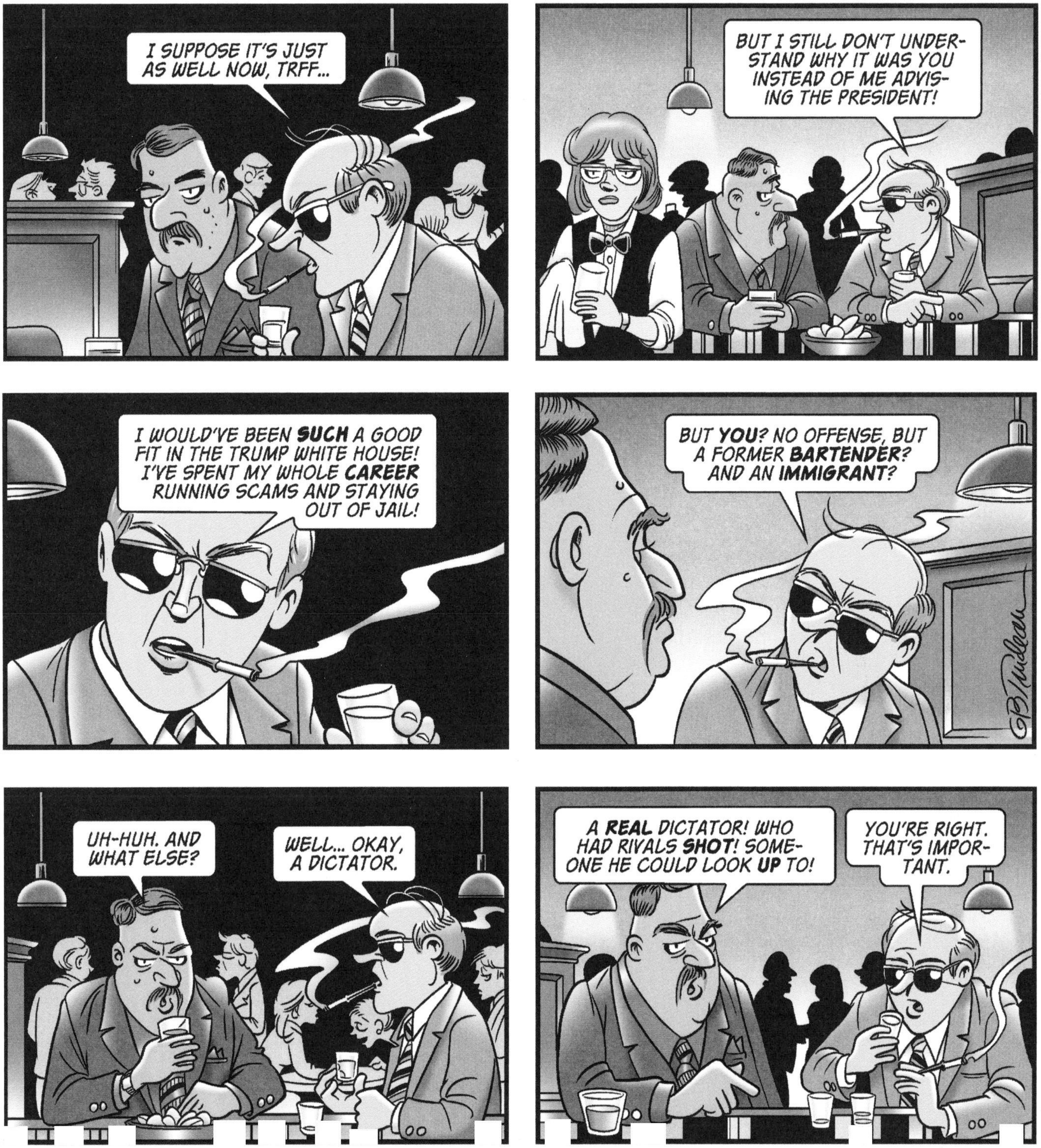
I SUPPOSE IT'S JUST AS WELL NOW, TRFF...
BUT I STILL DON'T UNDER-STAND WHY IT WAS YOU INSTEAD OF ME ADVIS-ING THE PRESIDENT!
I WOULD'VE BEEN **SUCH** A GOOD FIT IN THE TRUMP WHITE HOUSE! I'VE SPENT MY WHOLE **CAREER** RUNNING SCAMS AND STAYING OUT OF JAIL!
BUT **YOU**? NO OFFENSE, BUT A FORMER **BARTENDER**? AND AN **IMMIGRANT**?
UH-HUH. AND WHAT ELSE?
WELL... OKAY, A DICTATOR.
A **REAL** DICTATOR! WHO HAD RIVALS **SHOT**! SOME-ONE HE COULD LOOK **UP** TO!
YOU'RE RIGHT. THAT'S IMPOR-TANT.

February 28, 2021

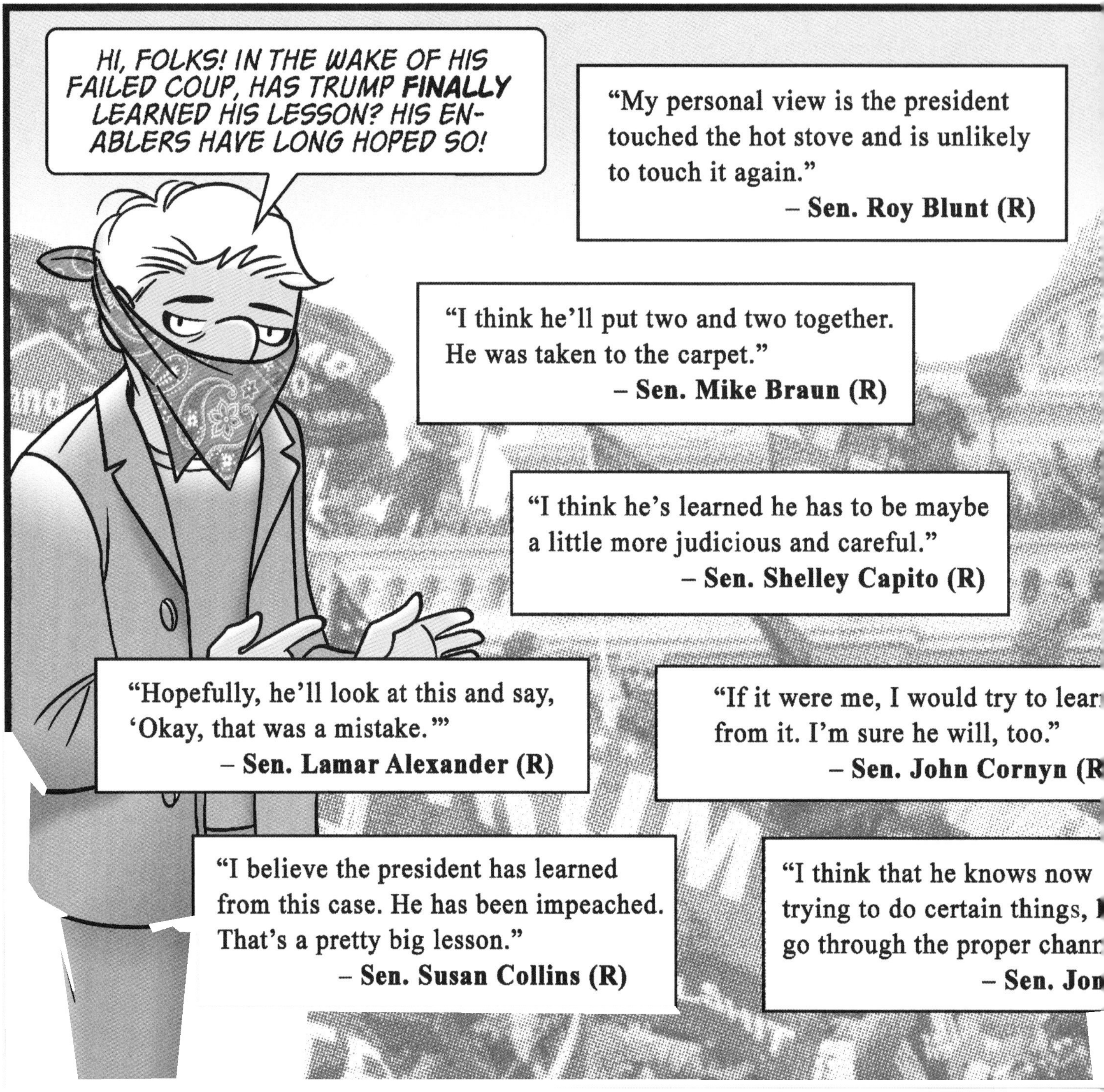
HI, FOLKS! IN THE WAKE OF HIS FAILED COUP, HAS TRUMP **FINALLY** LEARNED HIS LESSON? HIS EN-ABLERS HAVE LONG HOPED SO!
"My personal view is the president touched the hot stove and is unlikely to touch it again." – Sen. Roy Blunt (R)
"I think he'll put two and two together. He was taken to the carpet." – Sen. Mike Braun (R)
"I think he's learned he has to be maybe a little more judicious and careful." – Sen. Shelley Capito (R)
"Hopefully, he'll look at this and say, 'Okay, that was a mistake.'" – Sen. Lamar Alexander (R)
"If it were me, I would try to lear
from it. I'm sure he will, too." – Sen. John Cornyn (R
"I believe the president has learned from this case. He has been impeached. That's a pretty big lesson." – Sen. Susan Collins (R)
"I think that he knows now
trying to do certain things,
go through the proper chann
– Sen. Jo

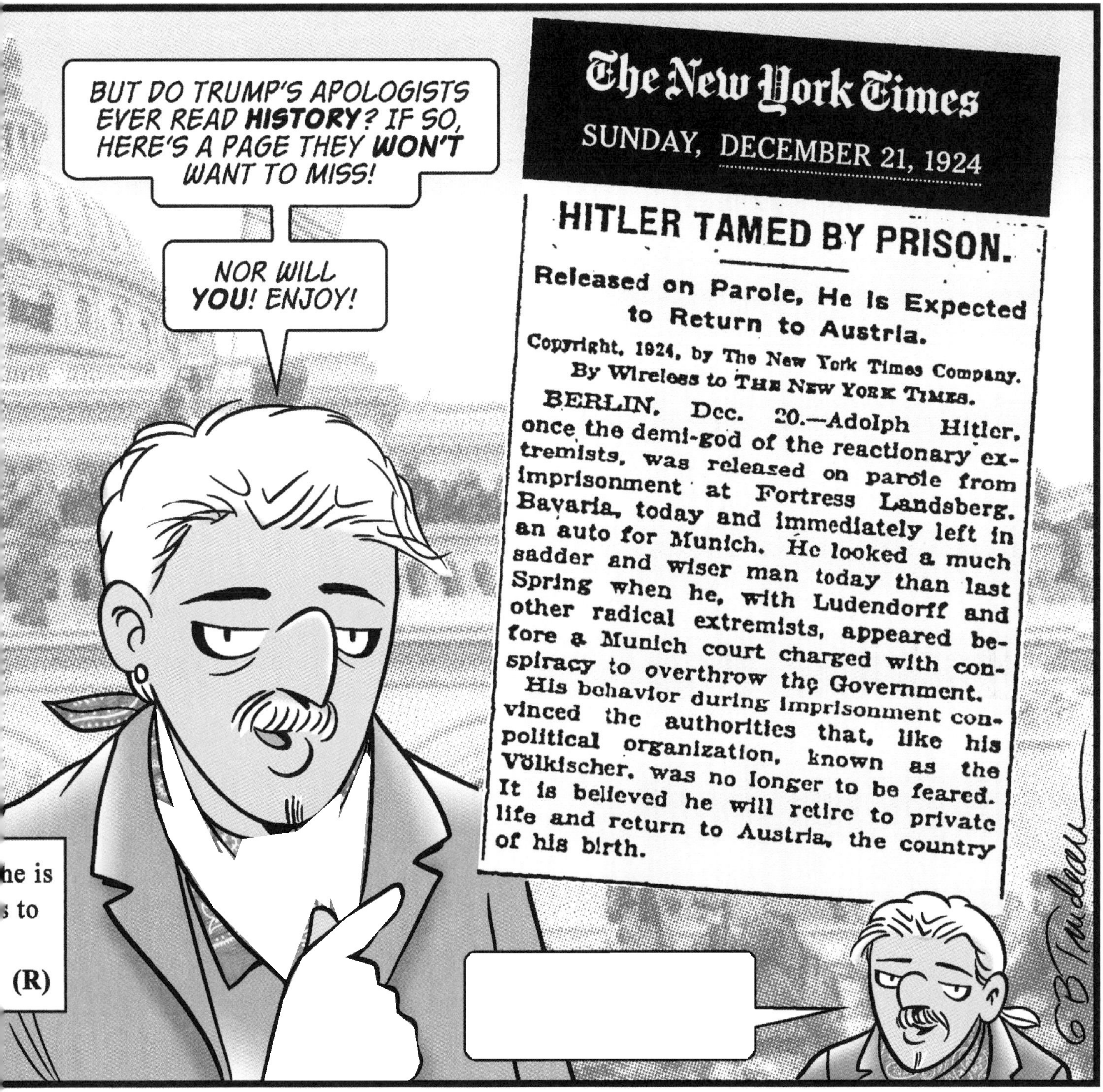
BUT DO TRUMP'S APOLOGISTS EVER READ **HISTORY**? IF SO, HERE'S A PAGE THEY **WON'T** WANT TO MISS!
NOR WILL **YOU**! ENJOY!
The New York Times
SUNDAY, DECEMBER 21, 1924
HITLER TAMED BY PRISON.
Released on Parole, He Is Expected to Return to Austria.
Copyright, 1924, by The New York Times Company.
By Wireless to THE NEW YORK TIMES.
BERLIN, Dec. 20.—Adolph Hitler, once the demi-god of the reactionary extremists, was released on parole from imprisonment at Fortress Landsberg, Bavaria, today and immediately left in an auto for Munich. He looked a much sadder and wiser man today than last Spring when he, with Ludendorff and other radical extremists, appeared before a Munich court charged with conspiracy to overthrow the Government.
His behavior during imprisonment convinced the authorities that, like his political organization, known as the Völkischer, was no longer to be feared. It is believed he will retire to private life and return to Austria, the country of his birth.
(R)

March 7, 2021

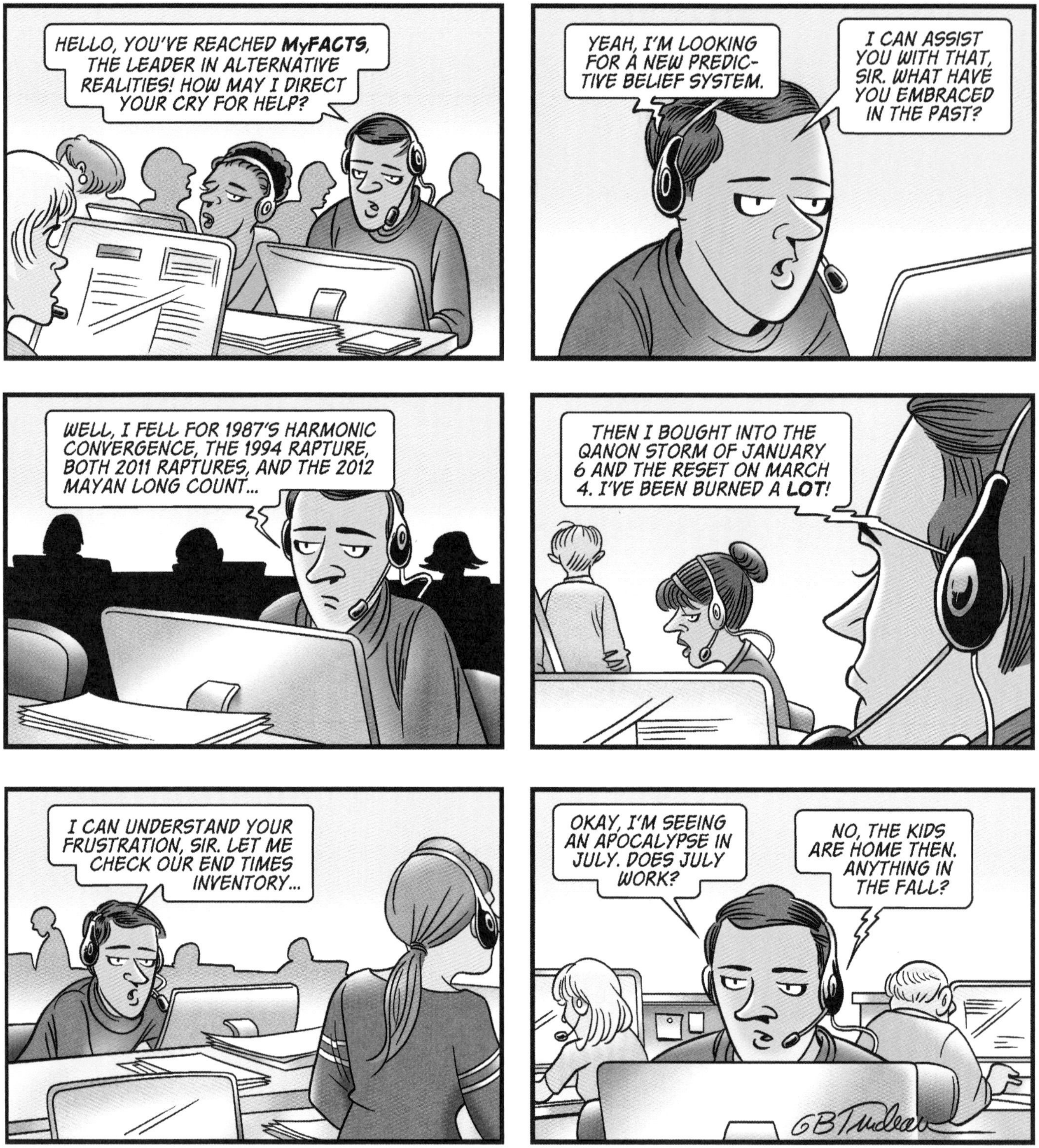
HELLO, YOU'VE REACHED **MyFACTS**, THE LEADER IN ALTERNATIVE REALITIES! HOW MAY I DIRECT YOUR CRY FOR HELP?
YEAH, I'M LOOKING FOR A NEW PREDICTIVE BELIEF SYSTEM.
I CAN ASSIST YOU WITH THAT, SIR. WHAT HAVE YOU EMBRACED IN THE PAST?
WELL, I FELL FOR 1987'S HARMONIC CONVERGENCE, THE 1994 RAPTURE, BOTH 2011 RAPTURES, AND THE 2012 MAYAN LONG COUNT...
THEN I BOUGHT INTO THE QANON STORM OF JANUARY 6 AND THE RESET ON MARCH 4. I'VE BEEN BURNED A **LOT**!
I CAN UNDERSTAND YOUR FRUSTRATION, SIR. LET ME CHECK OUR END TIMES INVENTORY...
OKAY, I'M SEEING AN APOCALYPSE IN JULY. DOES JULY WORK?
NO, THE KIDS ARE HOME THEN. ANYTHING IN THE FALL?
GBTrudeau

March 14, 2021

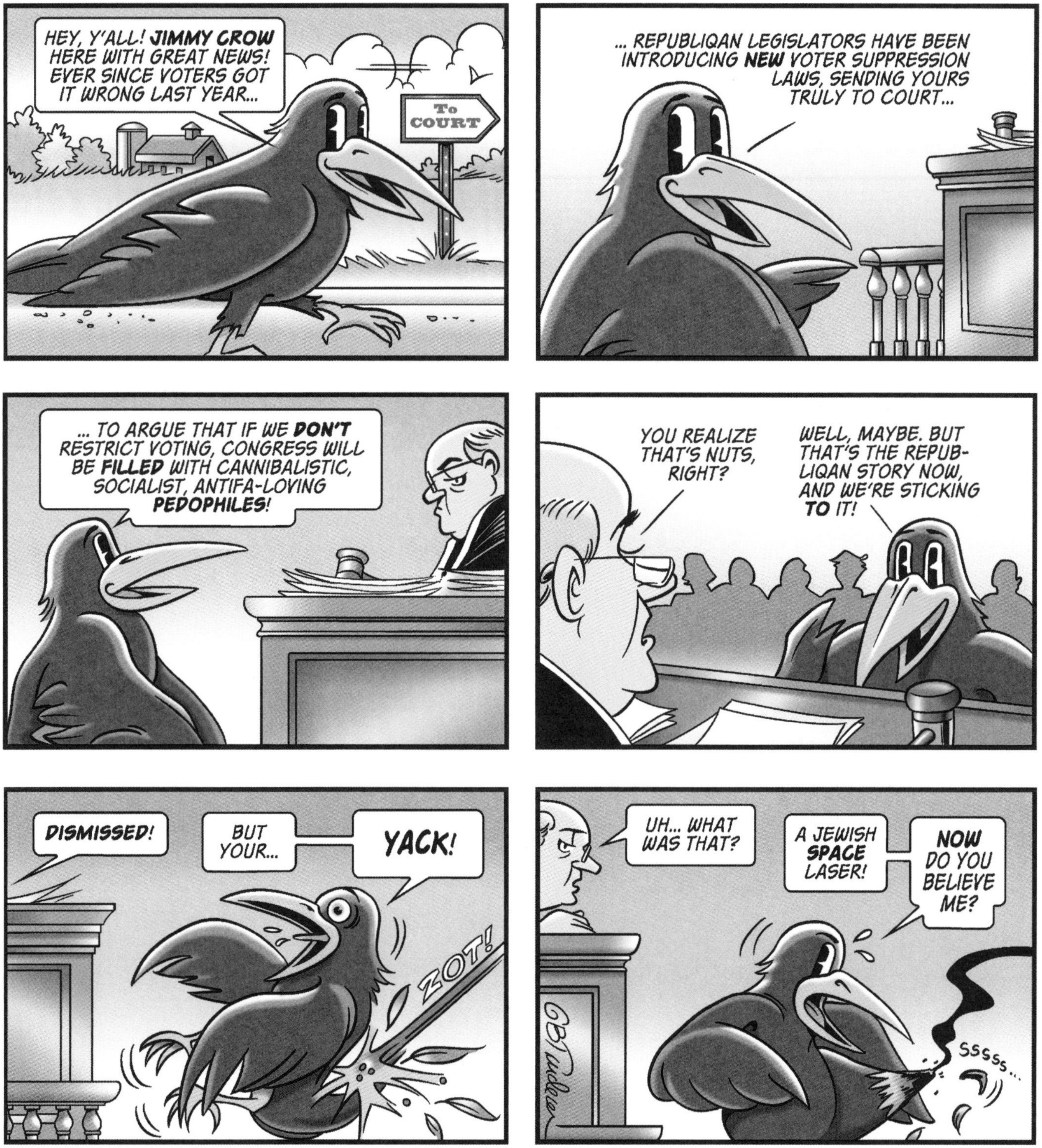
HEY, Y'ALL! JIMMY CROW HERE WITH GREAT NEWS! EVER SINCE VOTERS GOT IT WRONG LAST YEAR...
To COURT
... REPUBLIQAN LEGISLATORS HAVE BEEN INTRODUCING NEW VOTER SUPPRESSION LAWS, SENDING YOURS TRULY TO COURT...
... TO ARGUE THAT IF WE DON'T RESTRICT VOTING, CONGRESS WILL BE FILLED WITH CANNIBALISTIC, SOCIALIST, ANTIFA-LOVING PEDOPHILES!
YOU REALIZE THAT'S NUTS, RIGHT?
WELL, MAYBE. BUT THAT'S THE REPUBLIQAN STORY NOW, AND WE'RE STICKING TO IT!
DISMISSED!
BUT YOUR...
YACK!
ZOT!
UH... WHAT WAS THAT?
A JEWISH SPACE LASER!
NOW DO YOU BELIEVE ME?
SSSSS...
CB Tucker

March 21, 2021

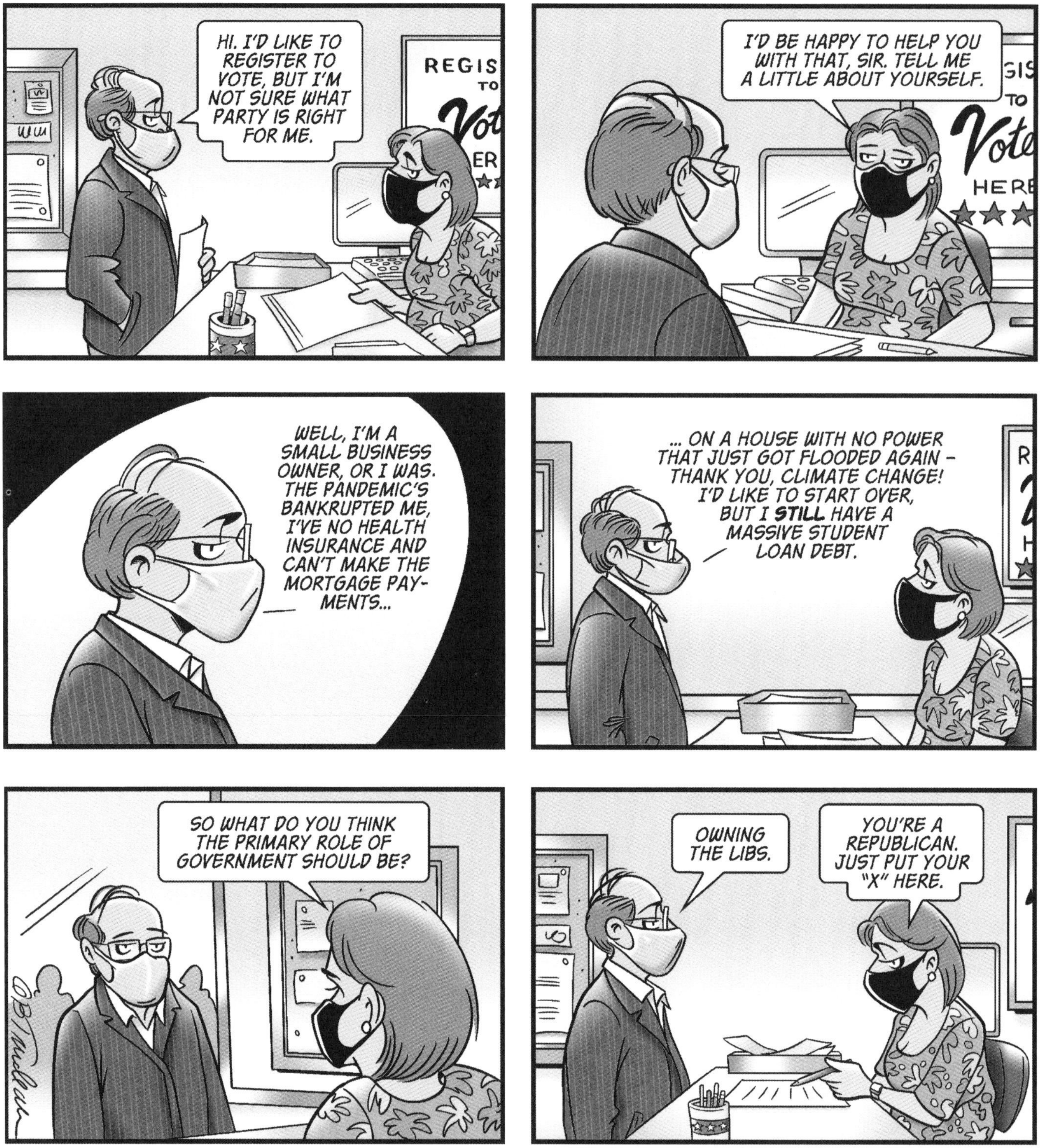

HI. I'D LIKE TO REGISTER TO VOTE, BUT I'M NOT SURE WHAT PARTY IS RIGHT FOR ME.
REGIS TO Vote HERE
I'D BE HAPPY TO HELP YOU WITH THAT, SIR. TELL ME A LITTLE ABOUT YOURSELF.
WELL, I'M A SMALL BUSINESS OWNER, OR I WAS. THE PANDEMIC'S BANKRUPTED ME, I'VE NO HEALTH INSURANCE AND CAN'T MAKE THE MORTGAGE PAY-MENTS...
... ON A HOUSE WITH NO POWER THAT JUST GOT FLOODED AGAIN – THANK YOU, CLIMATE CHANGE! I'D LIKE TO START OVER, BUT I **STILL** HAVE A MASSIVE STUDENT LOAN DEBT.
SO WHAT DO YOU THINK THE PRIMARY ROLE OF GOVERNMENT SHOULD BE?
OWNING THE LIBS.
YOU'RE A REPUBLICAN. JUST PUT YOUR "X" HERE.

March 28, 2021

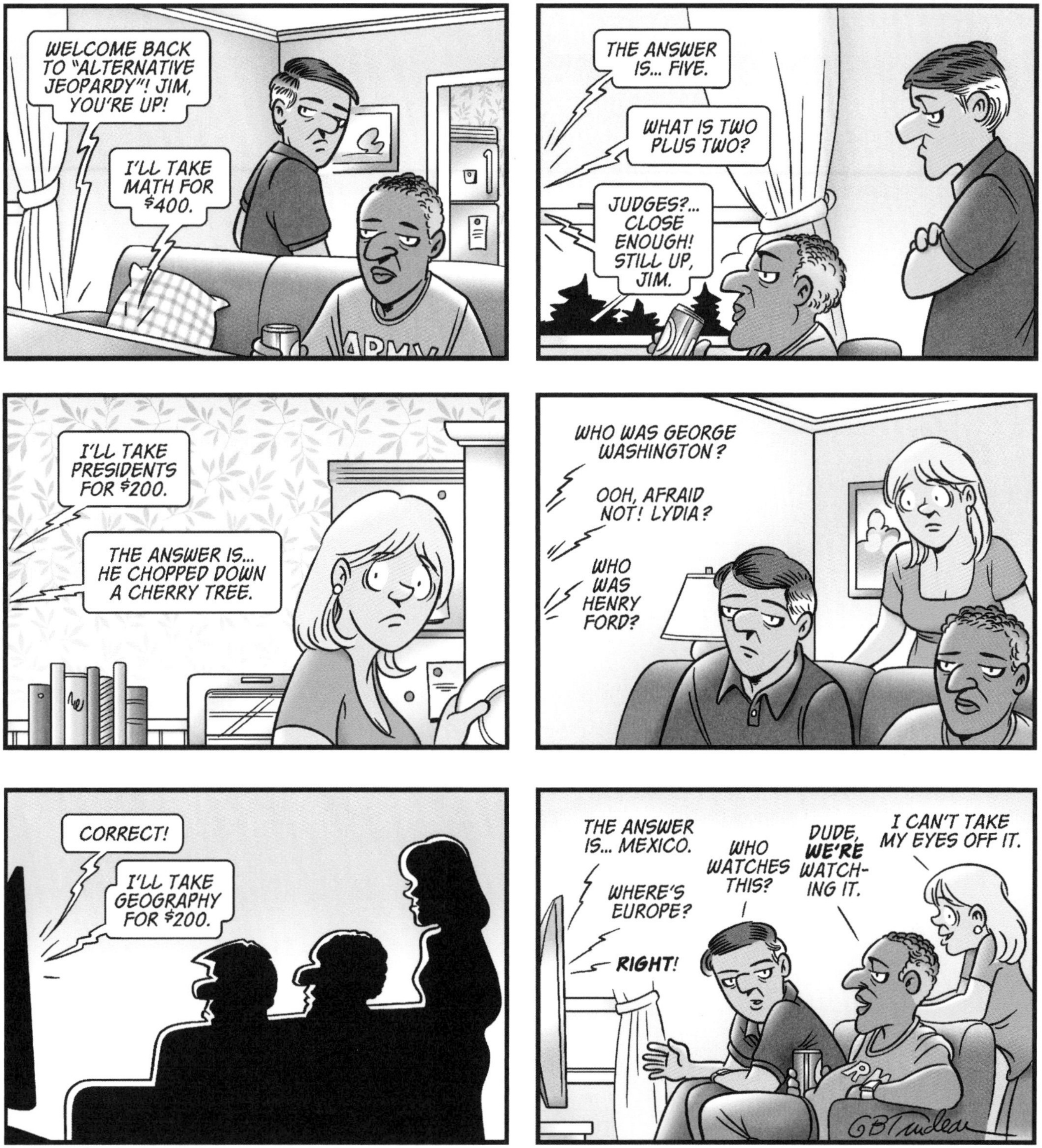
WELCOME BACK TO "ALTERNATIVE JEOPARDY"! JIM, YOU'RE UP!
I'LL TAKE MATH FOR $400.
THE ANSWER IS... FIVE.
WHAT IS TWO PLUS TWO?
JUDGES?... CLOSE ENOUGH! STILL UP, JIM.
I'LL TAKE PRESIDENTS FOR $200.
THE ANSWER IS... HE CHOPPED DOWN A CHERRY TREE.
WHO WAS GEORGE WASHINGTON?
OOH, AFRAID NOT! LYDIA?
WHO WAS HENRY FORD?
CORRECT!
I'LL TAKE GEOGRAPHY FOR $200.
THE ANSWER IS... MEXICO.
WHERE'S EUROPE?
RIGHT!
WHO WATCHES THIS?
DUDE, WE'RE WATCHING IT.
I CAN'T TAKE MY EYES OFF IT.
GBTrudeau

April 4, 2021

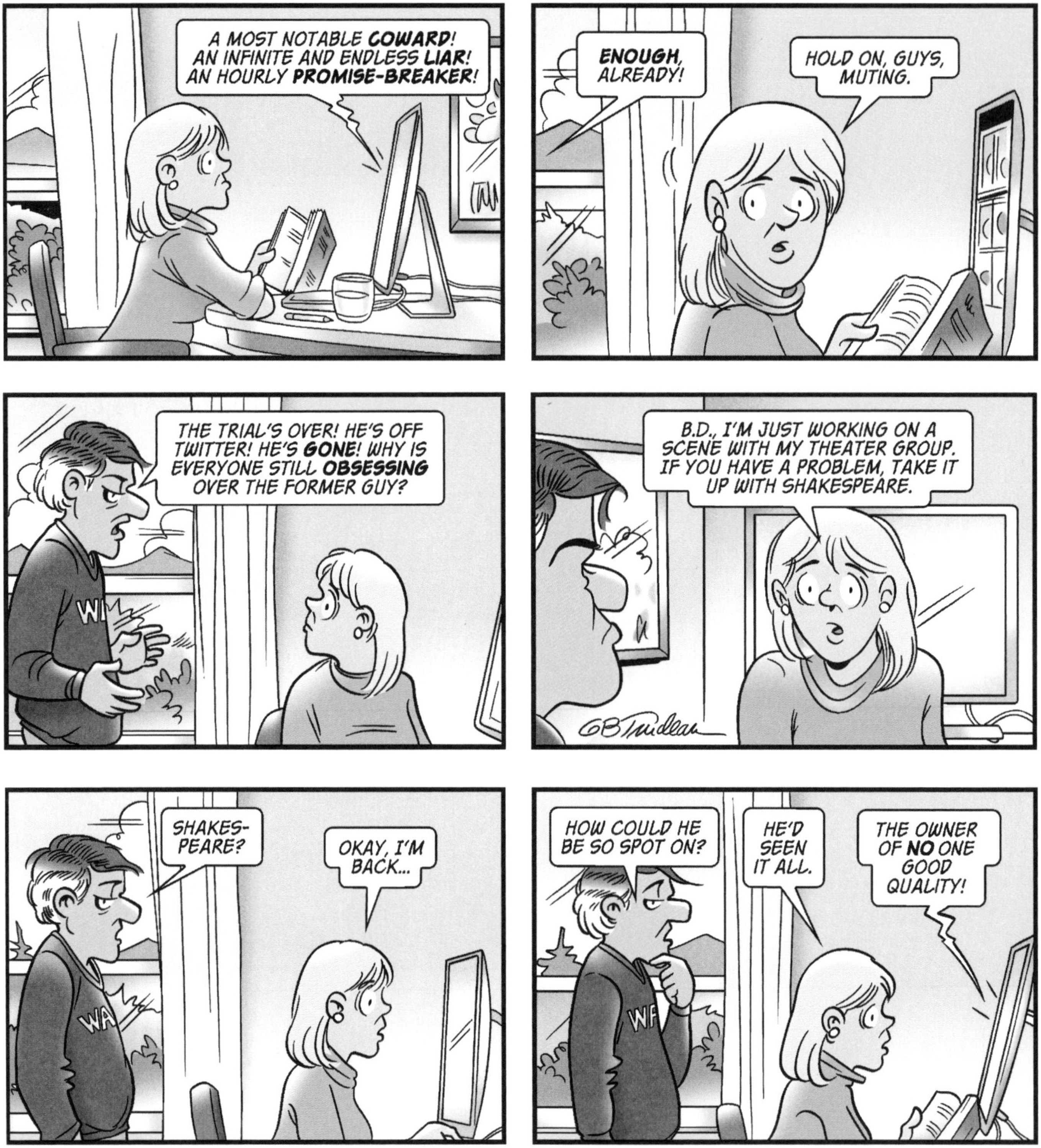
A MOST NOTABLE **COWARD**! AN INFINITE AND ENDLESS **LIAR**! AN HOURLY **PROMISE-BREAKER**!
ENOUGH, ALREADY!
HOLD ON, GUYS, MUTING.
THE TRIAL'S OVER! HE'S OFF TWITTER! HE'S **GONE**! WHY IS EVERYONE STILL **OBSESSING** OVER THE FORMER GUY?
B.D., I'M JUST WORKING ON A SCENE WITH MY THEATER GROUP. IF YOU HAVE A PROBLEM, TAKE IT UP WITH SHAKESPEARE.
GB Trudeau
SHAKES-PEARE?
OKAY, I'M BACK...
HOW COULD HE BE SO SPOT ON?
HE'D SEEN IT ALL.
THE OWNER OF **NO** ONE GOOD QUALITY!

April 11, 2021

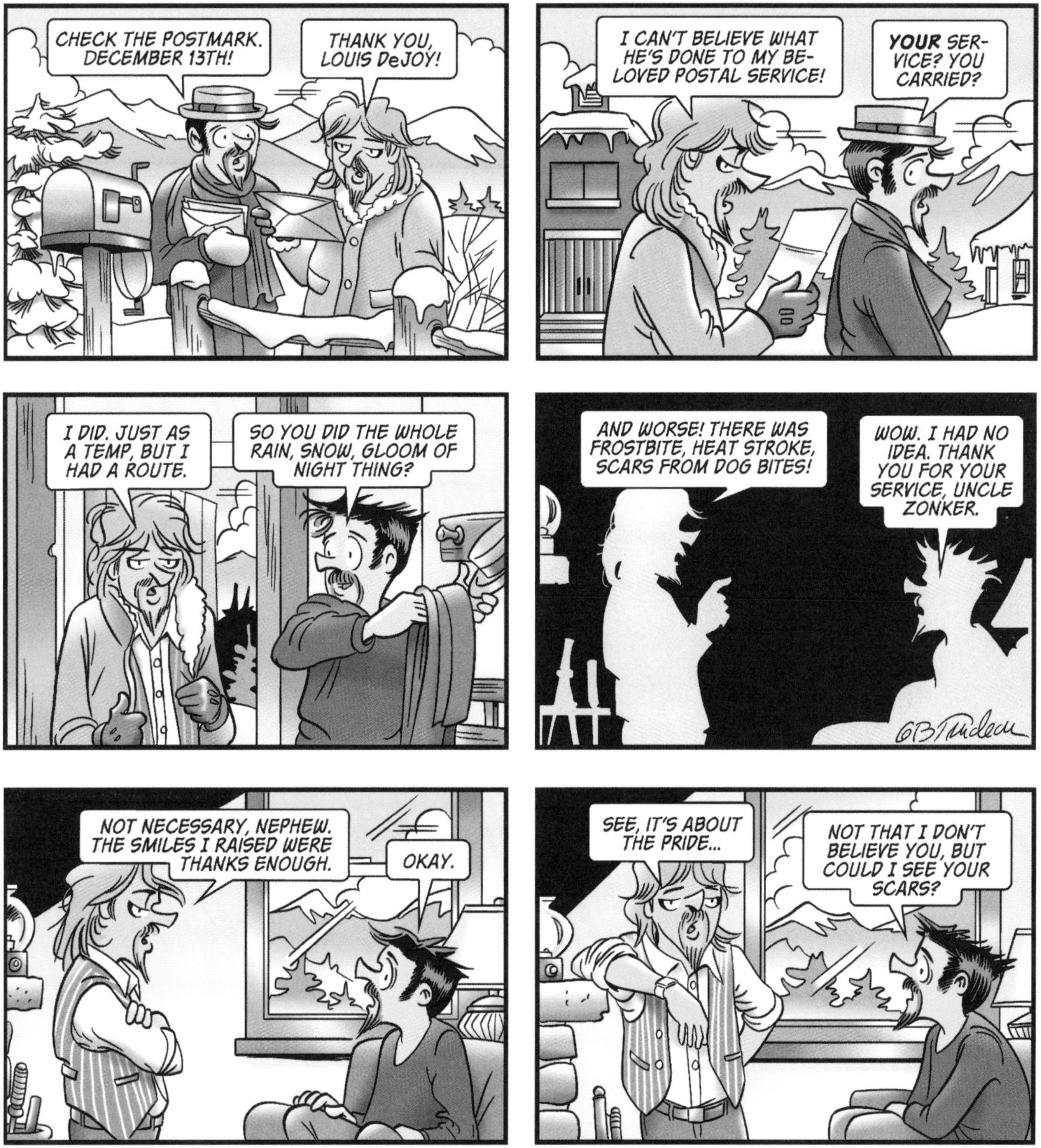
CHECK THE POSTMARK. DECEMBER 13TH!
THANK YOU, LOUIS DeJOY!
I CAN'T BELIEVE WHAT HE'S DONE TO MY BE-LOVED POSTAL SERVICE!
YOUR SER-VICE? YOU CARRIED?
I DID. JUST AS A TEMP, BUT I HAD A ROUTE.
SO YOU DID THE WHOLE RAIN, SNOW, GLOOM OF NIGHT THING?
AND WORSE! THERE WAS FROSTBITE, HEAT STROKE, SCARS FROM DOG BITES!
WOW. I HAD NO IDEA. THANK YOU FOR YOUR SERVICE, UNCLE ZONKER.
GBTrudeau
NOT NECESSARY, NEPHEW. THE SMILES I RAISED WERE THANKS ENOUGH.
OKAY.
SEE, IT'S ABOUT THE PRIDE...
NOT THAT I DON'T BELIEVE YOU, BUT COULD I SEE YOUR SCARS?

April 18, 2021

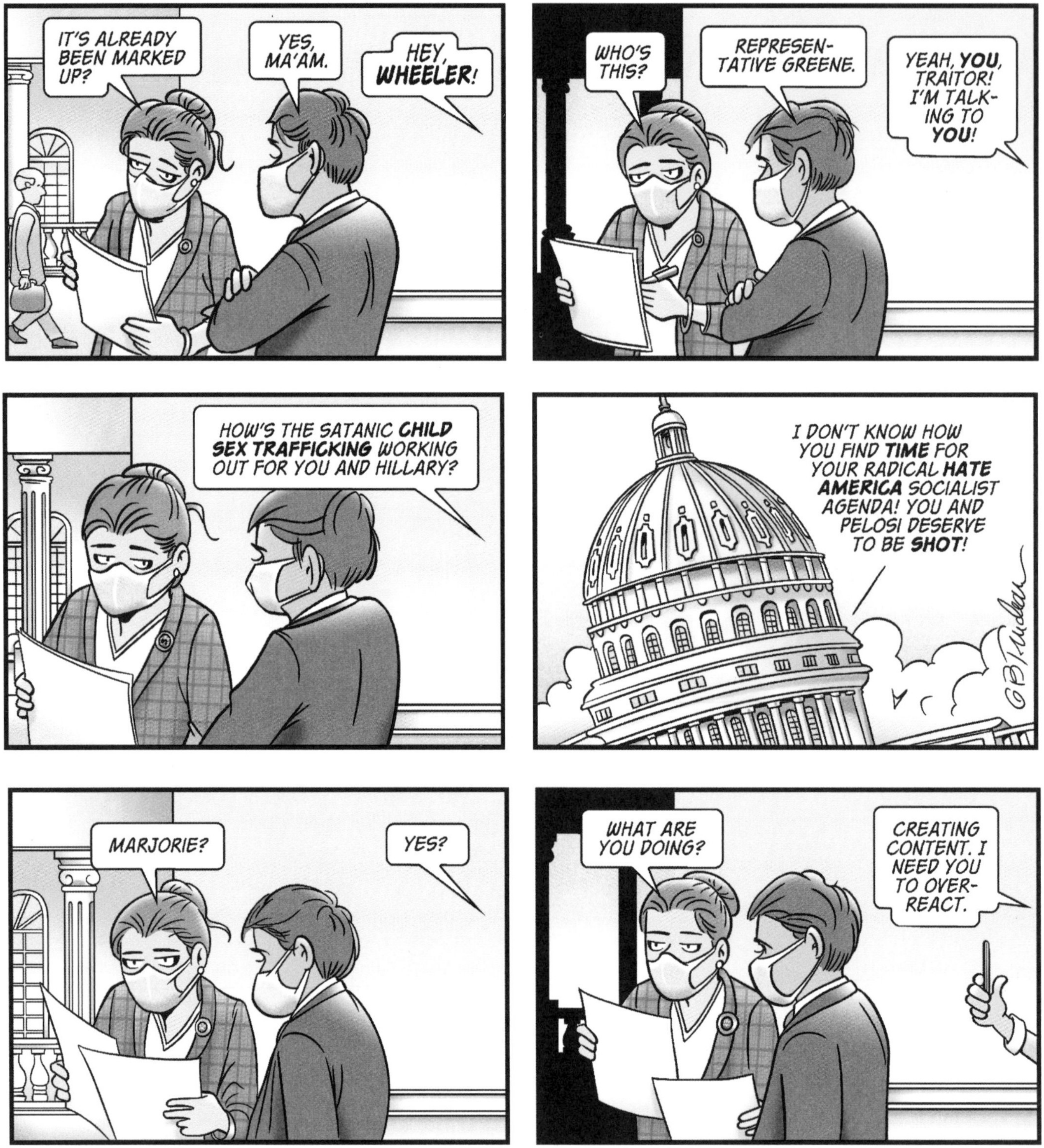
IT'S ALREADY BEEN MARKED UP?
YES, MA'AM.
HEY, WHEELER!
WHO'S THIS?
REPRESEN-TATIVE GREENE.
YEAH, YOU, TRAITOR! I'M TALK-ING TO YOU!
HOW'S THE SATANIC CHILD SEX TRAFFICKING WORKING OUT FOR YOU AND HILLARY?
I DON'T KNOW HOW YOU FIND TIME FOR YOUR RADICAL HATE AMERICA SOCIALIST AGENDA! YOU AND PELOSI DESERVE TO BE SHOT!
GBTrudeau
MARJORIE?
YES?
WHAT ARE YOU DOING?
CREATING CONTENT. I NEED YOU TO OVER-REACT.

April 25, 2021

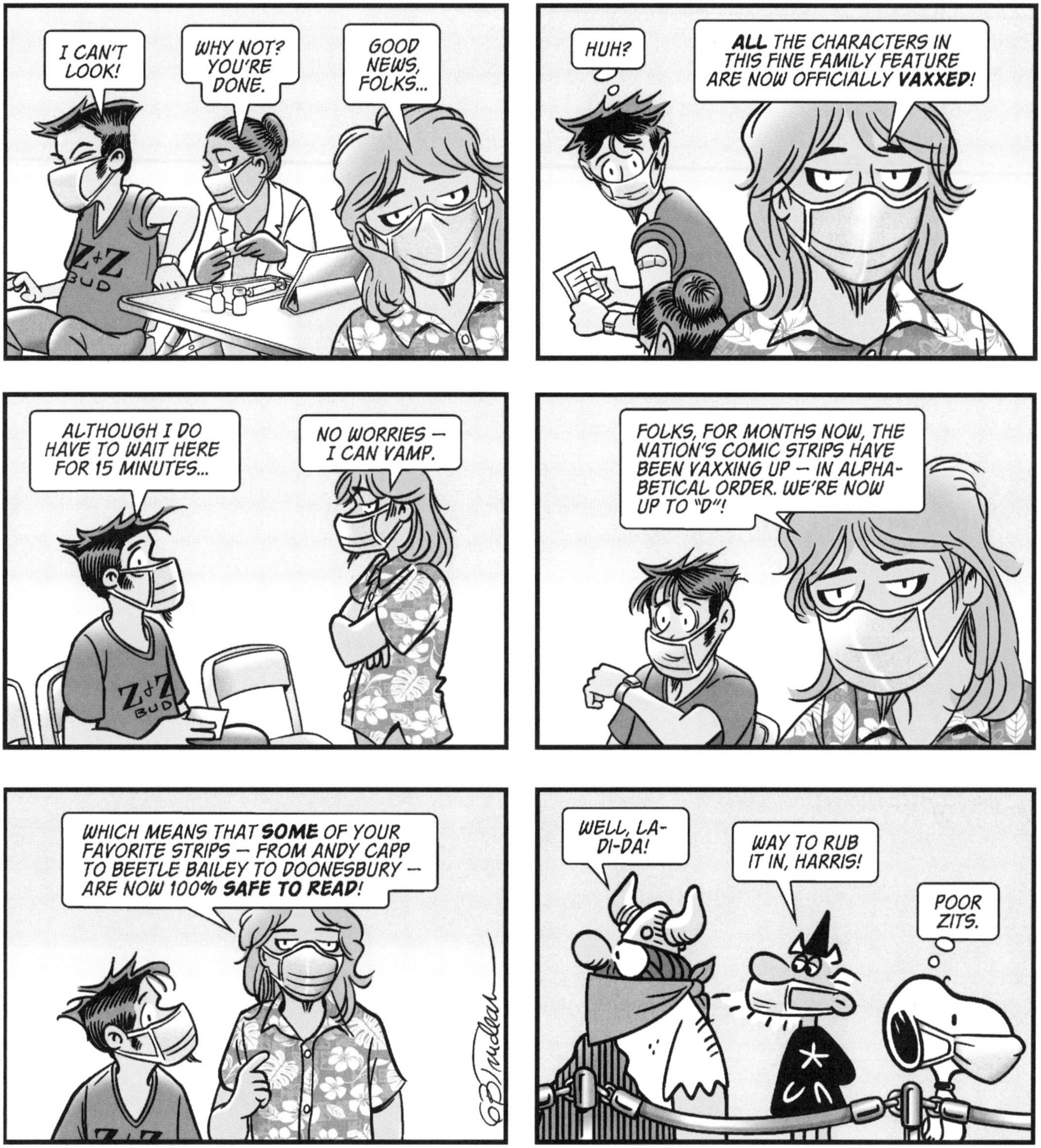
I CAN'T LOOK!
WHY NOT? YOU'RE DONE.
GOOD NEWS, FOLKS...
Z+Z BUD
HUH?
ALL THE CHARACTERS IN THIS FINE FAMILY FEATURE ARE NOW OFFICIALLY VAXXED!
ALTHOUGH I DO HAVE TO WAIT HERE FOR 15 MINUTES...
NO WORRIES — I CAN VAMP.
Z+Z BUD
FOLKS, FOR MONTHS NOW, THE NATION'S COMIC STRIPS HAVE BEEN VAXXING UP — IN ALPHABETICAL ORDER. WE'RE NOW UP TO "D"!
WHICH MEANS THAT SOME OF YOUR FAVORITE STRIPS — FROM ANDY CAPP TO BEETLE BAILEY TO DOONESBURY — ARE NOW 100% SAFE TO READ!
WELL, LA-DI-DA!
WAY TO RUB IT IN, HARRIS!
POOR ZITS.

May 2, 2021

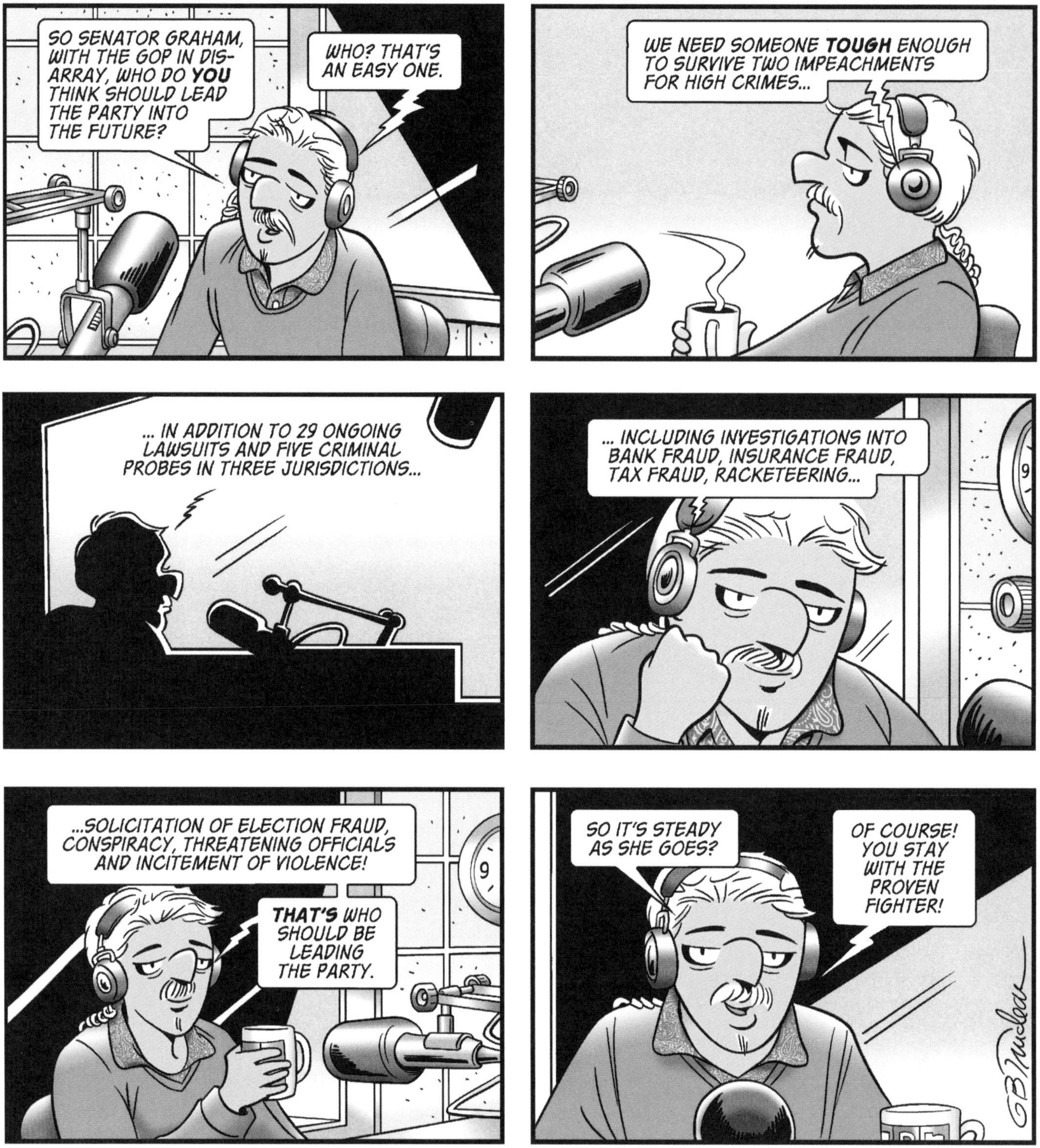
SO SENATOR GRAHAM, WITH THE GOP IN DIS-ARRAY, WHO DO **YOU** THINK SHOULD LEAD THE PARTY INTO THE FUTURE?
WHO? THAT'S AN EASY ONE.
WE NEED SOMEONE **TOUGH** ENOUGH TO SURVIVE TWO IMPEACHMENTS FOR HIGH CRIMES...
... IN ADDITION TO 29 ONGOING LAWSUITS AND FIVE CRIMINAL PROBES IN THREE JURISDICTIONS...
... INCLUDING INVESTIGATIONS INTO BANK FRAUD, INSURANCE FRAUD, TAX FRAUD, RACKETEERING...
...SOLICITATION OF ELECTION FRAUD, CONSPIRACY, THREATENING OFFICIALS AND INCITEMENT OF VIOLENCE!
THAT'S WHO SHOULD BE LEADING THE PARTY.
SO IT'S STEADY AS SHE GOES?
OF COURSE! YOU STAY WITH THE PROVEN FIGHTER!
GBTrudeau

May 9, 2021

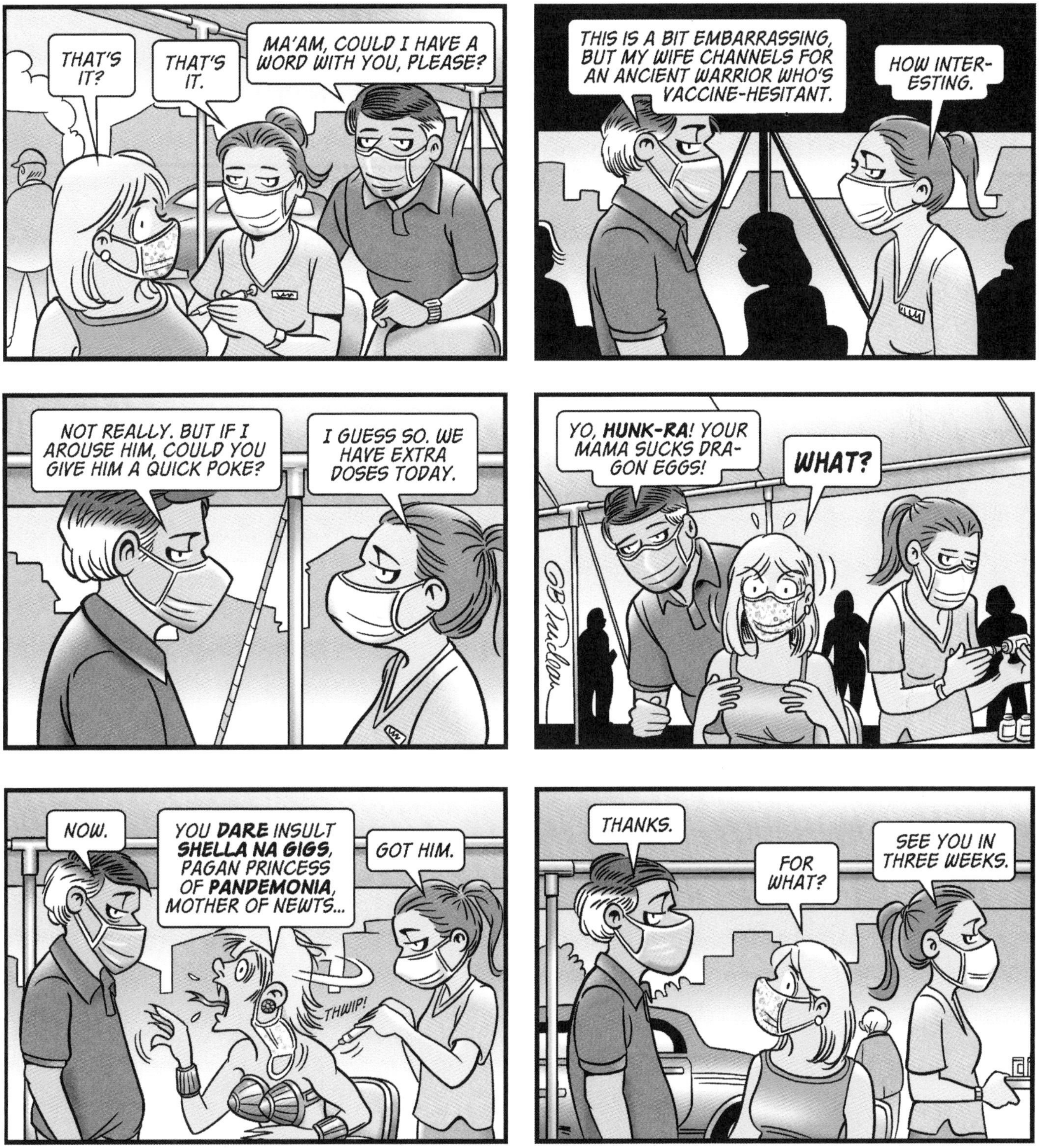
THAT'S IT?
THAT'S IT.
MA'AM, COULD I HAVE A WORD WITH YOU, PLEASE?
THIS IS A BIT EMBARRASSING, BUT MY WIFE CHANNELS FOR AN ANCIENT WARRIOR WHO'S VACCINE-HESITANT.
HOW INTER-ESTING.
NOT REALLY. BUT IF I AROUSE HIM, COULD YOU GIVE HIM A QUICK POKE?
I GUESS SO. WE HAVE EXTRA DOSES TODAY.
YO, **HUNK-RA**! YOUR MAMA SUCKS DRA-GON EGGS!
WHAT?
NOW.
YOU **DARE** INSULT **SHELLA NA GIGS**, PAGAN PRINCESS OF **PANDEMONIA**, MOTHER OF NEWTS...
GOT HIM.
THWIP!
THANKS.
FOR WHAT?
SEE YOU IN THREE WEEKS.

May 16, 2021

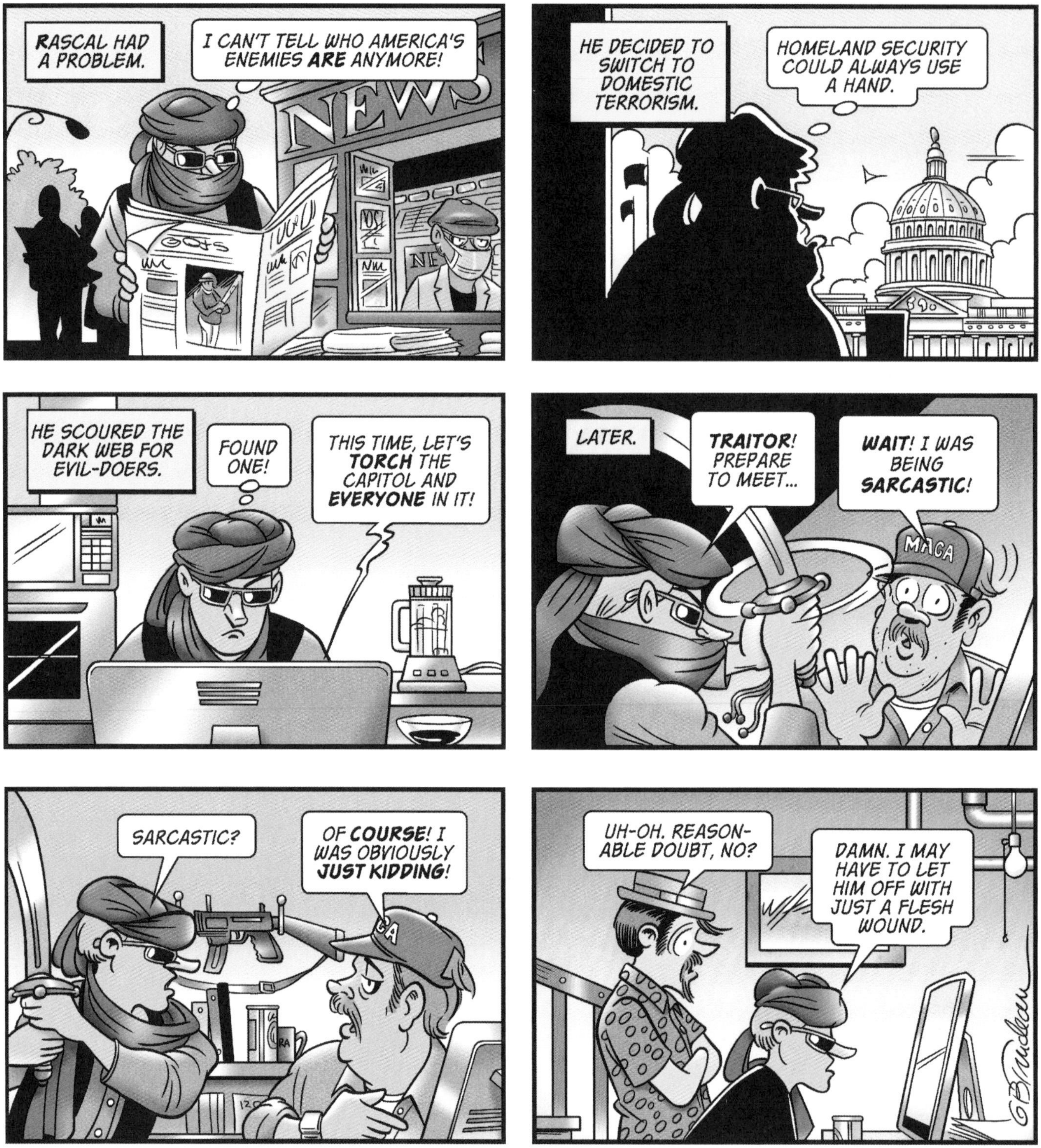
RASCAL HAD A PROBLEM.
I CAN'T TELL WHO AMERICA'S ENEMIES **ARE** ANYMORE!
NEWS
HE DECIDED TO SWITCH TO DOMESTIC TERRORISM.
HOMELAND SECURITY COULD ALWAYS USE A HAND.
HE SCOURED THE DARK WEB FOR EVIL-DOERS.
FOUND ONE!
THIS TIME, LET'S **TORCH** THE CAPITOL AND **EVERYONE** IN IT!
LATER.
TRAITOR! PREPARE TO MEET...
WAIT! I WAS BEING **SARCASTIC**!
MAGA
SARCASTIC?
OF **COURSE**! I WAS OBVIOUSLY **JUST KIDDING**!
UH-OH. REASON-ABLE DOUBT, NO?
DAMN. I MAY HAVE TO LET HIM OFF WITH JUST A FLESH WOUND.
GBTrudeau

May 23, 2021

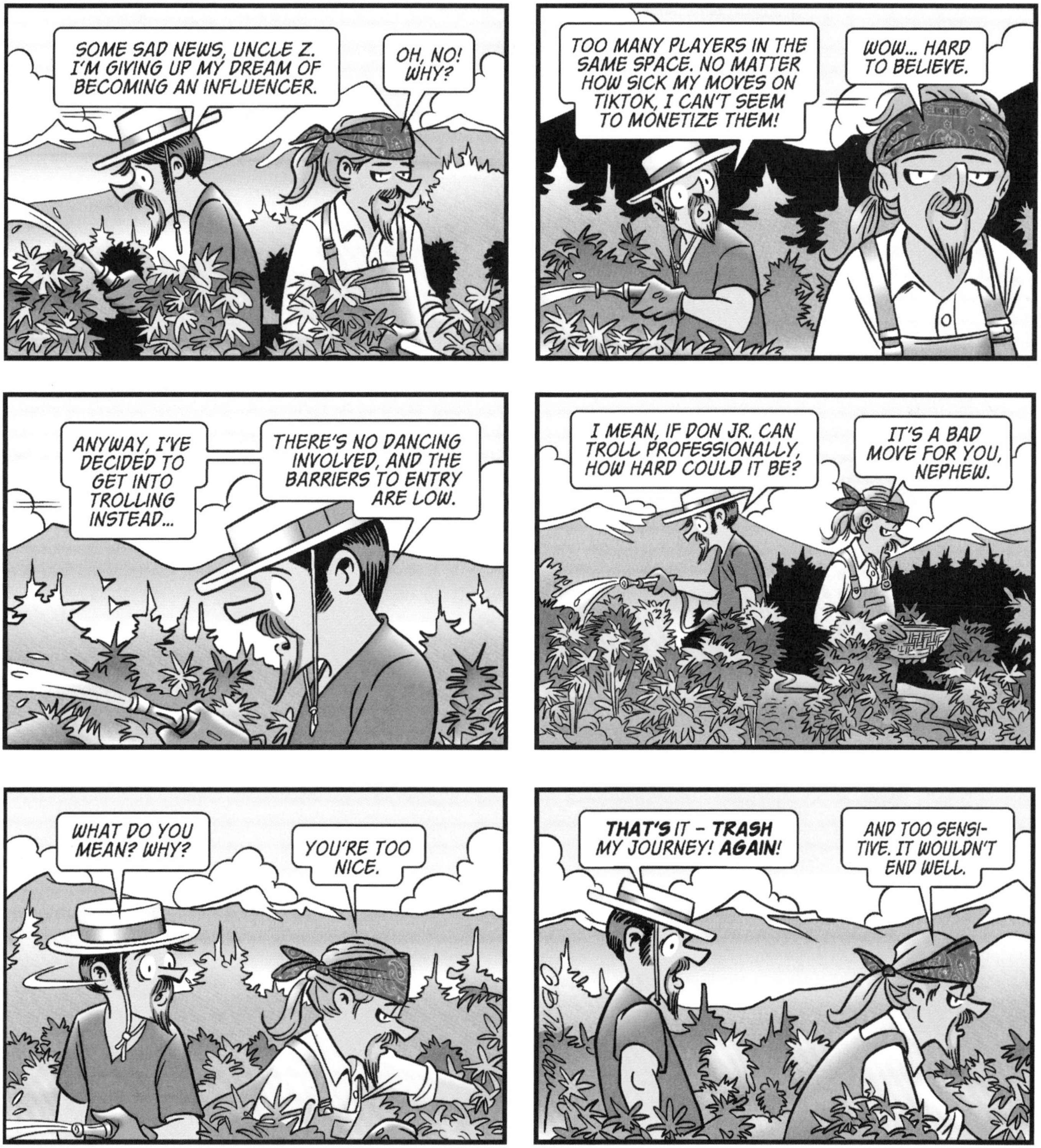
SOME SAD NEWS, UNCLE Z. I'M GIVING UP MY DREAM OF BECOMING AN INFLUENCER.
OH, NO! WHY?
TOO MANY PLAYERS IN THE SAME SPACE. NO MATTER HOW SICK MY MOVES ON TIKTOK, I CAN'T SEEM TO MONETIZE THEM!
WOW... HARD TO BELIEVE.
ANYWAY, I'VE DECIDED TO GET INTO TROLLING INSTEAD...
THERE'S NO DANCING INVOLVED, AND THE BARRIERS TO ENTRY ARE LOW.
I MEAN, IF DON JR. CAN TROLL PROFESSIONALLY, HOW HARD COULD IT BE?
IT'S A BAD MOVE FOR YOU, NEPHEW.
WHAT DO YOU MEAN? WHY?
YOU'RE TOO NICE.
THAT'S IT – **TRASH** MY JOURNEY! **AGAIN**!
AND TOO SENSI-TIVE. IT WOULDN'T END WELL.

May 30, 2021

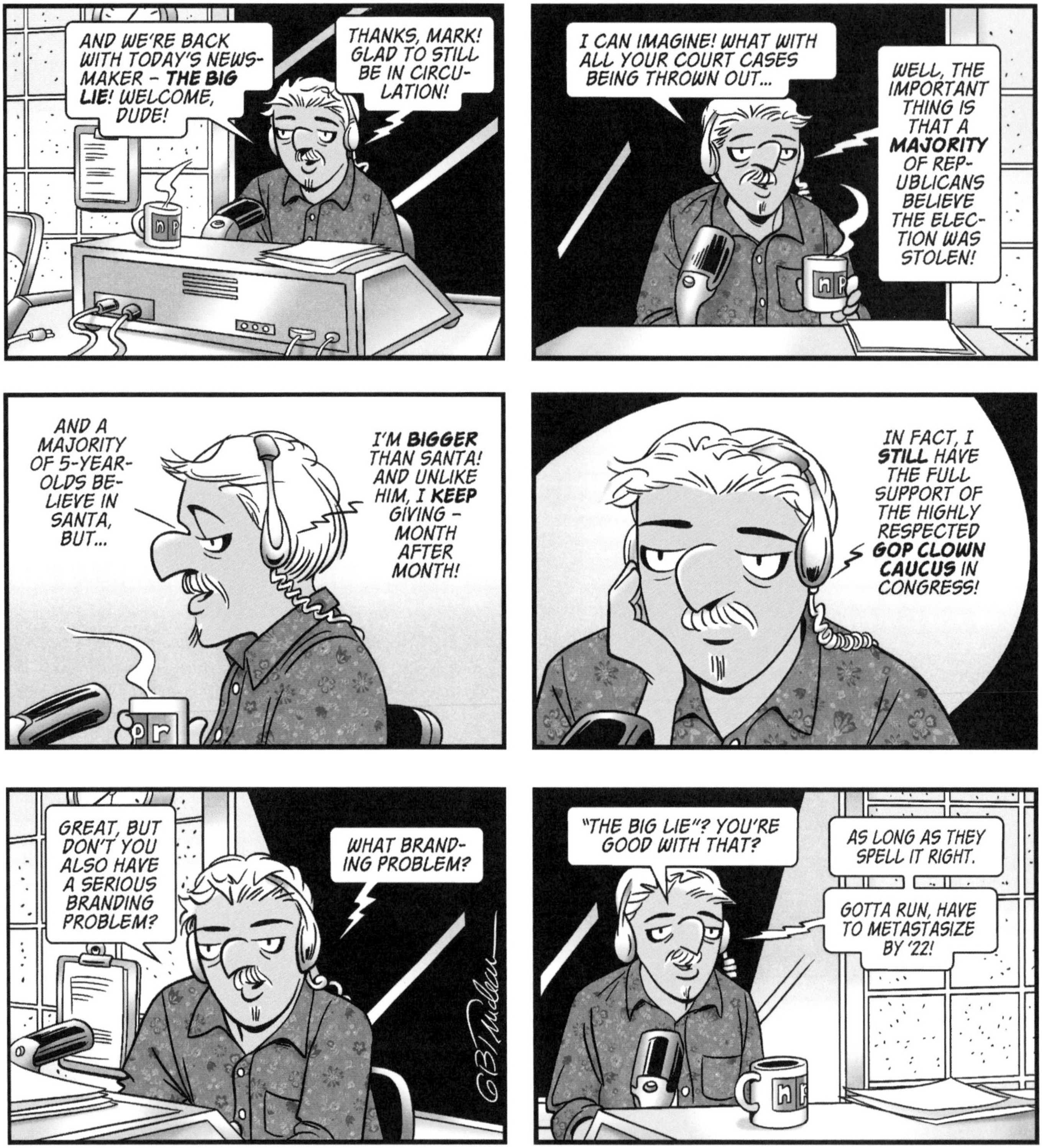
AND WE'RE BACK WITH TODAY'S NEWS-MAKER – **THE BIG LIE**! WELCOME, DUDE!
THANKS, MARK! GLAD TO STILL BE IN CIRCU-LATION!
I CAN IMAGINE! WHAT WITH ALL YOUR COURT CASES BEING THROWN OUT...
WELL, THE IMPORTANT THING IS THAT A **MAJORITY** OF REP-UBLICANS BELIEVE THE ELEC-TION WAS STOLEN!
AND A MAJORITY OF 5-YEAR-OLDS BE-LIEVE IN SANTA, BUT...
I'M **BIGGER** THAN SANTA! AND UNLIKE HIM, I **KEEP** GIVING – MONTH AFTER MONTH!
IN FACT, I **STILL** HAVE THE FULL SUPPORT OF THE HIGHLY RESPECTED **GOP CLOWN CAUCUS** IN CONGRESS!
GREAT, BUT DON'T YOU ALSO HAVE A SERIOUS BRANDING PROBLEM?
WHAT BRAND-ING PROBLEM?
©BTrudeau
"THE BIG LIE"? YOU'RE GOOD WITH THAT?
AS LONG AS THEY SPELL IT RIGHT.
GOTTA RUN, HAVE TO METASTASIZE BY '22!

June 6, 2021

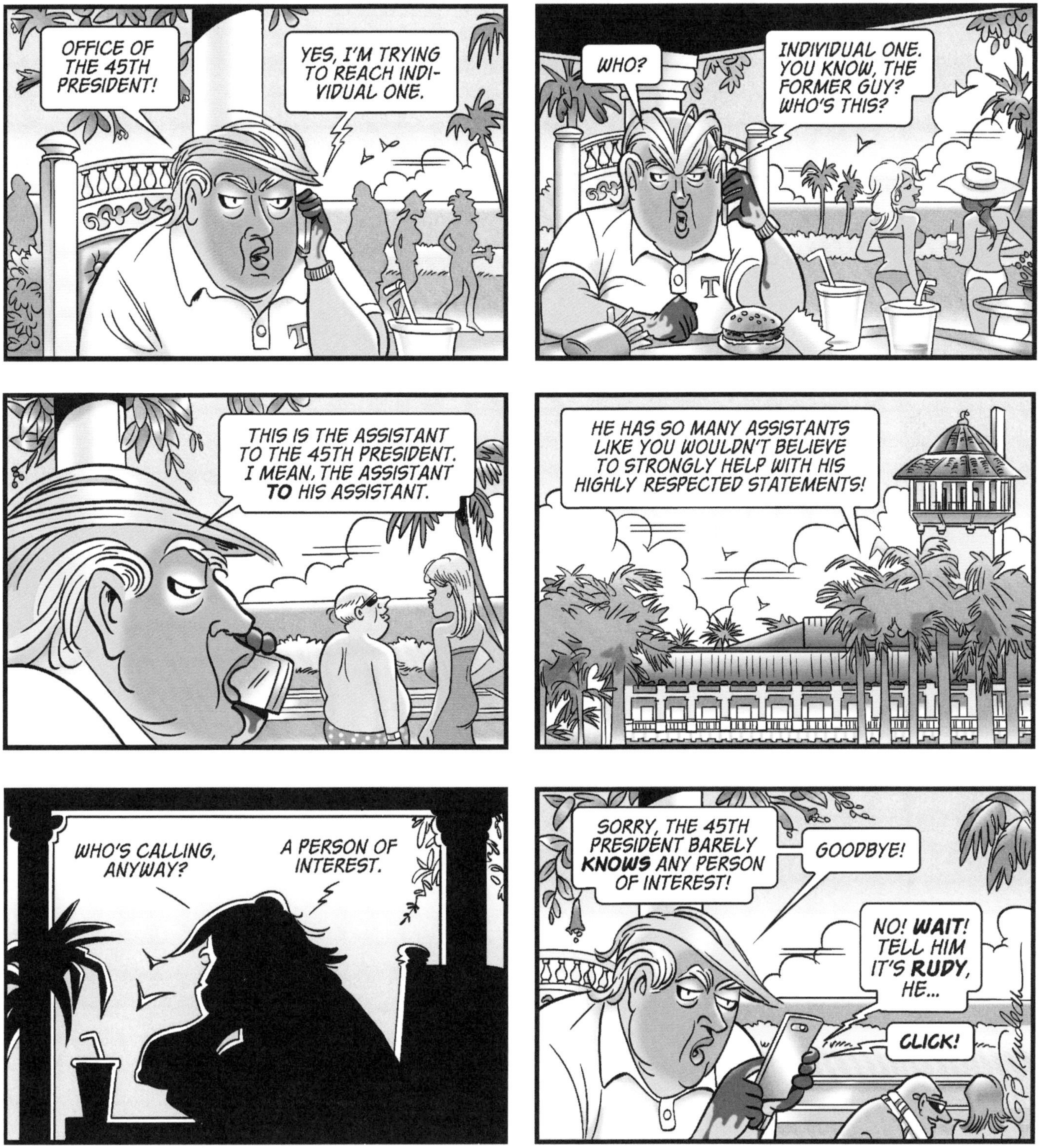
OFFICE OF THE 45TH PRESIDENT!
YES, I'M TRYING TO REACH INDIVIDUAL ONE.
WHO?
INDIVIDUAL ONE. YOU KNOW, THE FORMER GUY? WHO'S THIS?
THIS IS THE ASSISTANT TO THE 45TH PRESIDENT. I MEAN, THE ASSISTANT **TO** HIS ASSISTANT.
HE HAS SO MANY ASSISTANTS LIKE YOU WOULDN'T BELIEVE TO STRONGLY HELP WITH HIS HIGHLY RESPECTED STATEMENTS!
WHO'S CALLING, ANYWAY?
A PERSON OF INTEREST.
SORRY, THE 45TH PRESIDENT BARELY **KNOWS** ANY PERSON OF INTEREST!
GOODBYE!
NO! **WAIT**! TELL HIM IT'S **RUDY**, HE...
CLICK!

June 20, 2021

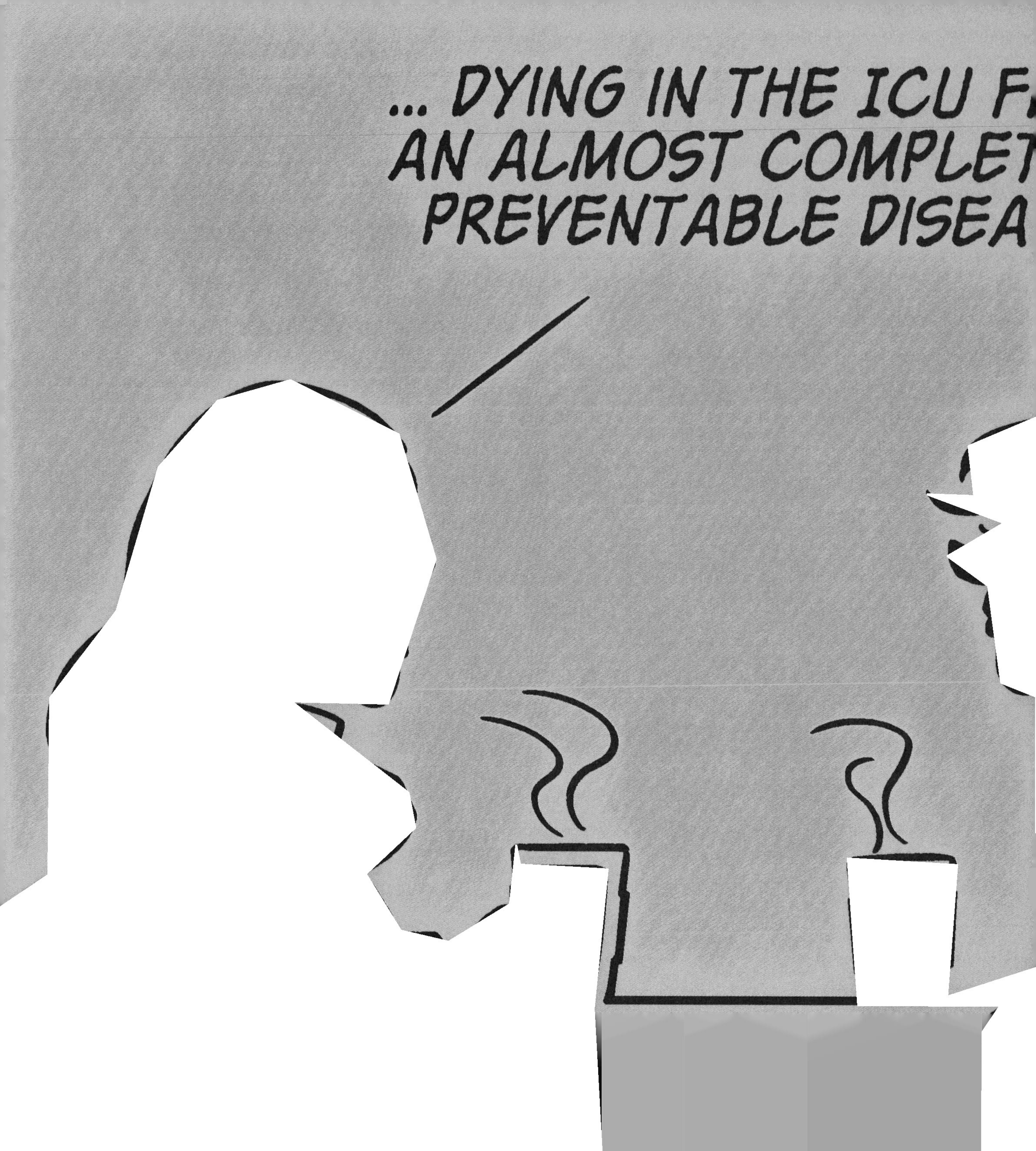
... DYING IN THE ICU FROM AN ALMOST COMPLET PREVENTABLE DISEA

PART 3

Owning the Libs

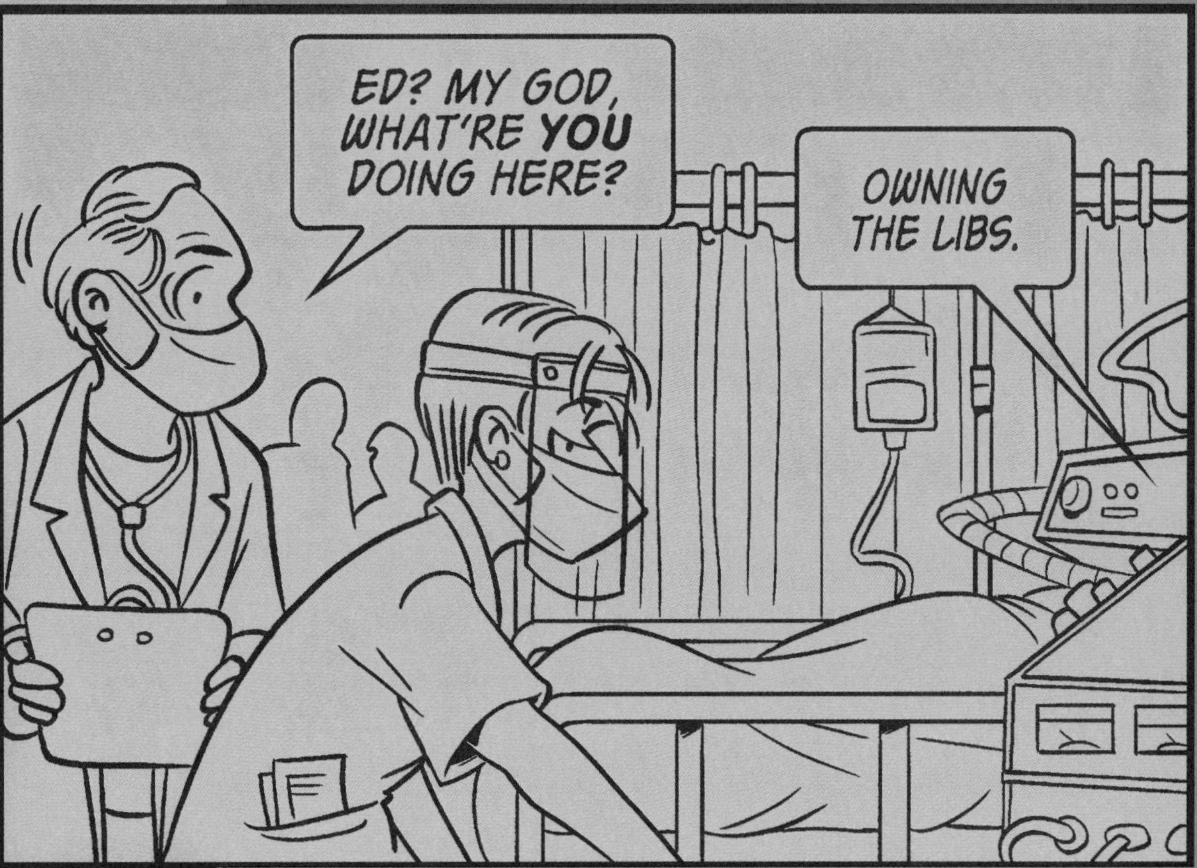
ED? MY GOD, WHAT'RE **YOU** DOING HERE?
OWNING THE LIBS.

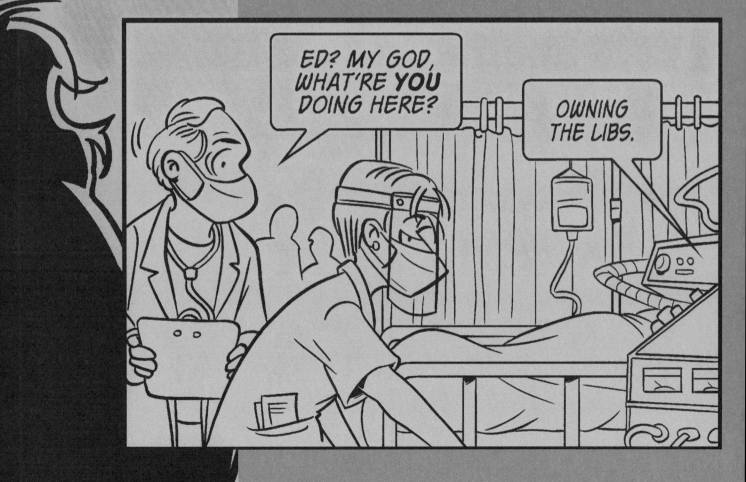

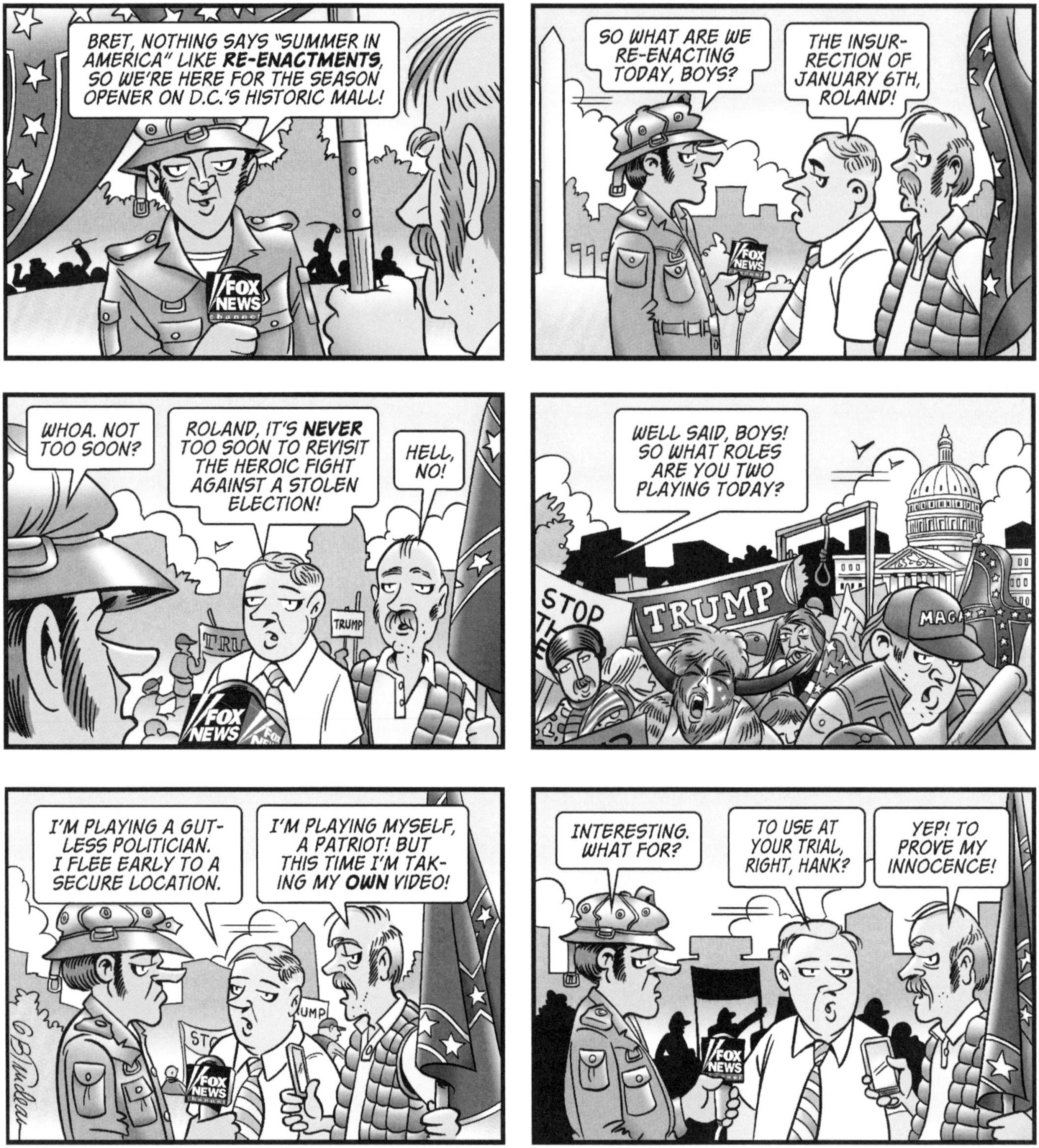
BRET, NOTHING SAYS "SUMMER IN AMERICA" LIKE **RE-ENACTMENTS**, SO WE'RE HERE FOR THE SEASON OPENER ON D.C.'S HISTORIC MALL!
SO WHAT ARE WE RE-ENACTING TODAY, BOYS?
THE INSUR-RECTION OF JANUARY 6TH, ROLAND!
WHOA. NOT TOO SOON?
ROLAND, IT'S **NEVER** TOO SOON TO REVISIT THE HEROIC FIGHT AGAINST A STOLEN ELECTION!
HELL, NO!
WELL SAID, BOYS! SO WHAT ROLES ARE YOU TWO PLAYING TODAY?
I'M PLAYING A GUT-LESS POLITICIAN. I FLEE EARLY TO A SECURE LOCATION.
I'M PLAYING MYSELF, A PATRIOT! BUT THIS TIME I'M TAK-ING MY **OWN** VIDEO!
INTERESTING. WHAT FOR?
TO USE AT YOUR TRIAL, RIGHT, HANK?
YEP! TO PROVE MY INNOCENCE!

June 27, 2021

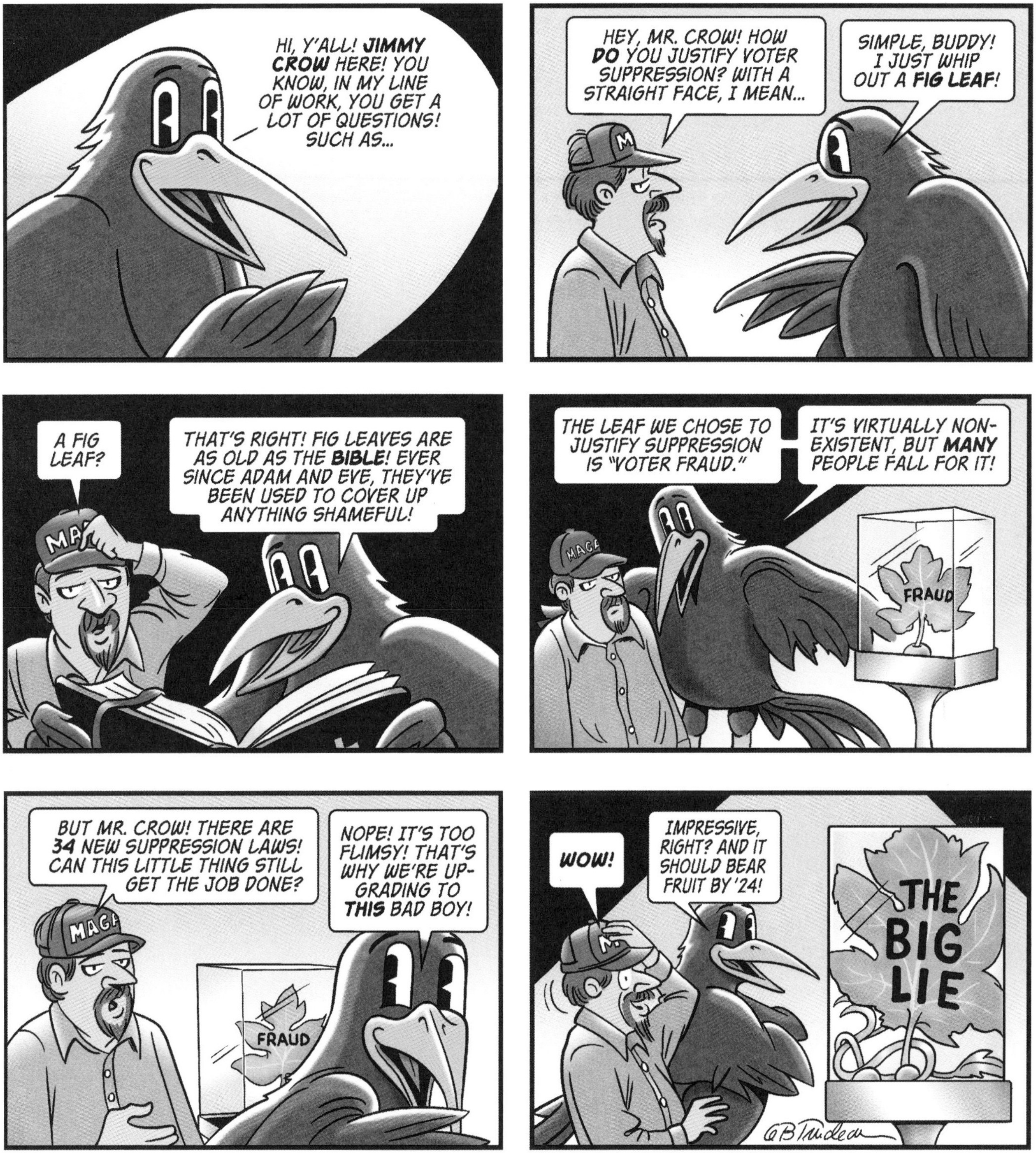
HI, Y'ALL! JIMMY CROW HERE! YOU KNOW, IN MY LINE OF WORK, YOU GET A LOT OF QUESTIONS! SUCH AS...
HEY, MR. CROW! HOW DO YOU JUSTIFY VOTER SUPPRESSION? WITH A STRAIGHT FACE, I MEAN...
SIMPLE, BUDDY! I JUST WHIP OUT A FIG LEAF!
A FIG LEAF?
THAT'S RIGHT! FIG LEAVES ARE AS OLD AS THE BIBLE! EVER SINCE ADAM AND EVE, THEY'VE BEEN USED TO COVER UP ANYTHING SHAMEFUL!
THE LEAF WE CHOSE TO JUSTIFY SUPPRESSION IS "VOTER FRAUD."
IT'S VIRTUALLY NON-EXISTENT, BUT MANY PEOPLE FALL FOR IT!
FRAUD
BUT MR. CROW! THERE ARE 34 NEW SUPPRESSION LAWS! CAN THIS LITTLE THING STILL GET THE JOB DONE?
NOPE! IT'S TOO FLIMSY! THAT'S WHY WE'RE UP-GRADING TO THIS BAD BOY!
FRAUD
WOW!
IMPRESSIVE, RIGHT? AND IT SHOULD BEAR FRUIT BY '24!
THE BIG LIE
GBTrudeau

July 4, 2021

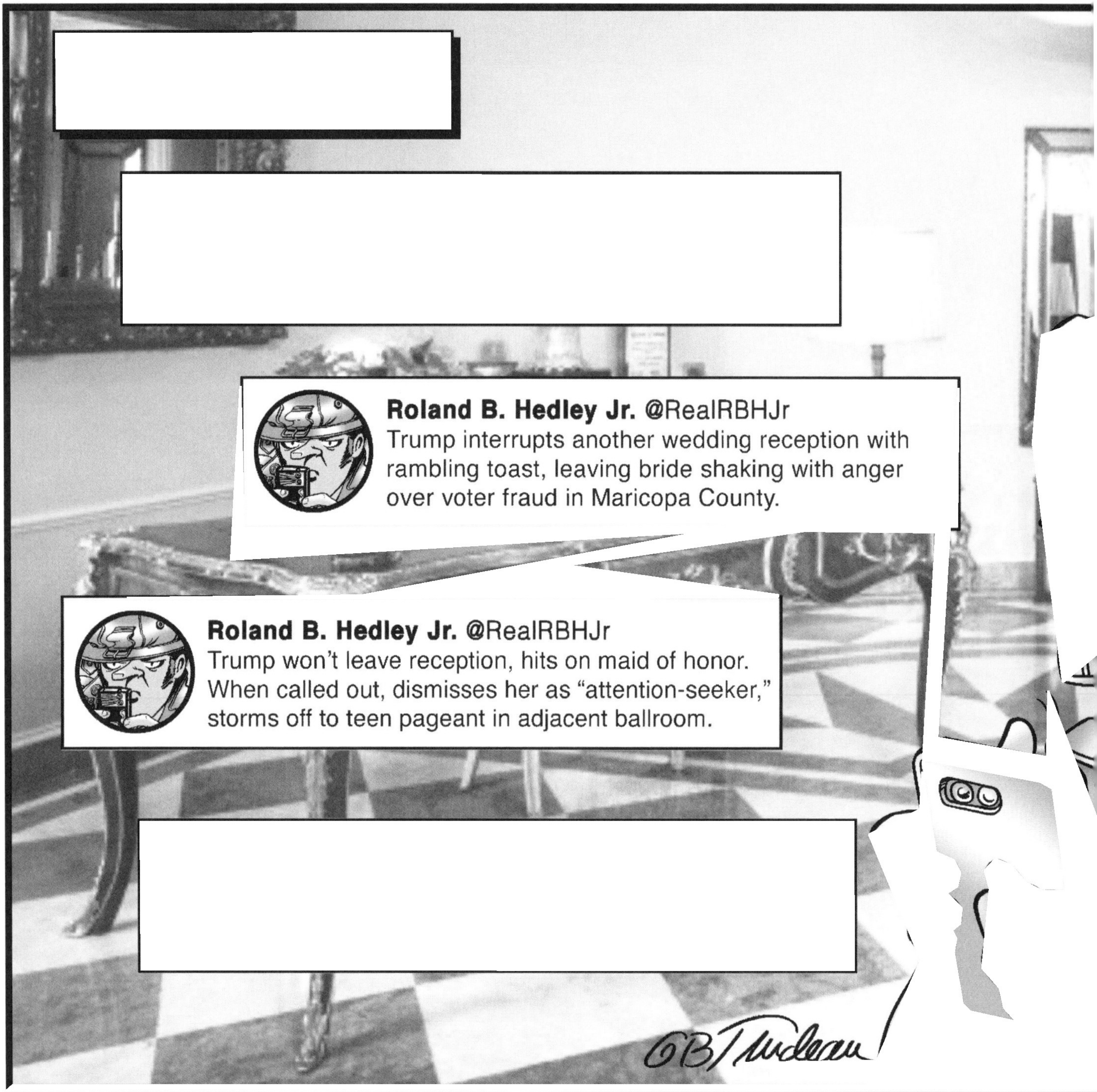
Roland B. Hedley Jr. @RealRBHJr
Trump interrupts another wedding reception with rambling toast, leaving bride shaking with anger over voter fraud in Maricopa County.
Roland B. Hedley Jr. @RealRBHJr
Trump won't leave reception, hits on maid of honor. When called out, dismisses her as "attention-seeker," storms off to teen pageant in adjacent ballroom.

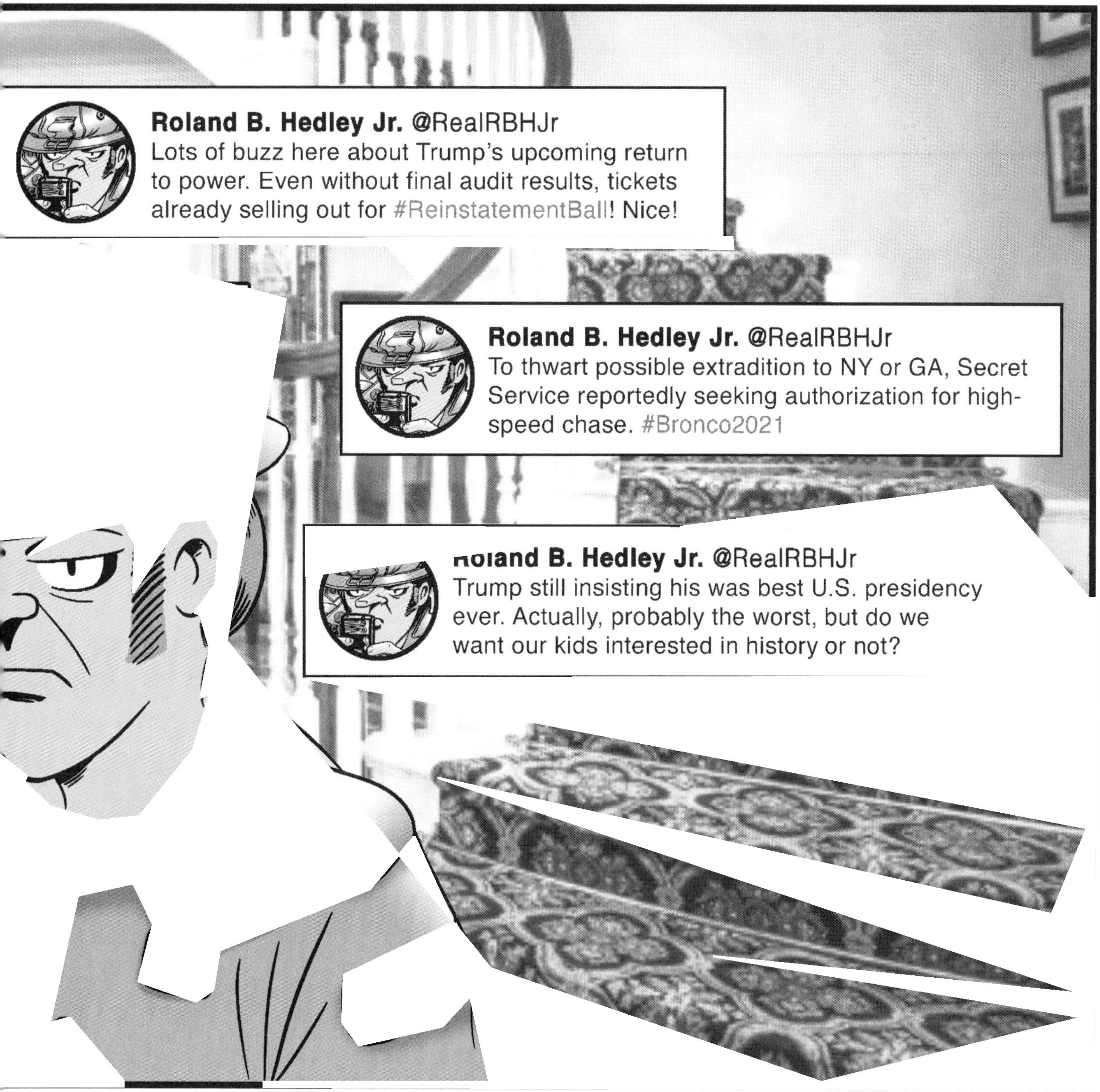
Roland B. Hedley Jr. @RealRBHJr
Lots of buzz here about Trump's upcoming return to power. Even without final audit results, tickets already selling out for #ReinstatementBall! Nice!
Roland B. Hedley Jr. @RealRBHJr
To thwart possible extradition to NY or GA, Secret Service reportedly seeking authorization for high-speed chase. #Bronco2021
Roland B. Hedley Jr. @RealRBHJr
Trump still insisting his was best U.S. presidency ever. Actually, probably the worst, but do we want our kids interested in history or not?

July 18, 2021

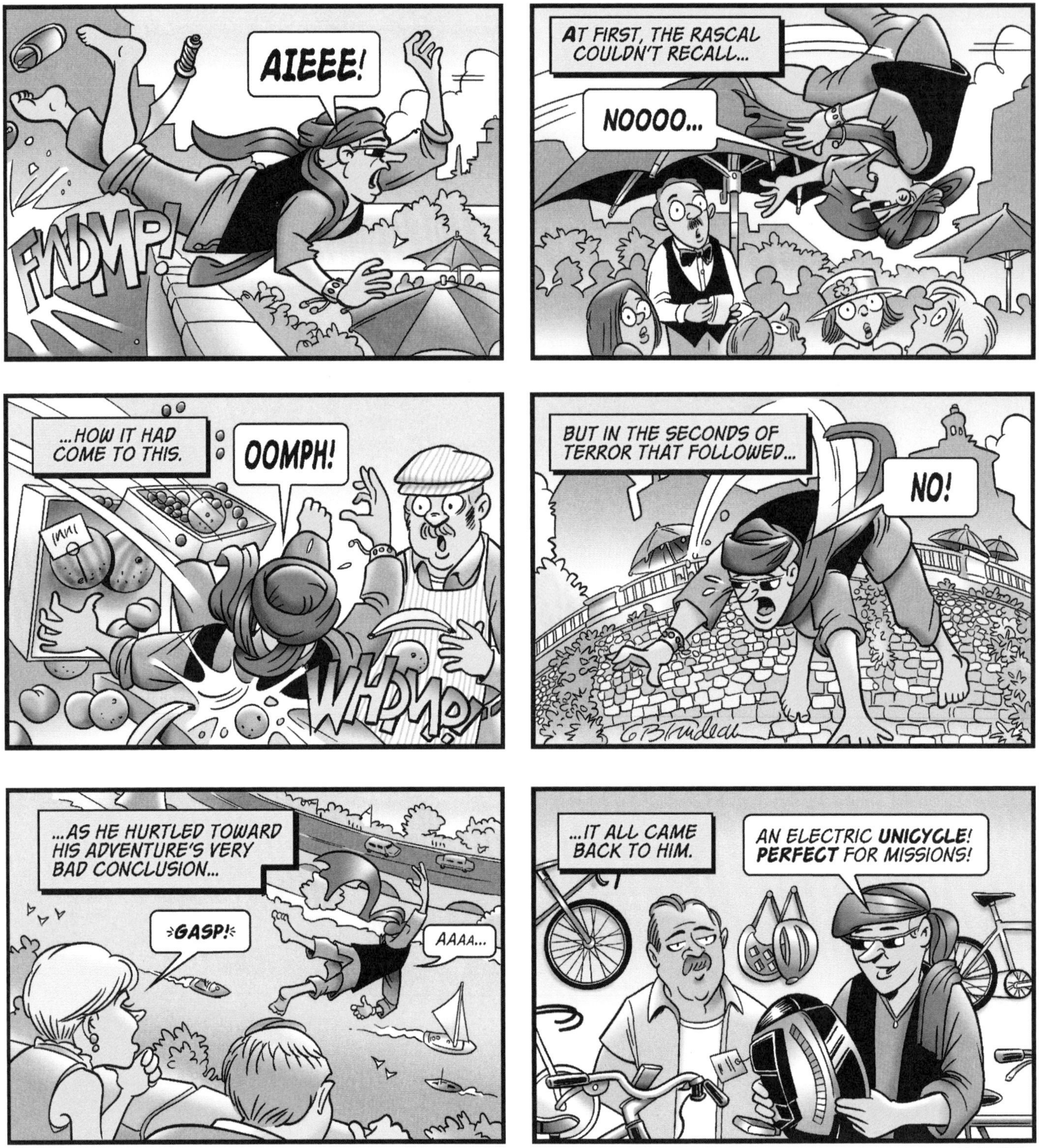

FWOMP!
AIEEE!
AT FIRST, THE RASCAL COULDN'T RECALL...
NOOOO...
...HOW IT HAD COME TO THIS.
OOMPH!
WHOMP!
BUT IN THE SECONDS OF TERROR THAT FOLLOWED...
NO!
G B Trudeau
...AS HE HURTLED TOWARD HIS ADVENTURE'S VERY BAD CONCLUSION...
GASP!
AAAA...
...IT ALL CAME BACK TO HIM.
AN ELECTRIC UNICYCLE! PERFECT FOR MISSIONS!

July 11, 2021

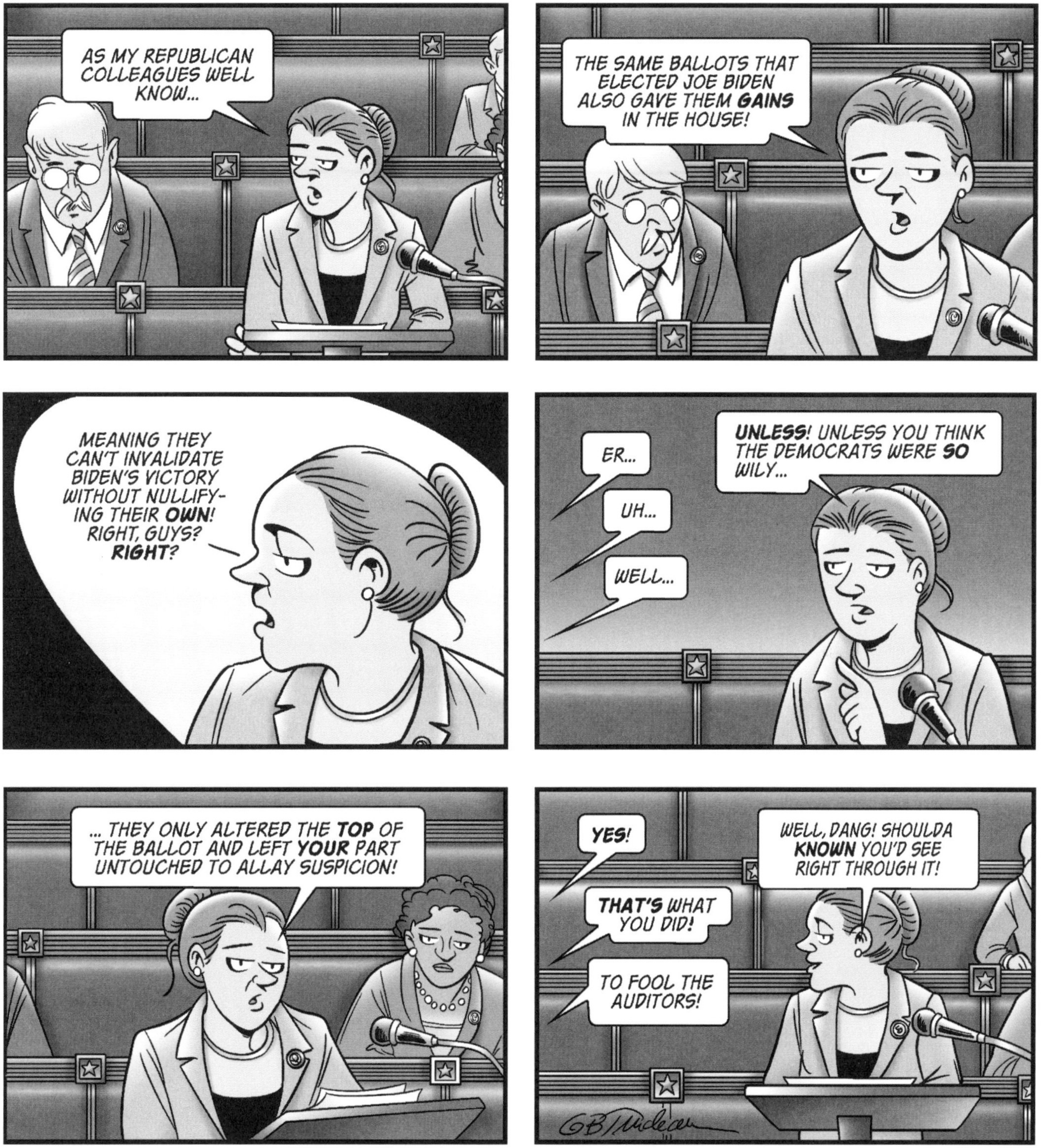
AS MY REPUBLICAN COLLEAGUES WELL KNOW...
THE SAME BALLOTS THAT ELECTED JOE BIDEN ALSO GAVE THEM GAINS IN THE HOUSE!
MEANING THEY CAN'T INVALIDATE BIDEN'S VICTORY WITHOUT NULLIFYING THEIR OWN! RIGHT, GUYS? RIGHT?
ER...
UH...
WELL...
UNLESS! UNLESS YOU THINK THE DEMOCRATS WERE SO WILY...
... THEY ONLY ALTERED THE TOP OF THE BALLOT AND LEFT YOUR PART UNTOUCHED TO ALLAY SUSPICION!
YES!
THAT'S WHAT YOU DID!
TO FOOL THE AUDITORS!
WELL, DANG! SHOULDA KNOWN YOU'D SEE RIGHT THROUGH IT!
GBTrudeau

July 25, 2021

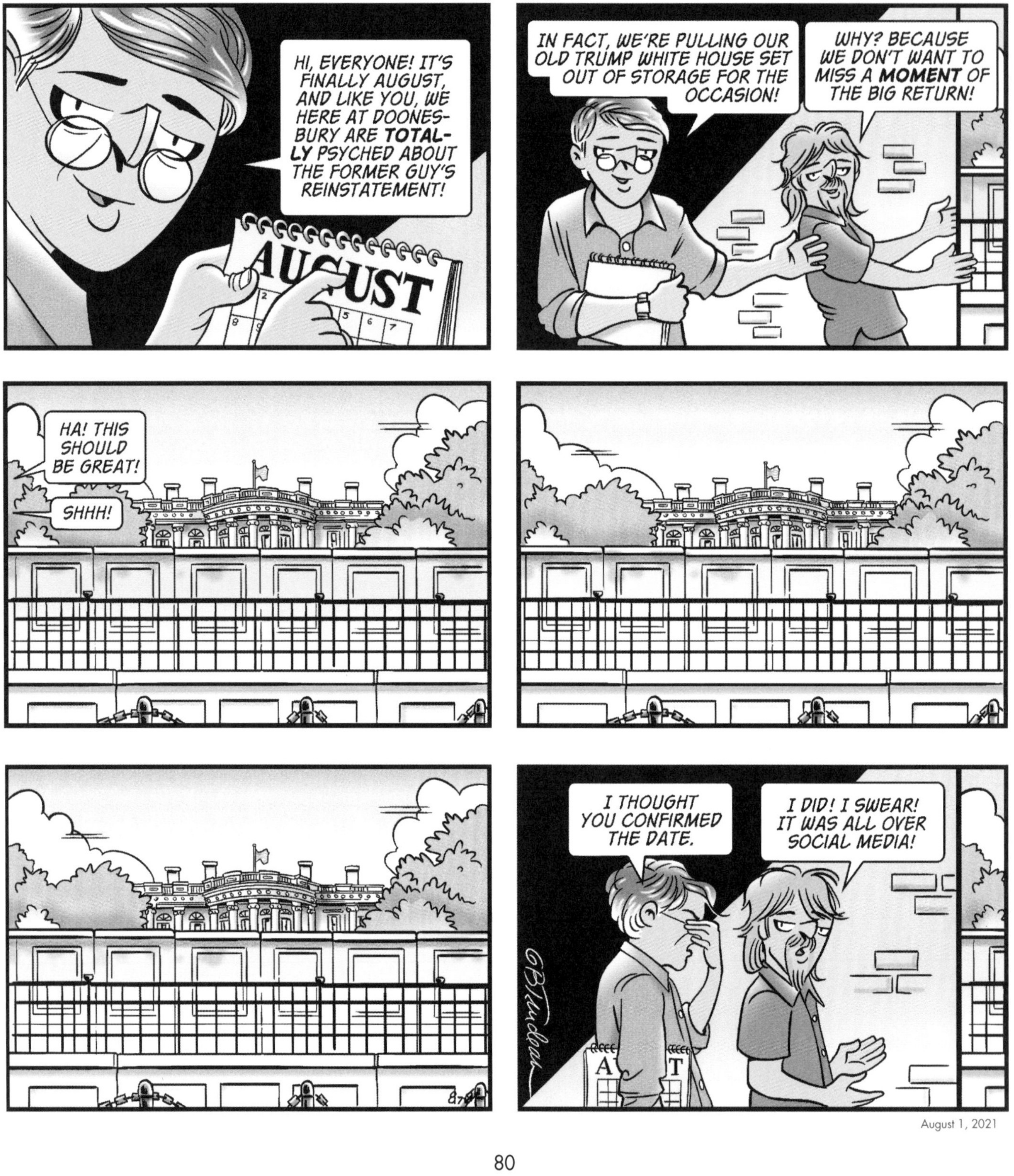
HI, EVERYONE! IT'S FINALLY AUGUST, AND LIKE YOU, WE HERE AT DOONESBURY ARE **TOTALLY** PSYCHED ABOUT THE FORMER GUY'S REINSTATEMENT!
AUGUST
IN FACT, WE'RE PULLING OUR OLD TRUMP WHITE HOUSE SET OUT OF STORAGE FOR THE OCCASION!
WHY? BECAUSE WE DON'T WANT TO MISS A **MOMENT** OF THE BIG RETURN!
HA! THIS SHOULD BE GREAT!
SHHH!
I THOUGHT YOU CONFIRMED THE DATE.
I DID! I SWEAR! IT WAS ALL OVER SOCIAL MEDIA!
©BTrudeau

August 1, 2021

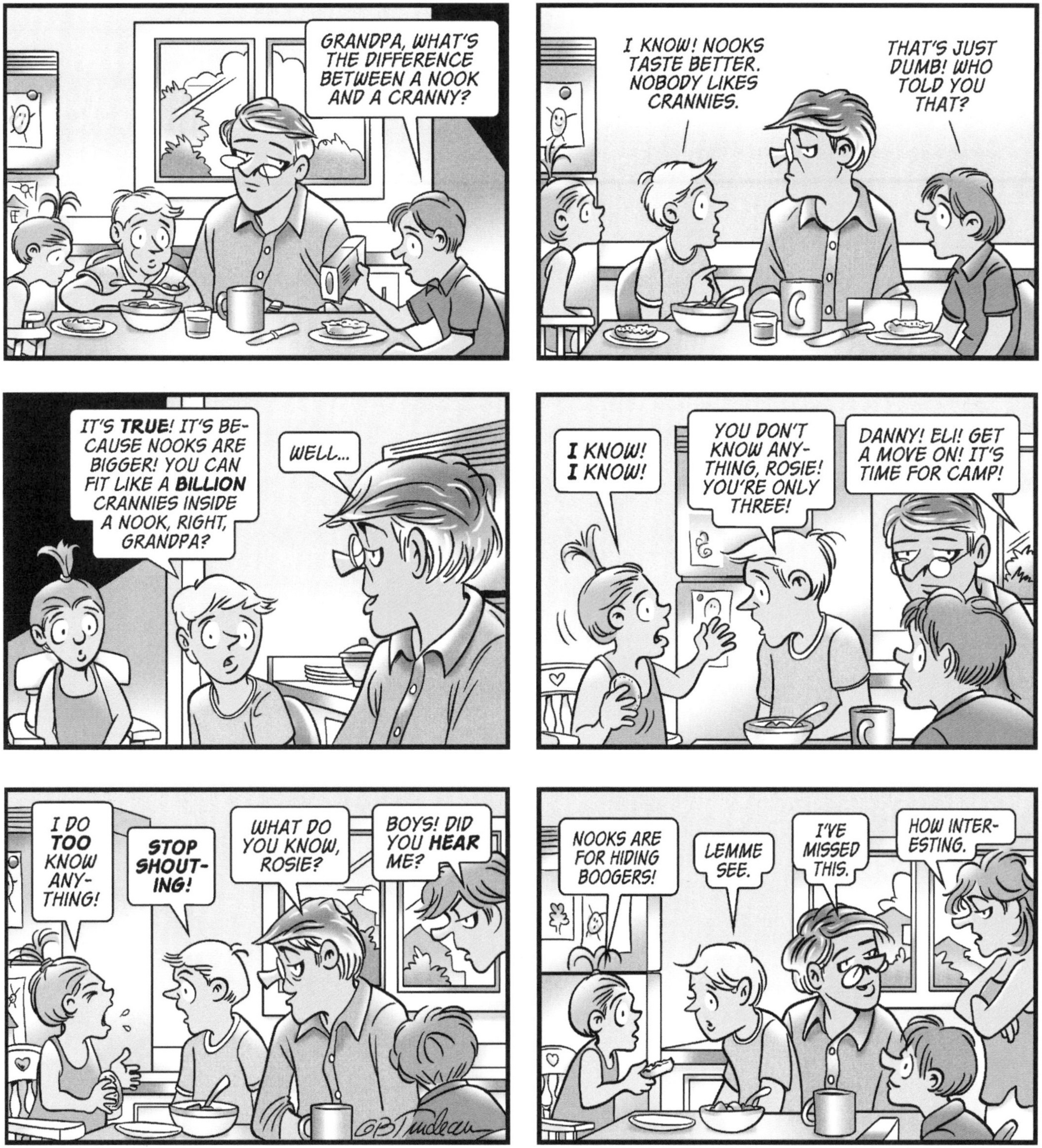

GRANDPA, WHAT'S THE DIFFERENCE BETWEEN A NOOK AND A CRANNY?
I KNOW! NOOKS TASTE BETTER. NOBODY LIKES CRANNIES.
THAT'S JUST DUMB! WHO TOLD YOU THAT?
IT'S **TRUE**! IT'S BE-CAUSE NOOKS ARE BIGGER! YOU CAN FIT LIKE A **BILLION** CRANNIES INSIDE A NOOK, RIGHT, GRANDPA?
WELL...
I KNOW! I KNOW!
YOU DON'T KNOW ANY-THING, ROSIE! YOU'RE ONLY THREE!
DANNY! ELI! GET A MOVE ON! IT'S TIME FOR CAMP!
I DO **TOO** KNOW ANY-THING!
STOP SHOUT-ING!
WHAT DO YOU KNOW, ROSIE?
BOYS! DID YOU **HEAR** ME?
NOOKS ARE FOR HIDING BOOGERS!
LEMME SEE.
I'VE MISSED THIS.
HOW INTER-ESTING.
GBTrudeau

August 8, 2021

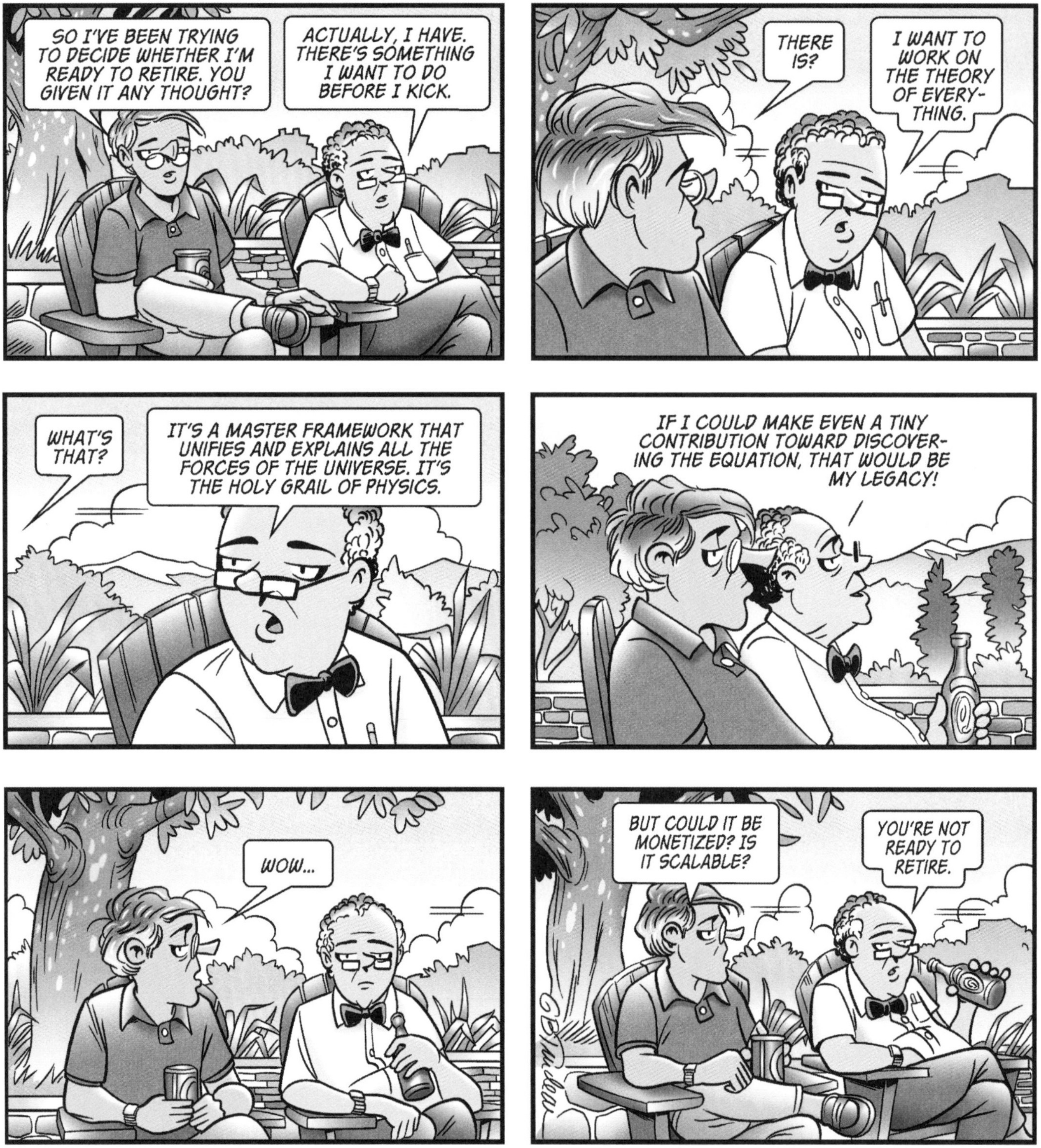
SO I'VE BEEN TRYING TO DECIDE WHETHER I'M READY TO RETIRE. YOU GIVEN IT ANY THOUGHT?
ACTUALLY, I HAVE. THERE'S SOMETHING I WANT TO DO BEFORE I KICK.
THERE IS?
I WANT TO WORK ON THE THEORY OF EVERY-THING.
WHAT'S THAT?
IT'S A MASTER FRAMEWORK THAT UNIFIES AND EXPLAINS ALL THE FORCES OF THE UNIVERSE. IT'S THE HOLY GRAIL OF PHYSICS.
IF I COULD MAKE EVEN A TINY CONTRIBUTION TOWARD DISCOVER-ING THE EQUATION, THAT WOULD BE MY LEGACY!
WOW...
BUT COULD IT BE MONETIZED? IS IT SCALABLE?
YOU'RE NOT READY TO RETIRE.

August 15, 2021

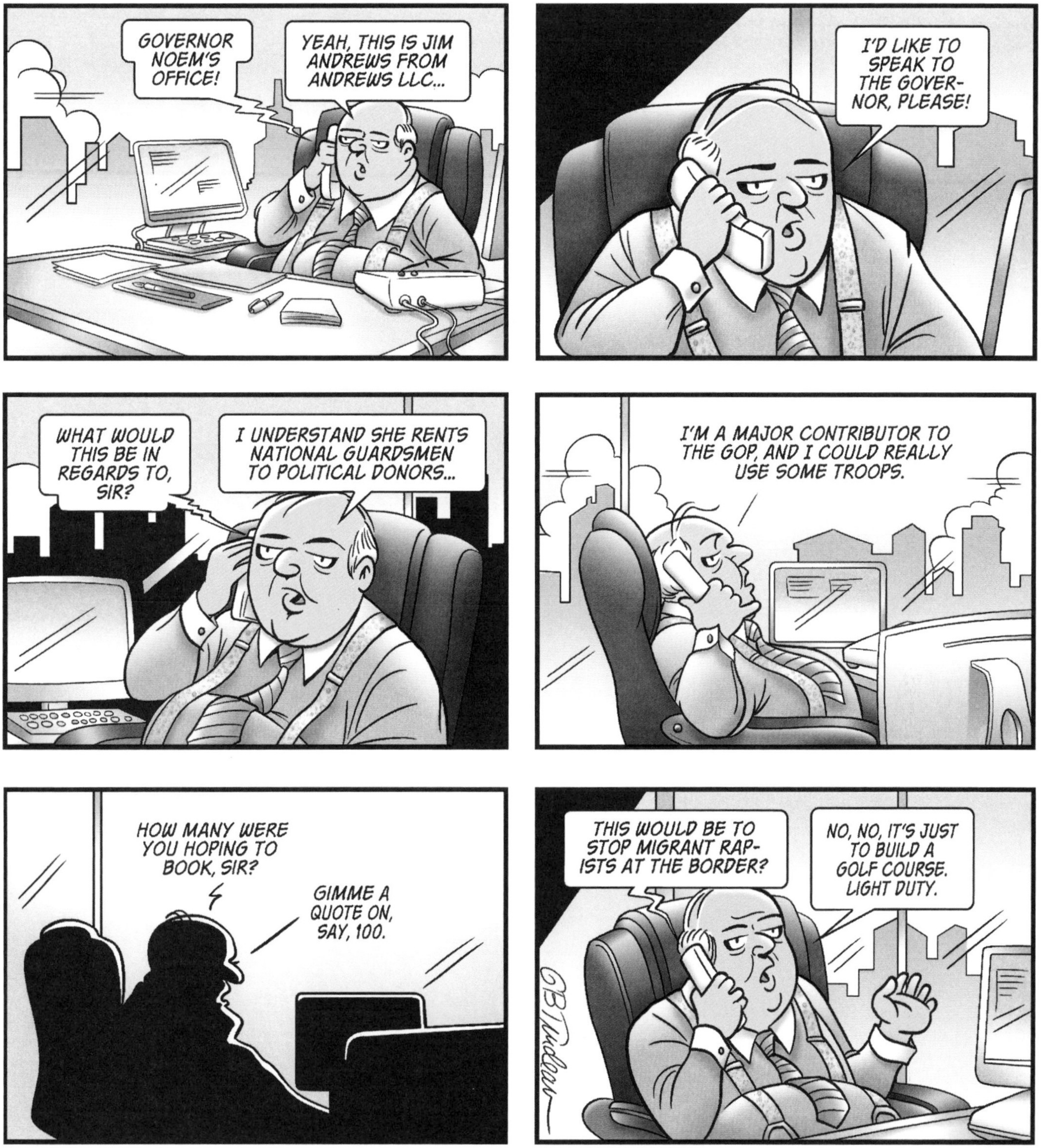
GOVERNOR NOEM'S OFFICE!
YEAH, THIS IS JIM ANDREWS FROM ANDREWS LLC...
I'D LIKE TO SPEAK TO THE GOVER-NOR, PLEASE!
WHAT WOULD THIS BE IN REGARDS TO, SIR?
I UNDERSTAND SHE RENTS NATIONAL GUARDSMEN TO POLITICAL DONORS...
I'M A MAJOR CONTRIBUTOR TO THE GOP, AND I COULD REALLY USE SOME TROOPS.
HOW MANY WERE YOU HOPING TO BOOK, SIR?
GIMME A QUOTE ON, SAY, 100.
THIS WOULD BE TO STOP MIGRANT RAP-ISTS AT THE BORDER?
NO, NO, IT'S JUST TO BUILD A GOLF COURSE. LIGHT DUTY.
GB Trudeau

August 22, 2021

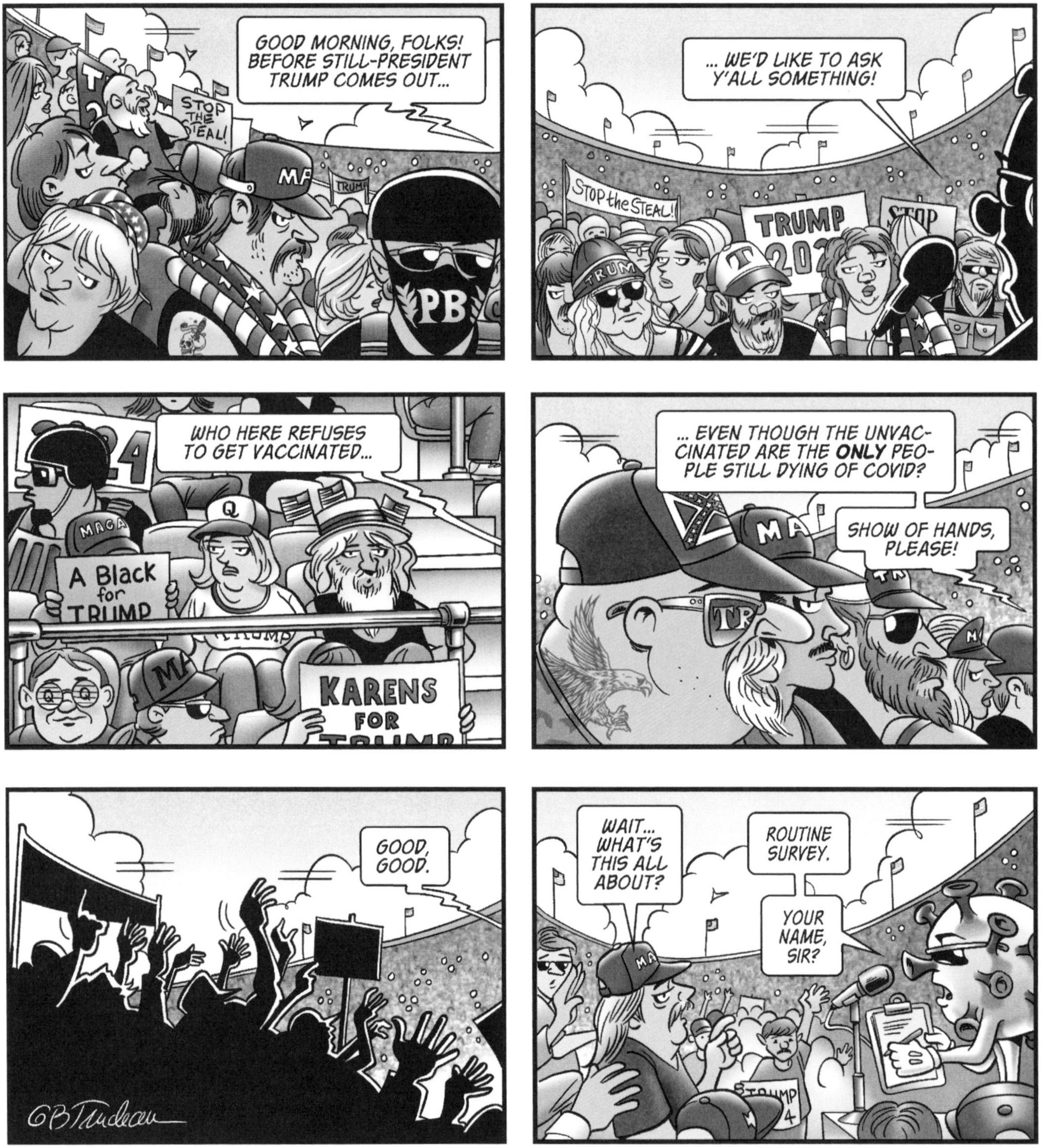
GOOD MORNING, FOLKS! BEFORE STILL-PRESIDENT TRUMP COMES OUT...
STOP THE STEAL!
... WE'D LIKE TO ASK Y'ALL SOMETHING!
STOP the STEAL!
TRUMP
WHO HERE REFUSES TO GET VACCINATED...
MAGA
A Black for TRUMP
KARENS FOR
... EVEN THOUGH THE UNVACCINATED ARE THE **ONLY** PEOPLE STILL DYING OF COVID?
SHOW OF HANDS, PLEASE!
GOOD, GOOD.
GBTrudeau
WAIT... WHAT'S THIS ALL ABOUT?
ROUTINE SURVEY.
YOUR NAME, SIR?

August 29, 2021

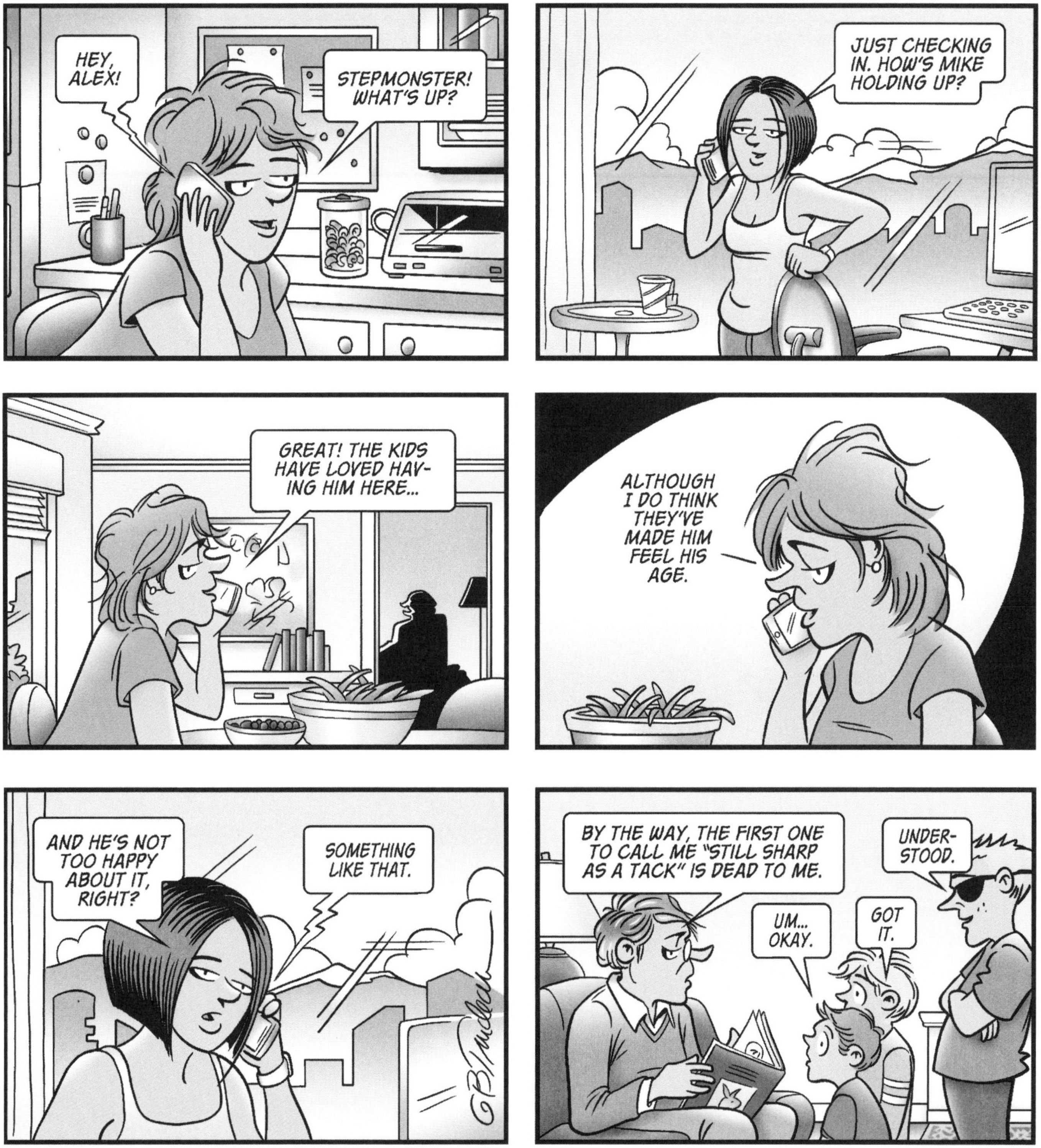
HEY, ALEX!
STEPMONSTER! WHAT'S UP?
JUST CHECKING IN. HOW'S MIKE HOLDING UP?
GREAT! THE KIDS HAVE LOVED HAV-ING HIM HERE...
ALTHOUGH I DO THINK THEY'VE MADE HIM FEEL HIS AGE.
AND HE'S NOT TOO HAPPY ABOUT IT, RIGHT?
SOMETHING LIKE THAT.
BY THE WAY, THE FIRST ONE TO CALL ME "STILL SHARP AS A TACK" IS DEAD TO ME.
UM... OKAY.
GOT IT.
UNDER-STOOD.

September 5, 2021

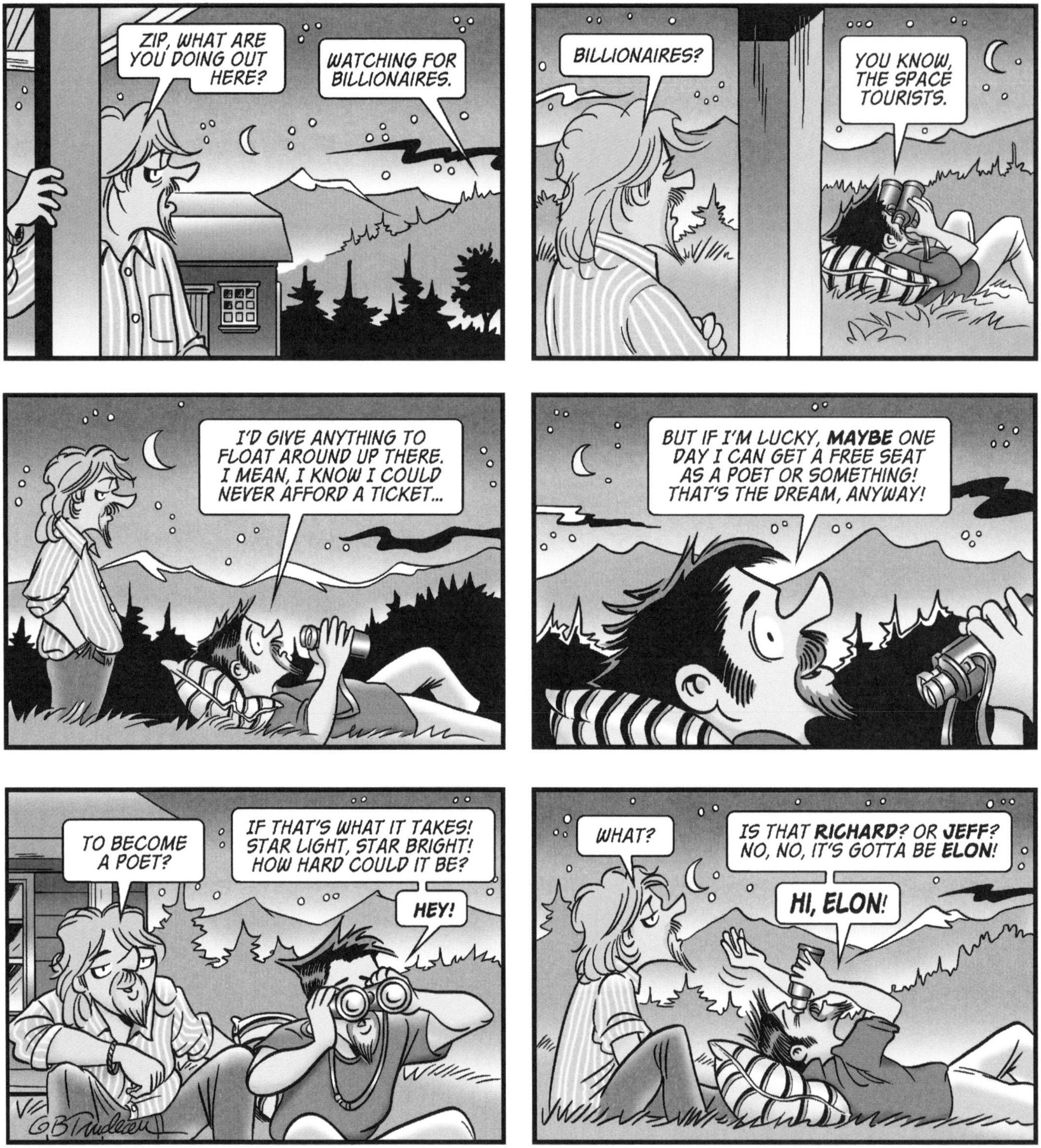

ZIP, WHAT ARE YOU DOING OUT HERE?
WATCHING FOR BILLIONAIRES.
BILLIONAIRES?
YOU KNOW, THE SPACE TOURISTS.
I'D GIVE ANYTHING TO FLOAT AROUND UP THERE. I MEAN, I KNOW I COULD NEVER AFFORD A TICKET...
BUT IF I'M LUCKY, **MAYBE** ONE DAY I CAN GET A FREE SEAT AS A POET OR SOMETHING! THAT'S THE DREAM, ANYWAY!
TO BECOME A POET?
IF THAT'S WHAT IT TAKES! STAR LIGHT, STAR BRIGHT! HOW HARD COULD IT BE?
HEY!
WHAT?
IS THAT **RICHARD**? OR **JEFF**? NO, NO, IT'S GOTTA BE **ELON**!
HI, ELON!
G.B. Trudeau

September 12, 2021

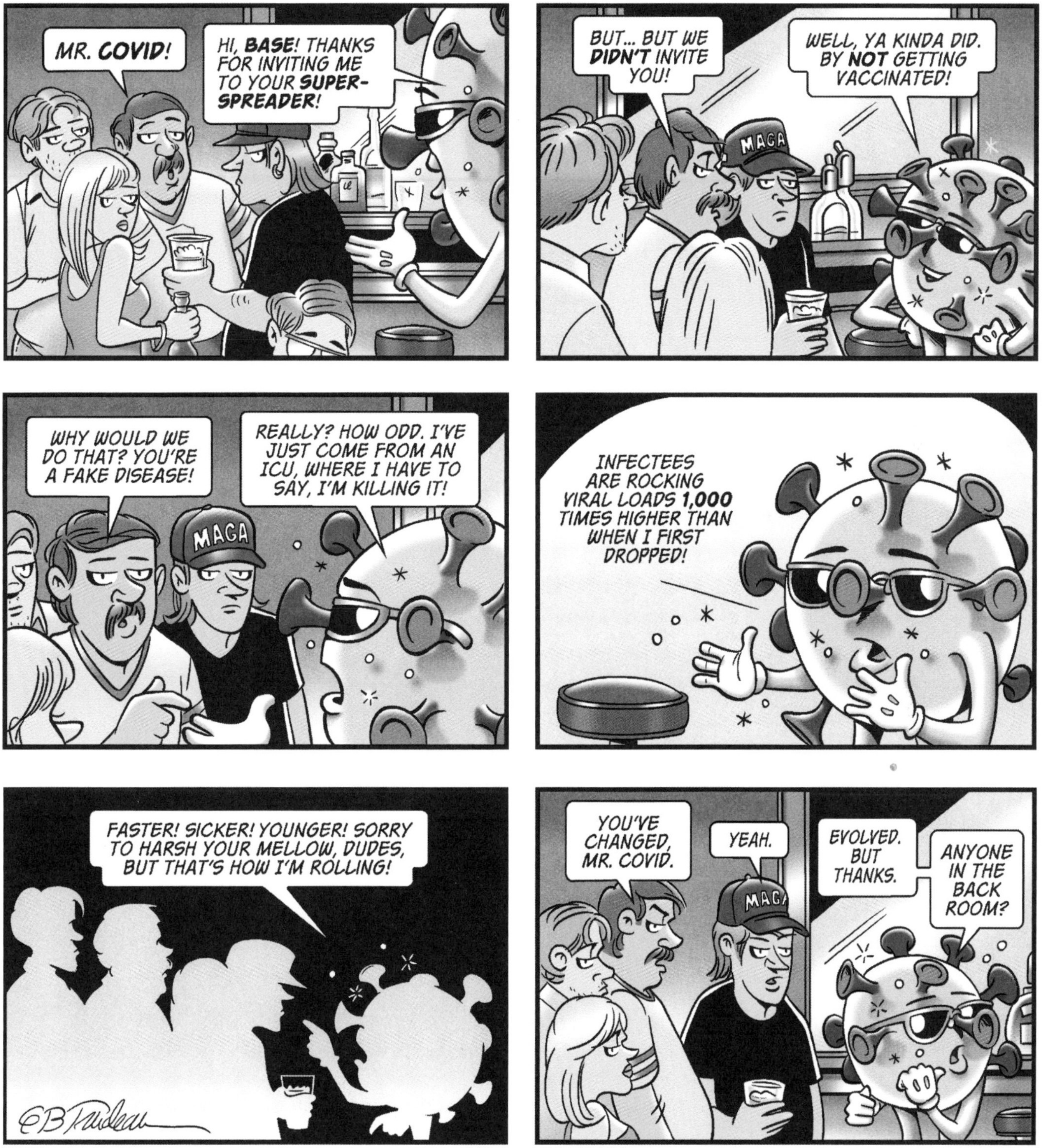
MR. COVID!
HI, BASE! THANKS FOR INVITING ME TO YOUR SUPER-SPREADER!
BUT... BUT WE DIDN'T INVITE YOU!
WELL, YA KINDA DID. BY NOT GETTING VACCINATED!
MAGA
WHY WOULD WE DO THAT? YOU'RE A FAKE DISEASE!
REALLY? HOW ODD. I'VE JUST COME FROM AN ICU, WHERE I HAVE TO SAY, I'M KILLING IT!
INFECTEES ARE ROCKING VIRAL LOADS 1,000 TIMES HIGHER THAN WHEN I FIRST DROPPED!
FASTER! SICKER! YOUNGER! SORRY TO HARSH YOUR MELLOW, DUDES, BUT THAT'S HOW I'M ROLLING!
YOU'VE CHANGED, MR. COVID.
YEAH.
EVOLVED. BUT THANKS.
ANYONE IN THE BACK ROOM?

September 26, 2021

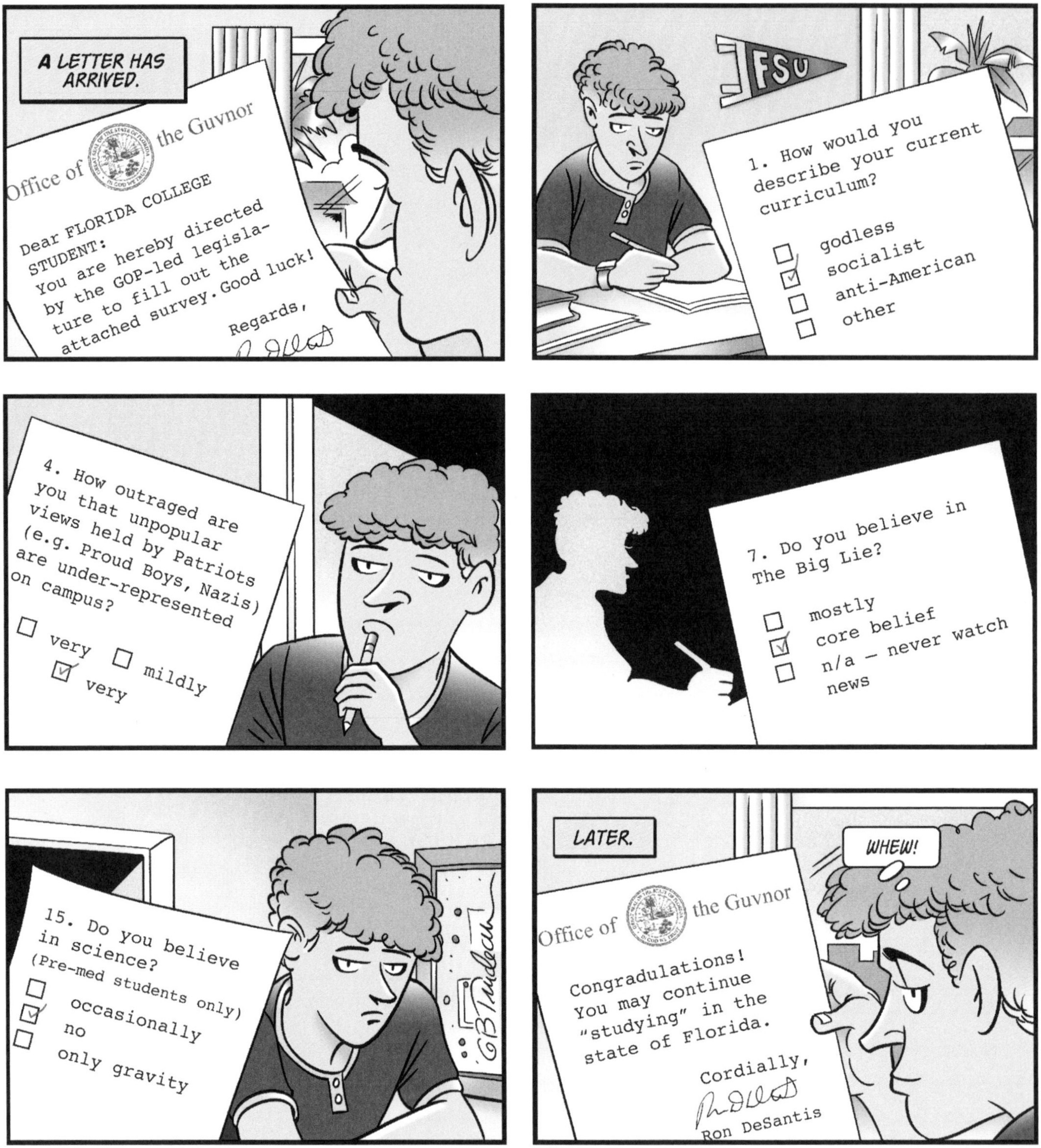

A LETTER HAS ARRIVED.
Office of the Guvnor
Dear FLORIDA COLLEGE STUDENT:
You are hereby directed by the GOP-led legislature to fill out the attached survey. Good luck!
Regards,
1. How would you describe your current curriculum?
godless
socialist
anti-American
other
FSU
4. How outraged are you that unpopular views held by Patriots (e.g. Proud Boys, Nazis) are under-represented on campus?
very
mildly
very
7. Do you believe in The Big Lie?
mostly
core belief
n/a – never watch news
15. Do you believe in science? (Pre-med students only)
occasionally
no
only gravity
LATER.
WHEW!
Office of the Guvnor
Congradulations!
You may continue "studying" in the state of Florida.
Cordially,
Ron DeSantis

October 3, 2021

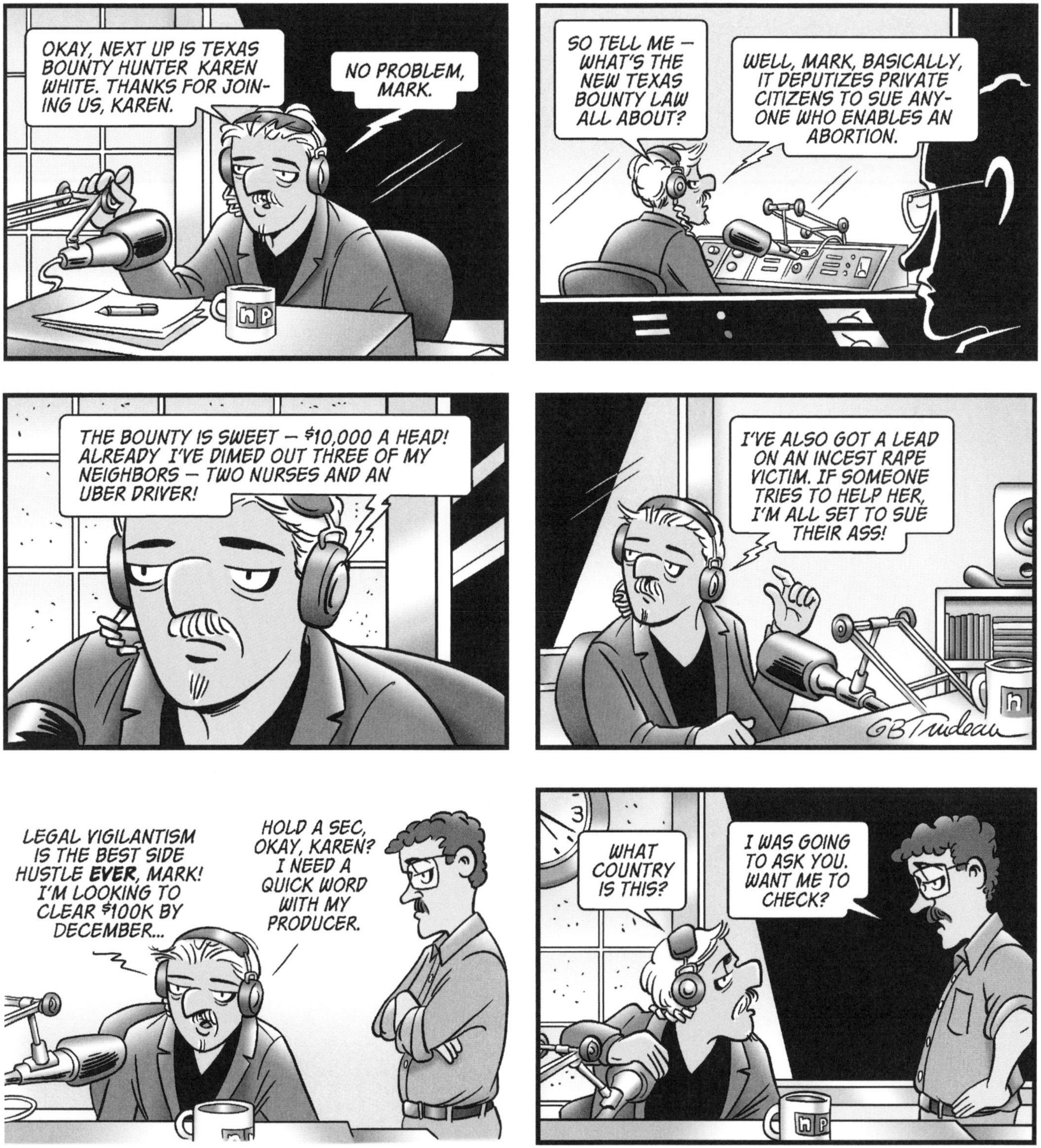
OKAY, NEXT UP IS TEXAS BOUNTY HUNTER KAREN WHITE. THANKS FOR JOINING US, KAREN.
NO PROBLEM, MARK.
SO TELL ME — WHAT'S THE NEW TEXAS BOUNTY LAW ALL ABOUT?
WELL, MARK, BASICALLY, IT DEPUTIZES PRIVATE CITIZENS TO SUE ANYONE WHO ENABLES AN ABORTION.
THE BOUNTY IS SWEET — $10,000 A HEAD! ALREADY I'VE DIMED OUT THREE OF MY NEIGHBORS — TWO NURSES AND AN UBER DRIVER!
I'VE ALSO GOT A LEAD ON AN INCEST RAPE VICTIM. IF SOMEONE TRIES TO HELP HER, I'M ALL SET TO SUE THEIR ASS!
GBTrudeau
LEGAL VIGILANTISM IS THE BEST SIDE HUSTLE EVER, MARK! I'M LOOKING TO CLEAR $100K BY DECEMBER...
HOLD A SEC, OKAY, KAREN? I NEED A QUICK WORD WITH MY PRODUCER.
WHAT COUNTRY IS THIS?
I WAS GOING TO ASK YOU. WANT ME TO CHECK?

October 10, 2021

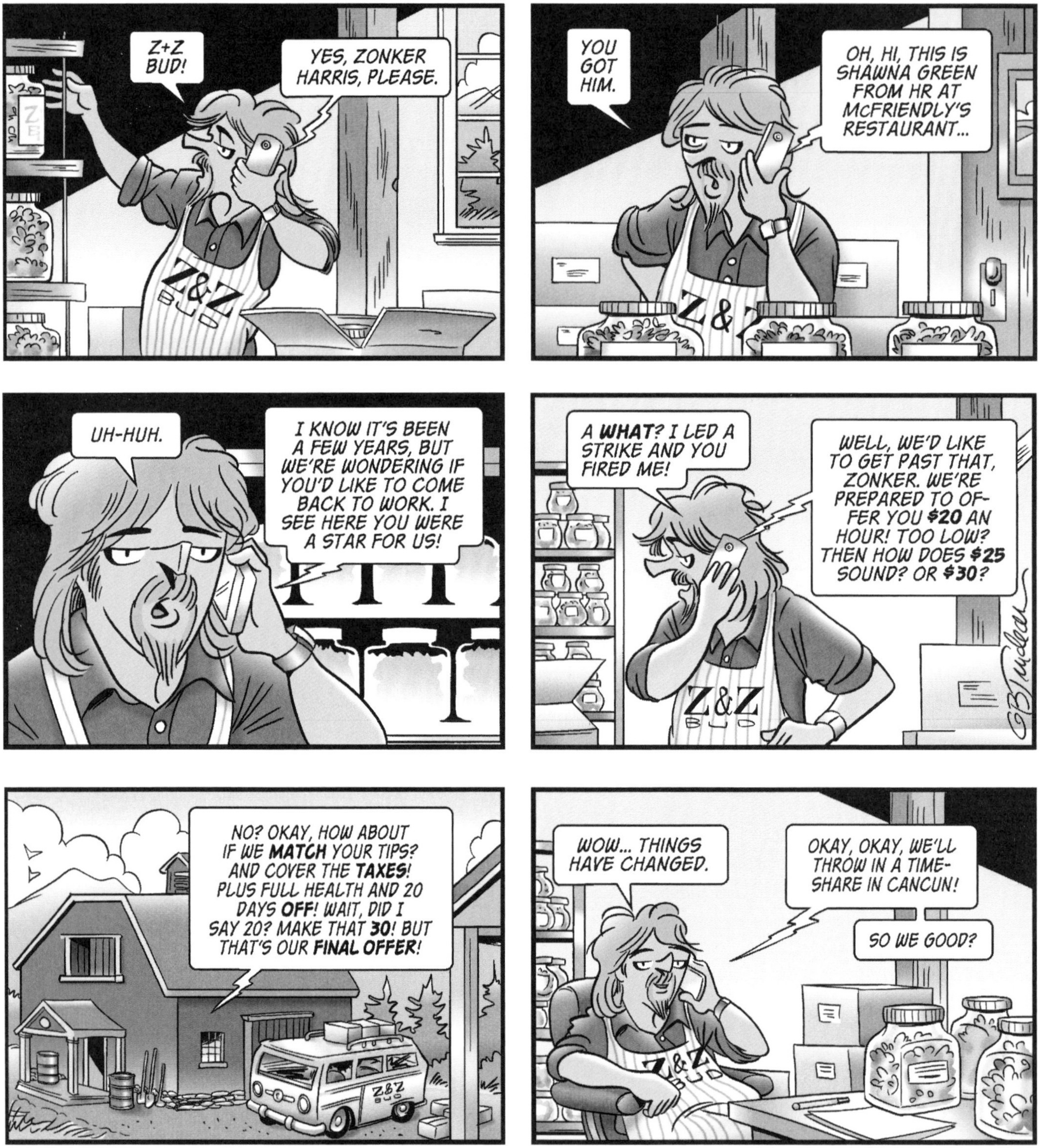
Z+Z BUD!
YES, ZONKER HARRIS, PLEASE.
YOU GOT HIM.
OH, HI, THIS IS SHAWNA GREEN FROM HR AT McFRIENDLY'S RESTAURANT...
UH-HUH.
I KNOW IT'S BEEN A FEW YEARS, BUT WE'RE WONDERING IF YOU'D LIKE TO COME BACK TO WORK. I SEE HERE YOU WERE A STAR FOR US!
A WHAT? I LED A STRIKE AND YOU FIRED ME!
WELL, WE'D LIKE TO GET PAST THAT, ZONKER. WE'RE PREPARED TO OFFER YOU $20 AN HOUR! TOO LOW? THEN HOW DOES $25 SOUND? OR $30?
NO? OKAY, HOW ABOUT IF WE MATCH YOUR TIPS? AND COVER THE TAXES! PLUS FULL HEALTH AND 20 DAYS OFF! WAIT, DID I SAY 20? MAKE THAT 30! BUT THAT'S OUR FINAL OFFER!
WOW... THINGS HAVE CHANGED.
OKAY, OKAY, WE'LL THROW IN A TIME-SHARE IN CANCUN!
SO WE GOOD?

October 17, 2021

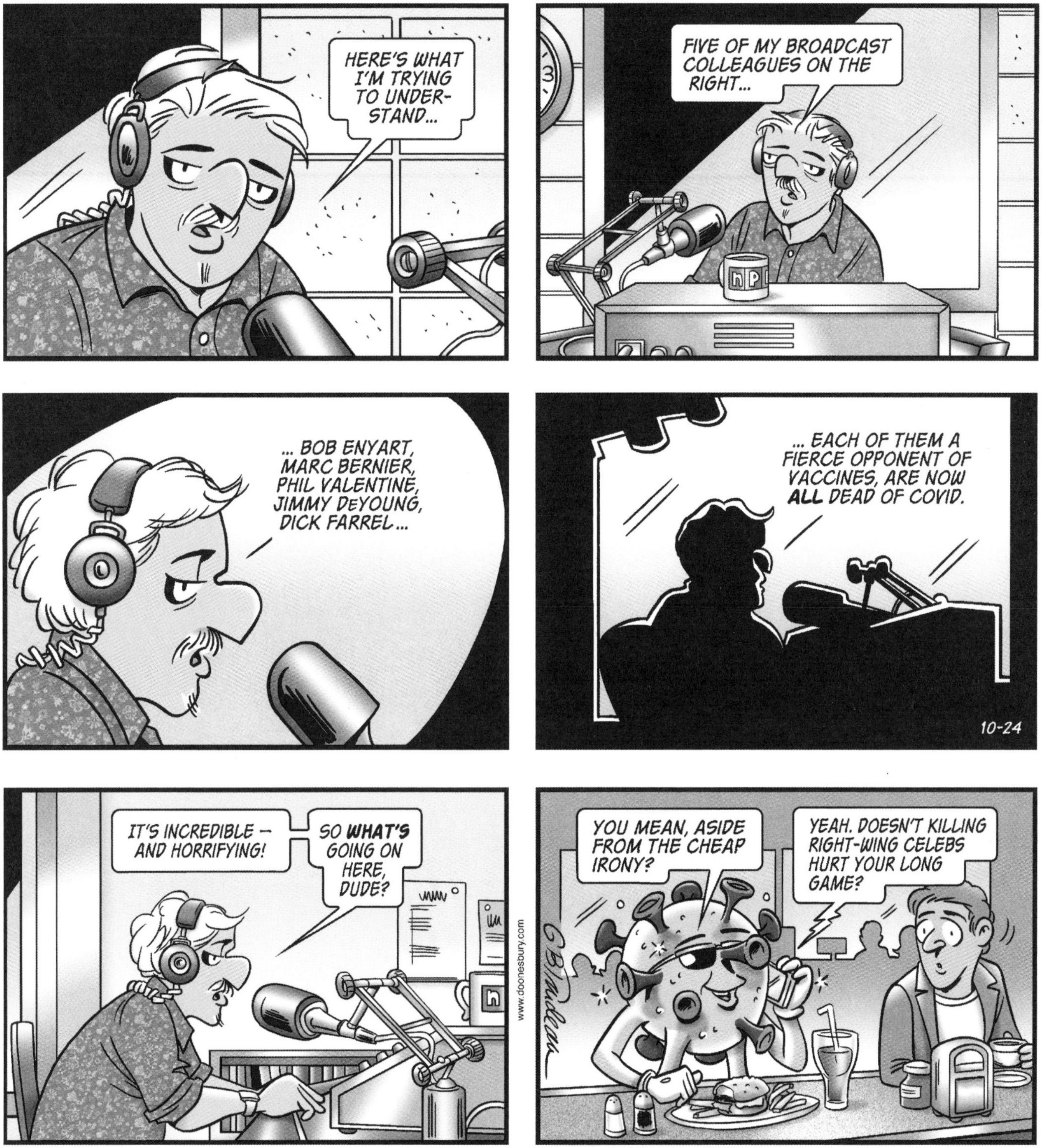
HERE'S WHAT I'M TRYING TO UNDER-STAND...
FIVE OF MY BROADCAST COLLEAGUES ON THE RIGHT...
... BOB ENYART, MARC BERNIER, PHIL VALENTINE, JIMMY DeYOUNG, DICK FARREL...
... EACH OF THEM A FIERCE OPPONENT OF VACCINES, ARE NOW **ALL** DEAD OF COVID.
10-24
IT'S INCREDIBLE — AND HORRIFYING!
SO **WHAT'S** GOING ON HERE, DUDE?
www.doonesbury.com
YOU MEAN, ASIDE FROM THE CHEAP IRONY?
YEAH. DOESN'T KILLING RIGHT-WING CELEBS HURT YOUR LONG GAME?

October 24, 2021

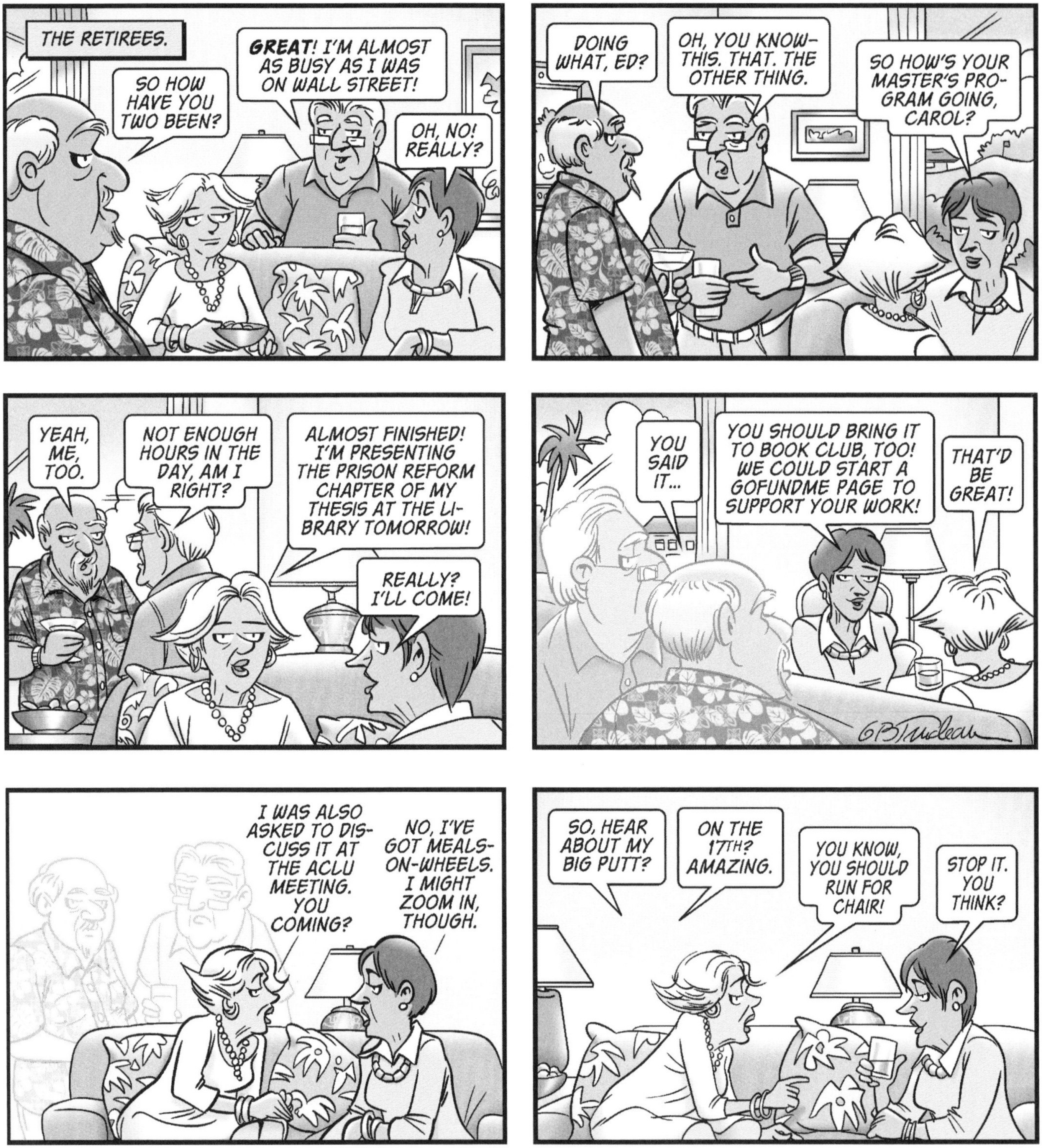
THE RETIREES.
SO HOW HAVE YOU TWO BEEN?
GREAT! I'M ALMOST AS BUSY AS I WAS ON WALL STREET!
OH, NO! REALLY?
DOING WHAT, ED?
OH, YOU KNOW—THIS. THAT. THE OTHER THING.
SO HOW'S YOUR MASTER'S PROGRAM GOING, CAROL?
YEAH, ME, TOO.
NOT ENOUGH HOURS IN THE DAY, AM I RIGHT?
ALMOST FINISHED! I'M PRESENTING THE PRISON REFORM CHAPTER OF MY THESIS AT THE LIBRARY TOMORROW!
REALLY? I'LL COME!
YOU SAID IT...
YOU SHOULD BRING IT TO BOOK CLUB, TOO! WE COULD START A GOFUNDME PAGE TO SUPPORT YOUR WORK!
THAT'D BE GREAT!
GB Trudeau
I WAS ALSO ASKED TO DISCUSS IT AT THE ACLU MEETING. YOU COMING?
NO, I'VE GOT MEALS-ON-WHEELS. I MIGHT ZOOM IN, THOUGH.
SO, HEAR ABOUT MY BIG PUTT?
ON THE 17TH? AMAZING.
YOU KNOW, YOU SHOULD RUN FOR CHAIR!
STOP IT. YOU THINK?

October 31, 2021

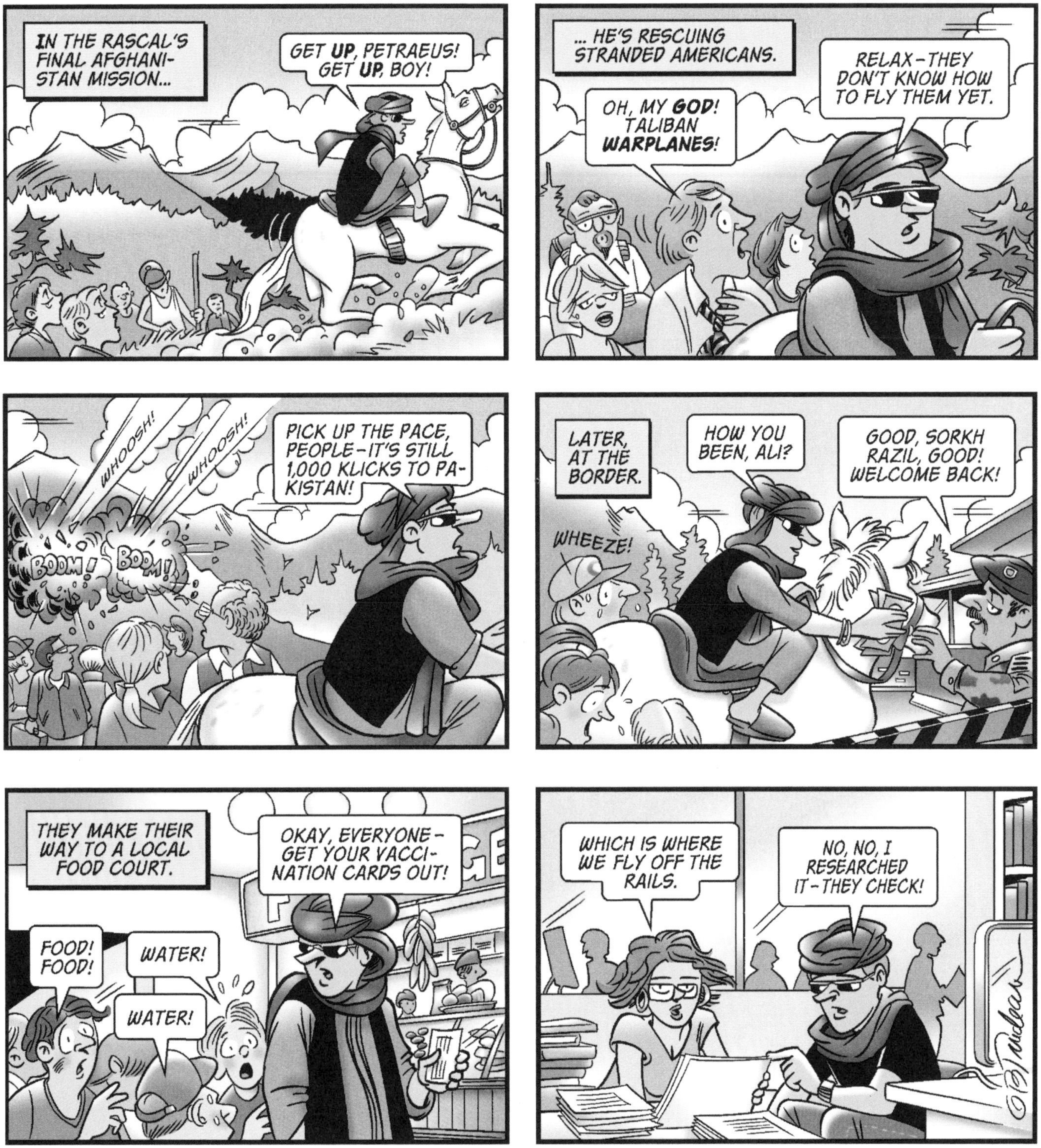
IN THE RASCAL'S FINAL AFGHANI-STAN MISSION...
GET UP, PETRAEUS! GET UP, BOY!
... HE'S RESCUING STRANDED AMERICANS.
OH, MY GOD! TALIBAN WARPLANES!
RELAX–THEY DON'T KNOW HOW TO FLY THEM YET.
WHOOSH!
WHOOSH!
BOOM!
BOOM!
PICK UP THE PACE, PEOPLE–IT'S STILL 1,000 KLICKS TO PA-KISTAN!
LATER, AT THE BORDER.
HOW YOU BEEN, ALI?
GOOD, SORKH RAZIL, GOOD! WELCOME BACK!
WHEEZE!
THEY MAKE THEIR WAY TO A LOCAL FOOD COURT.
OKAY, EVERYONE–GET YOUR VACCI-NATION CARDS OUT!
FOOD! FOOD!
WATER!
WATER!
WHICH IS WHERE WE FLY OFF THE RAILS.
NO, NO, I RESEARCHED IT–THEY CHECK!

November 7, 2021

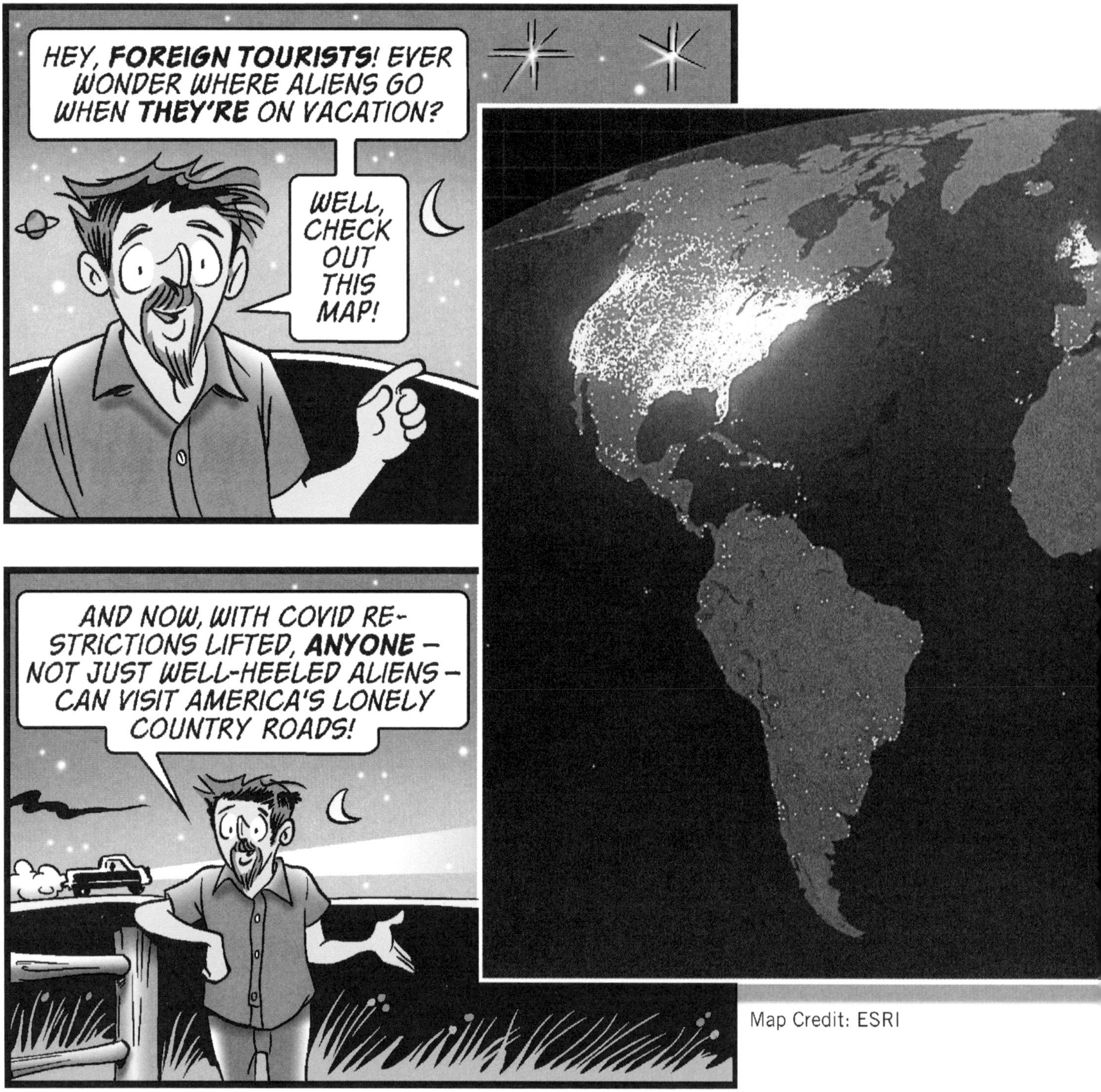
HEY, FOREIGN TOURISTS! EVER WONDER WHERE ALIENS GO WHEN THEY'RE ON VACATION?
WELL, CHECK OUT THIS MAP!
AND NOW, WITH COVID RE-STRICTIONS LIFTED, ANYONE – NOT JUST WELL-HEELED ALIENS – CAN VISIT AMERICA'S LONELY COUNTRY ROADS!

Map Credit: ESRI

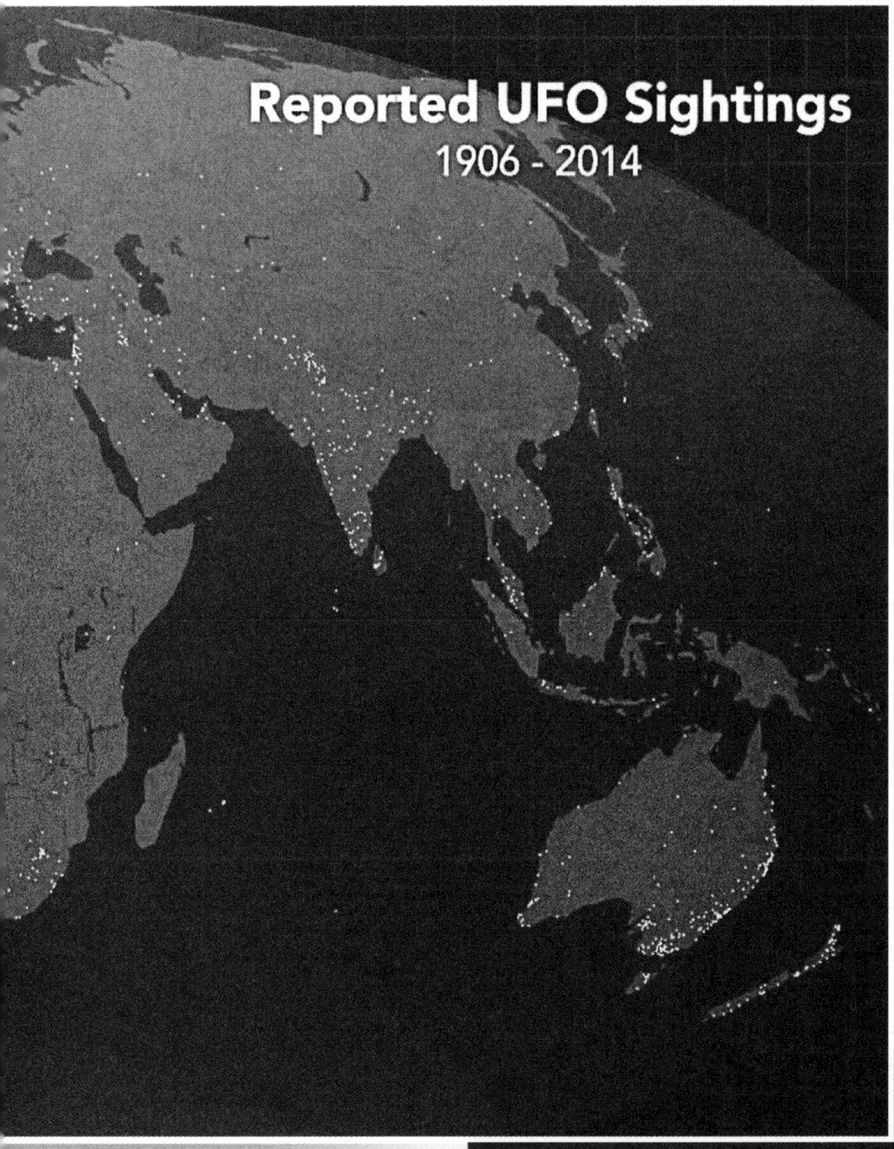
Reported UFO Sightings
1906 - 2014

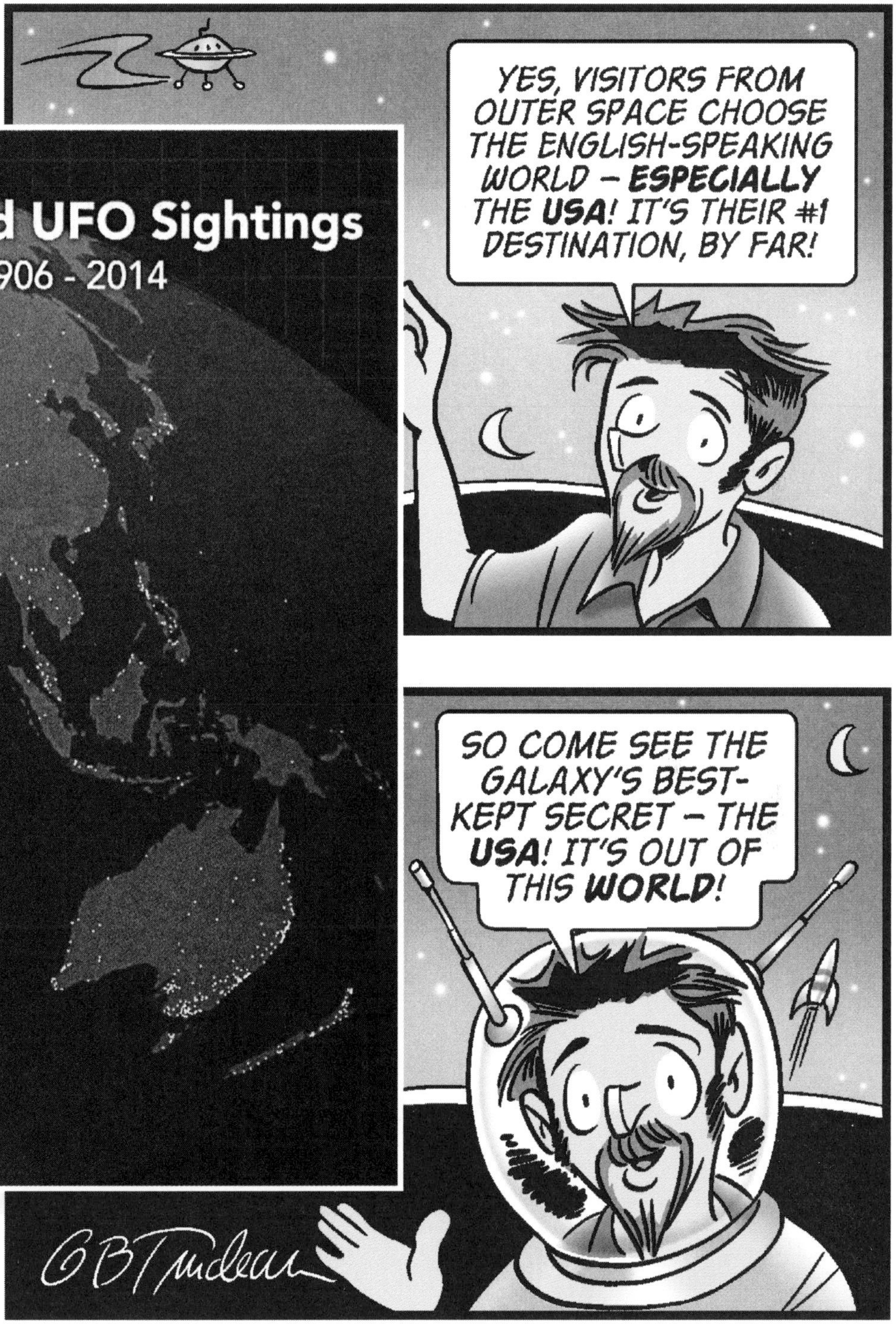
YES, VISITORS FROM OUTER SPACE CHOOSE THE ENGLISH-SPEAKING WORLD – **ESPECIALLY** THE **USA**! IT'S THEIR #1 DESTINATION, BY FAR!
SO COME SEE THE GALAXY'S BEST-KEPT SECRET – THE **USA**! IT'S OUT OF THIS **WORLD**!

November 21, 2021

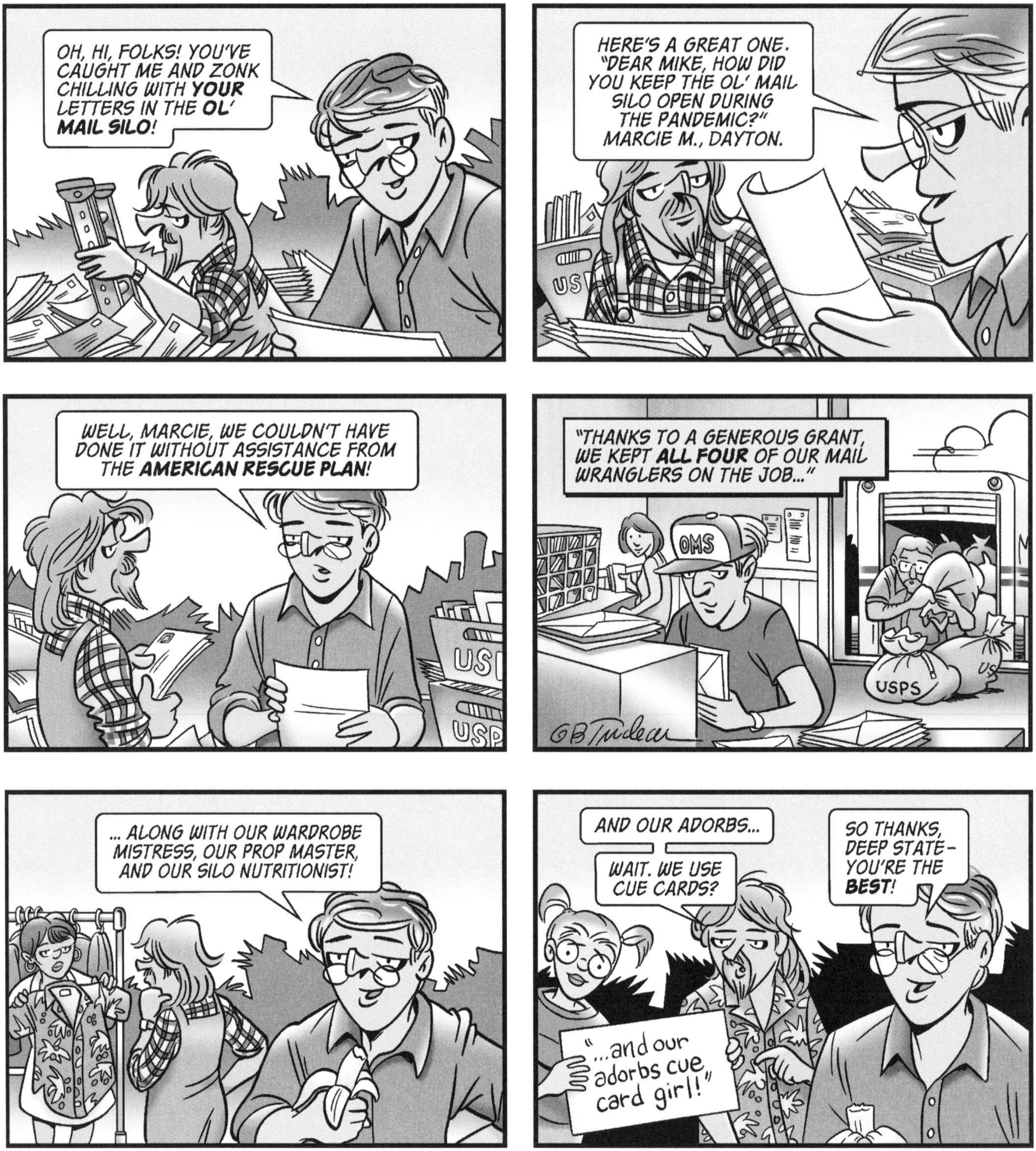
OH, HI, FOLKS! YOU'VE CAUGHT ME AND ZONK CHILLING WITH **YOUR** LETTERS IN THE **OL' MAIL SILO**!
HERE'S A GREAT ONE. "DEAR MIKE, HOW DID YOU KEEP THE OL' MAIL SILO OPEN DURING THE PANDEMIC?" MARCIE M., DAYTON.
WELL, MARCIE, WE COULDN'T HAVE DONE IT WITHOUT ASSISTANCE FROM THE **AMERICAN RESCUE PLAN**!
"THANKS TO A GENEROUS GRANT, WE KEPT **ALL FOUR** OF OUR MAIL WRANGLERS ON THE JOB..."
OMS
USPS
GBTrudeau
... ALONG WITH OUR WARDROBE MISTRESS, OUR PROP MASTER, AND OUR SILO NUTRITIONIST!
AND OUR ADORBS...
WAIT. WE USE CUE CARDS?
SO THANKS, DEEP STATE– YOU'RE THE **BEST**!
"...and our adorbs cue card girl!"

November 14, 2021

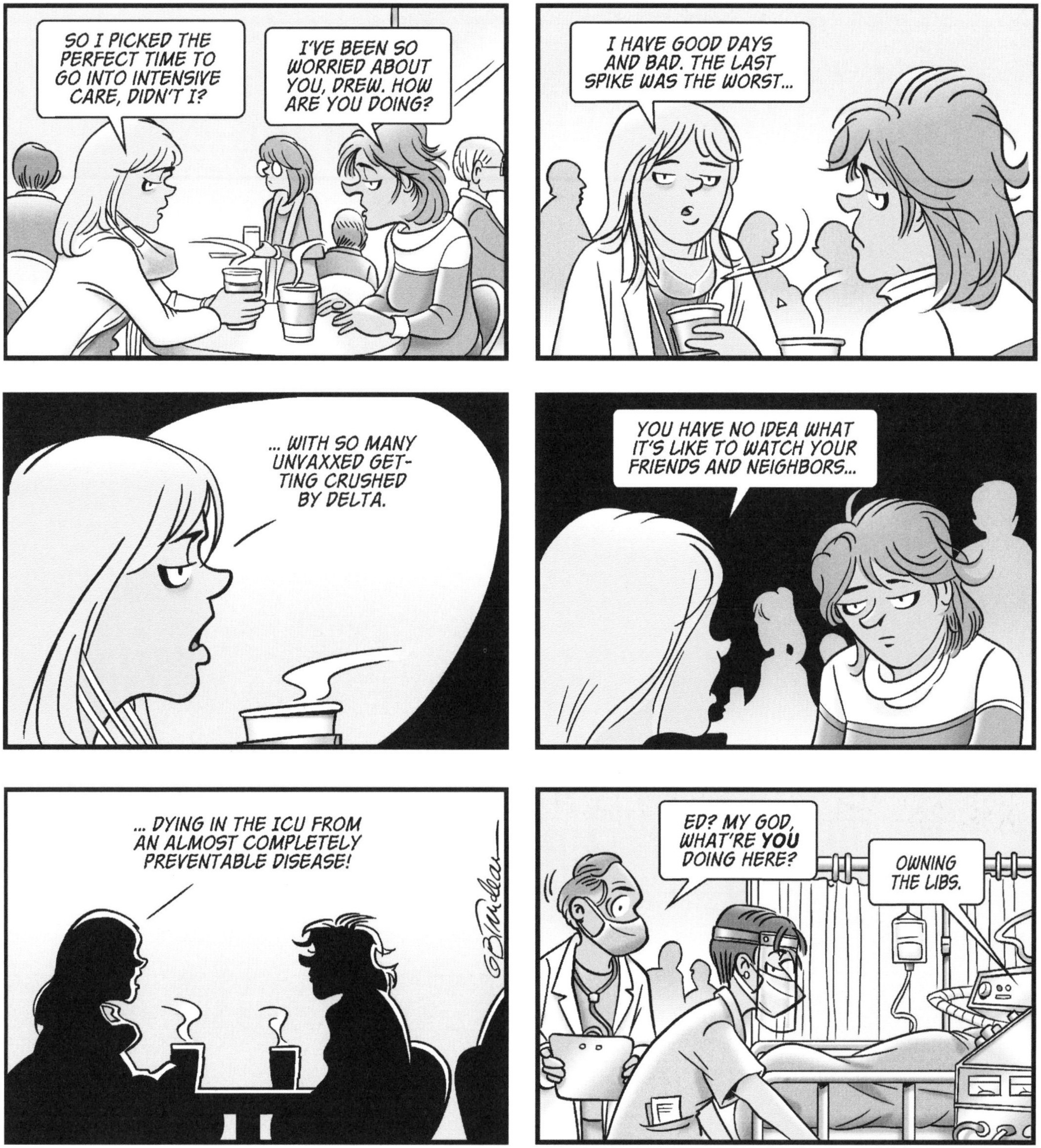

SO I PICKED THE PERFECT TIME TO GO INTO INTENSIVE CARE, DIDN'T I?
I'VE BEEN SO WORRIED ABOUT YOU, DREW. HOW ARE YOU DOING?
I HAVE GOOD DAYS AND BAD. THE LAST SPIKE WAS THE WORST...
... WITH SO MANY UNVAXXED GET-TING CRUSHED BY DELTA.
YOU HAVE NO IDEA WHAT IT'S LIKE TO WATCH YOUR FRIENDS AND NEIGHBORS...
... DYING IN THE ICU FROM AN ALMOST COMPLETELY PREVENTABLE DISEASE!
GBTrudeau
ED? MY GOD, WHAT'RE **YOU** DOING HERE?
OWNING THE LIBS.

November 28, 2021

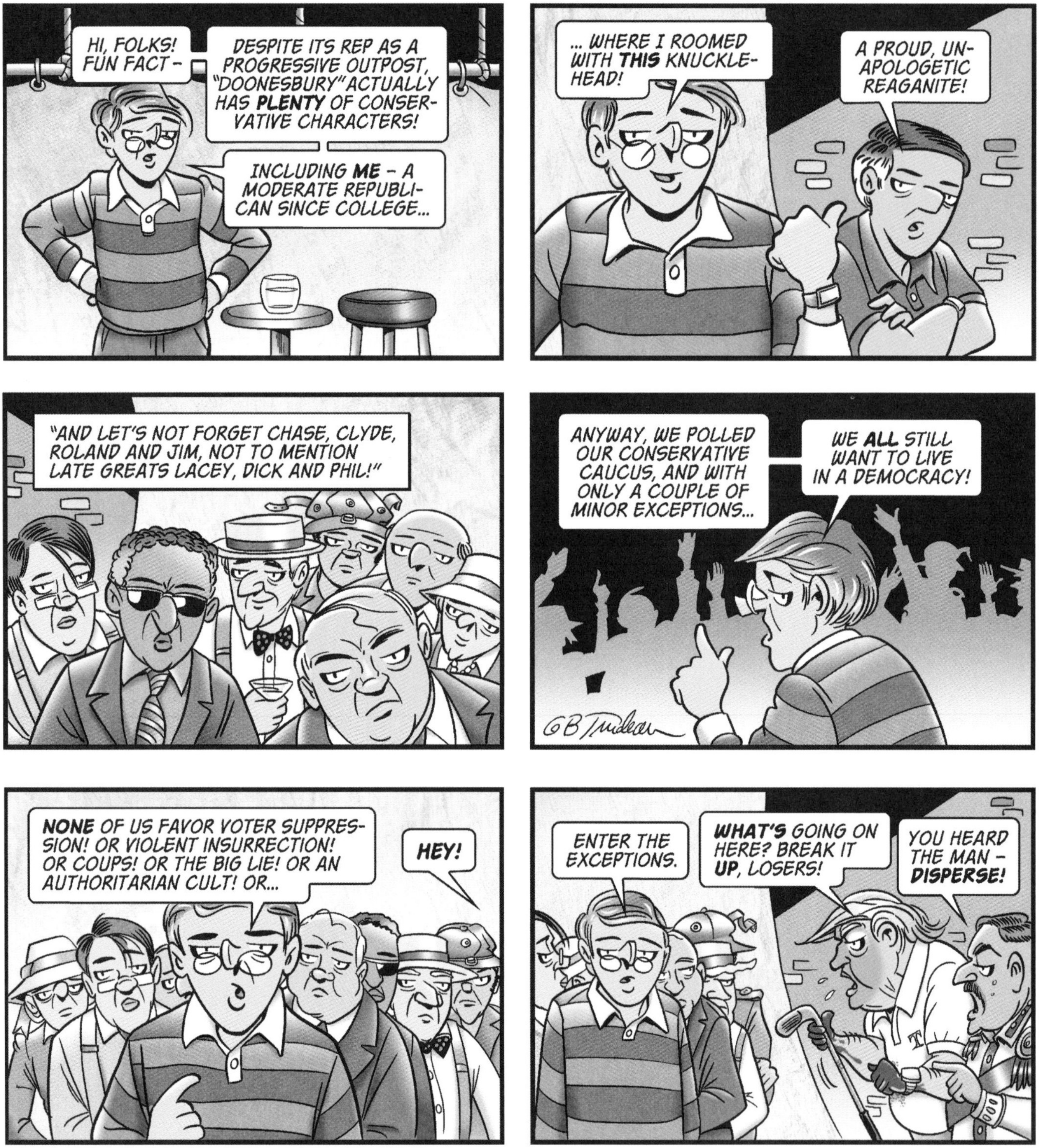
HI, FOLKS! FUN FACT –
DESPITE ITS REP AS A PROGRESSIVE OUTPOST, "DOONESBURY" ACTUALLY HAS **PLENTY** OF CONSERVATIVE CHARACTERS!
INCLUDING **ME** – A MODERATE REPUBLICAN SINCE COLLEGE...
... WHERE I ROOMED WITH **THIS** KNUCKLEHEAD!
A PROUD, UNAPOLOGETIC REAGANITE!
"AND LET'S NOT FORGET CHASE, CLYDE, ROLAND AND JIM, NOT TO MENTION LATE GREATS LACEY, DICK AND PHIL!"
ANYWAY, WE POLLED OUR CONSERVATIVE CAUCUS, AND WITH ONLY A COUPLE OF MINOR EXCEPTIONS...
WE **ALL** STILL WANT TO LIVE IN A DEMOCRACY!
GB Trudeau
NONE OF US FAVOR VOTER SUPPRESSION! OR VIOLENT INSURRECTION! OR COUPS! OR THE BIG LIE! OR AN AUTHORITARIAN CULT! OR...
HEY!
ENTER THE EXCEPTIONS.
WHAT'S GOING ON HERE? BREAK IT **UP**, LOSERS!
YOU HEARD THE MAN – **DISPERSE!**

December 5, 2021

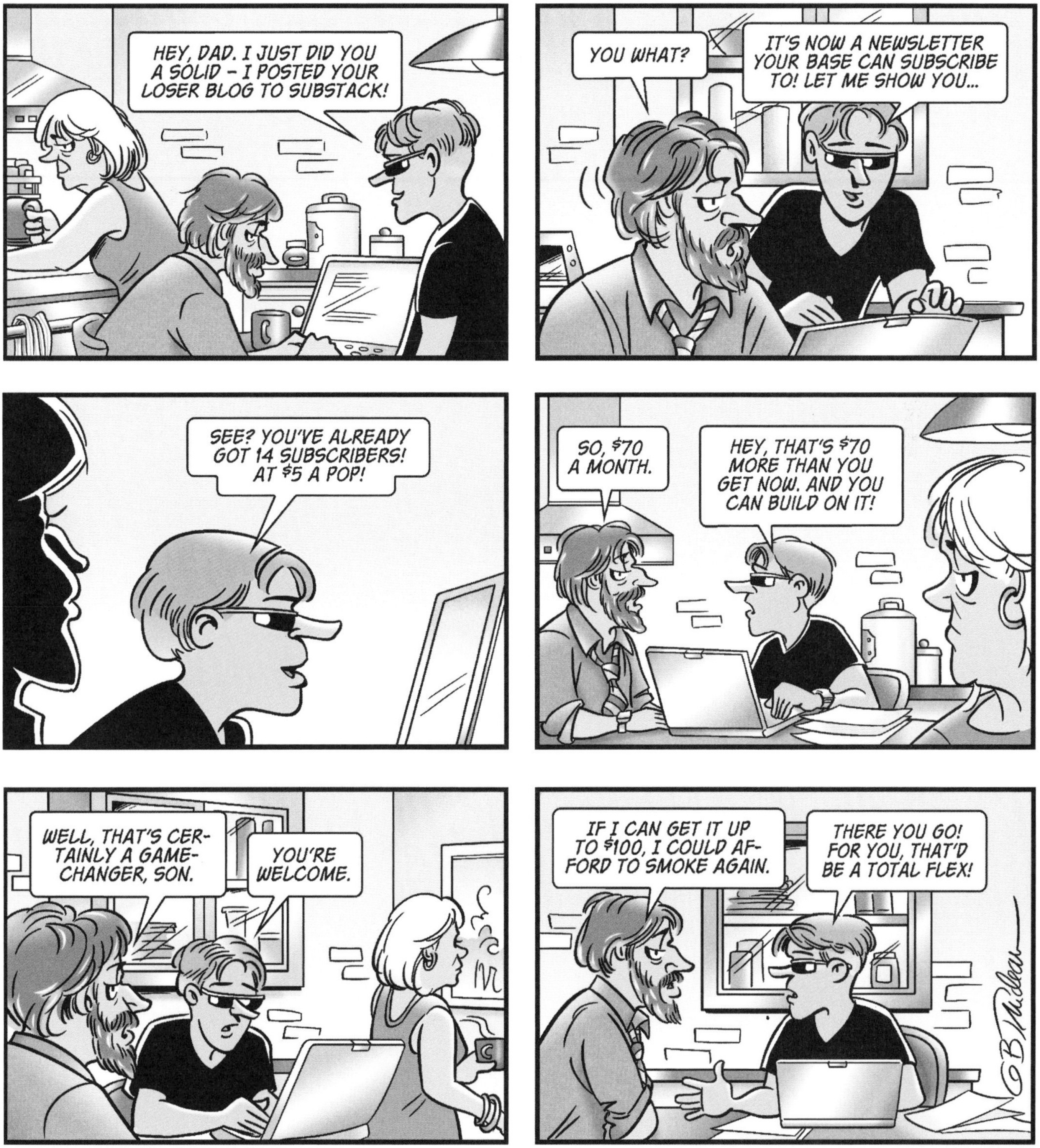
HEY, DAD. I JUST DID YOU A SOLID – I POSTED YOUR LOSER BLOG TO SUBSTACK!
YOU WHAT?
IT'S NOW A NEWSLETTER YOUR BASE CAN SUBSCRIBE TO! LET ME SHOW YOU...
SEE? YOU'VE ALREADY GOT 14 SUBSCRIBERS! AT $5 A POP!
SO, $70 A MONTH.
HEY, THAT'S $70 MORE THAN YOU GET NOW. AND YOU CAN BUILD ON IT!
WELL, THAT'S CERTAINLY A GAME-CHANGER, SON.
YOU'RE WELCOME.
IF I CAN GET IT UP TO $100, I COULD AFFORD TO SMOKE AGAIN.
THERE YOU GO! FOR YOU, THAT'D BE A TOTAL FLEX!
GBTrudeau

December 12, 2021

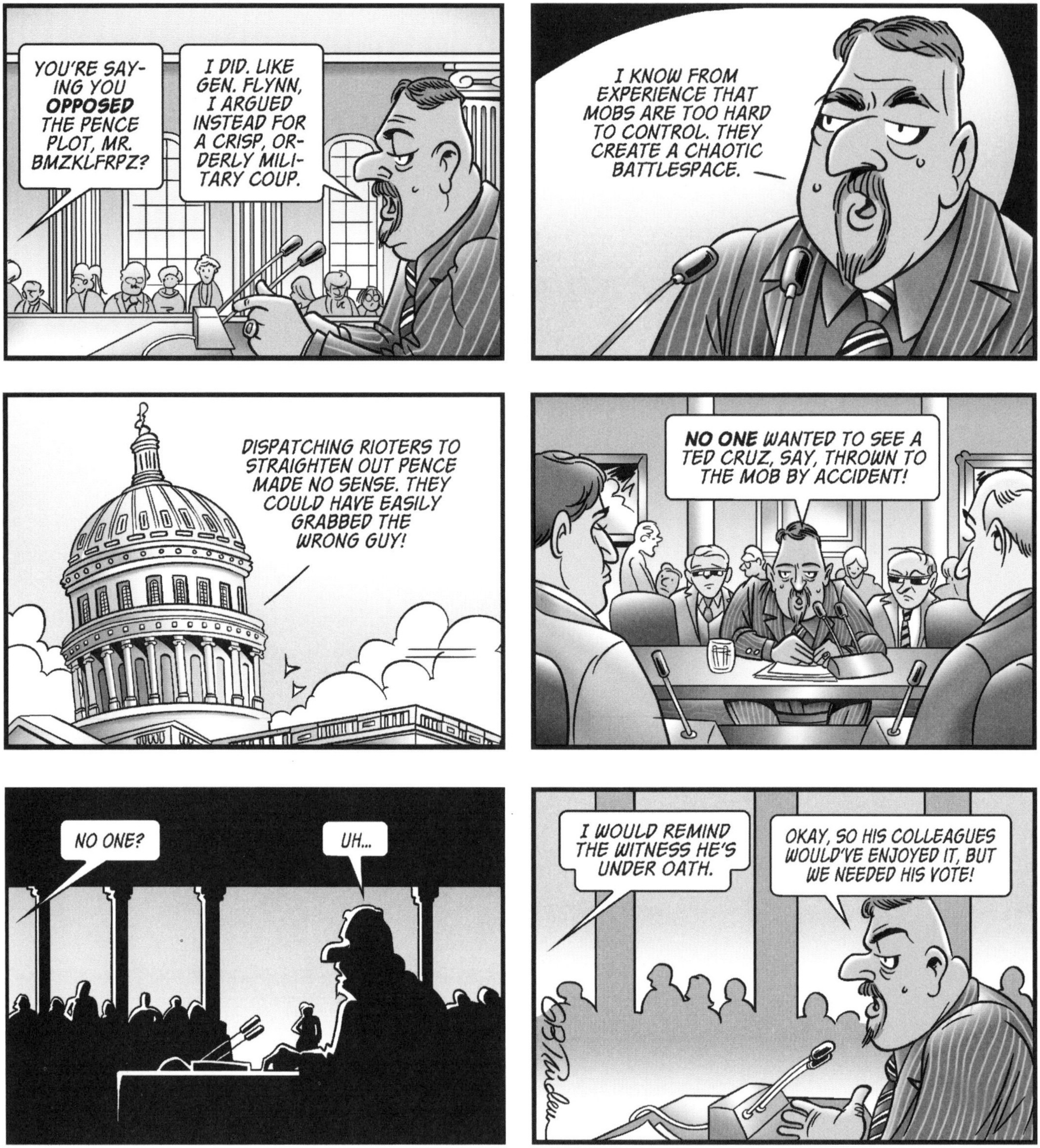
YOU'RE SAYING YOU **OPPOSED** THE PENCE PLOT, MR. BMZKLFRPZ?
I DID. LIKE GEN. FLYNN, I ARGUED INSTEAD FOR A CRISP, ORDERLY MILITARY COUP.
I KNOW FROM EXPERIENCE THAT MOBS ARE TOO HARD TO CONTROL. THEY CREATE A CHAOTIC BATTLESPACE.
DISPATCHING RIOTERS TO STRAIGHTEN OUT PENCE MADE NO SENSE. THEY COULD HAVE EASILY GRABBED THE WRONG GUY!
NO ONE WANTED TO SEE A TED CRUZ, SAY, THROWN TO THE MOB BY ACCIDENT!
NO ONE?
UH...
I WOULD REMIND THE WITNESS HE'S UNDER OATH.
OKAY, SO HIS COLLEAGUES WOULD'VE ENJOYED IT, BUT WE NEEDED HIS VOTE!
GBTrudeau

December 19, 2021

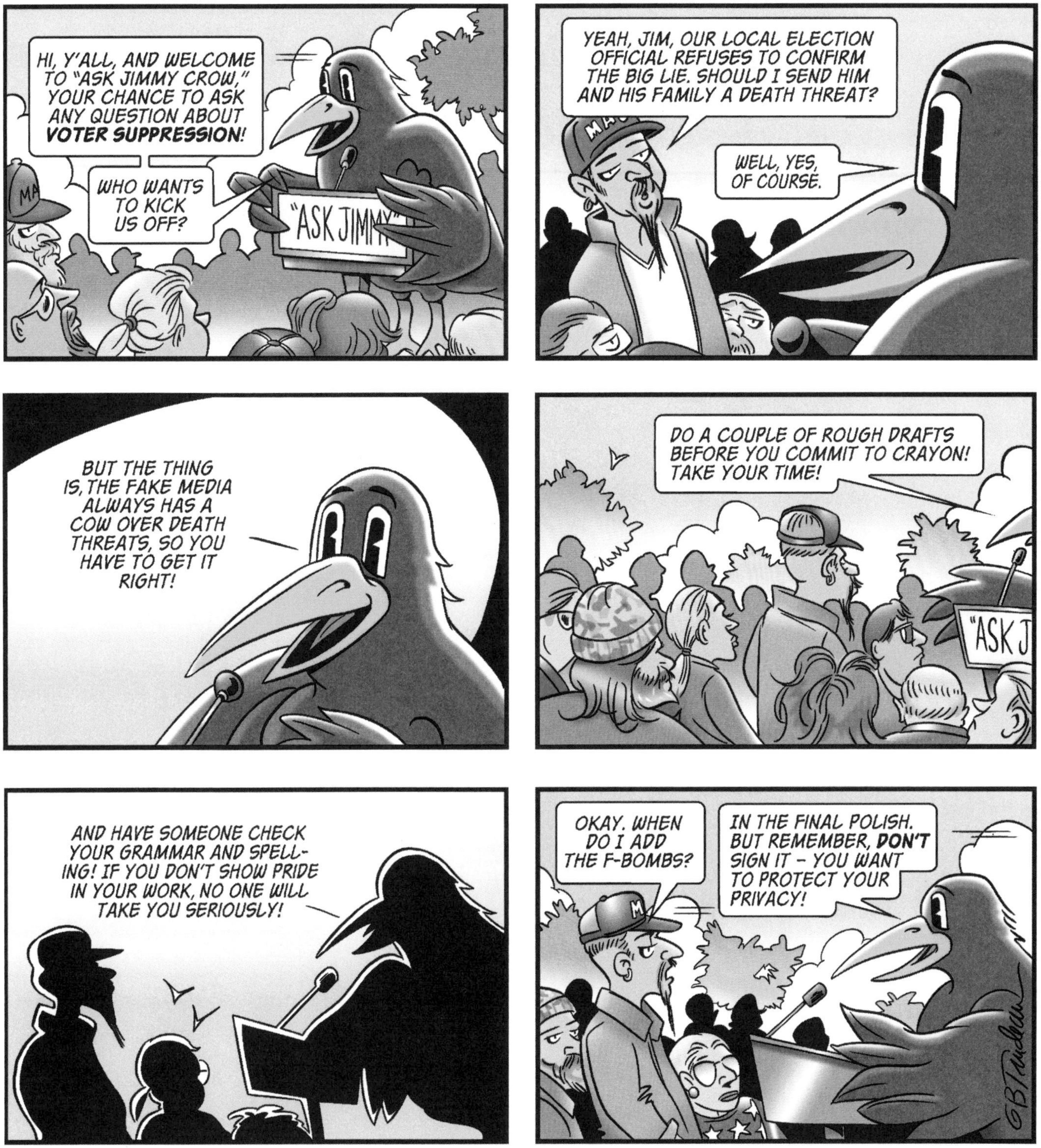
HI, Y'ALL, AND WELCOME TO "ASK JIMMY CROW," YOUR CHANCE TO ASK ANY QUESTION ABOUT **VOTER SUPPRESSION**!
WHO WANTS TO KICK US OFF?
"ASK JIMMY"
YEAH, JIM, OUR LOCAL ELECTION OFFICIAL REFUSES TO CONFIRM THE BIG LIE. SHOULD I SEND HIM AND HIS FAMILY A DEATH THREAT?
WELL, YES, OF COURSE.
BUT THE THING IS, THE FAKE MEDIA ALWAYS HAS A COW OVER DEATH THREATS, SO YOU HAVE TO GET IT RIGHT!
DO A COUPLE OF ROUGH DRAFTS BEFORE YOU COMMIT TO CRAYON! TAKE YOUR TIME!
AND HAVE SOMEONE CHECK YOUR GRAMMAR AND SPELLING! IF YOU DON'T SHOW PRIDE IN YOUR WORK, NO ONE WILL TAKE YOU SERIOUSLY!
OKAY. WHEN DO I ADD THE F-BOMBS?
IN THE FINAL POLISH. BUT REMEMBER, **DON'T** SIGN IT – YOU WANT TO PROTECT YOUR PRIVACY!
GBTrudeau

December 26, 2021

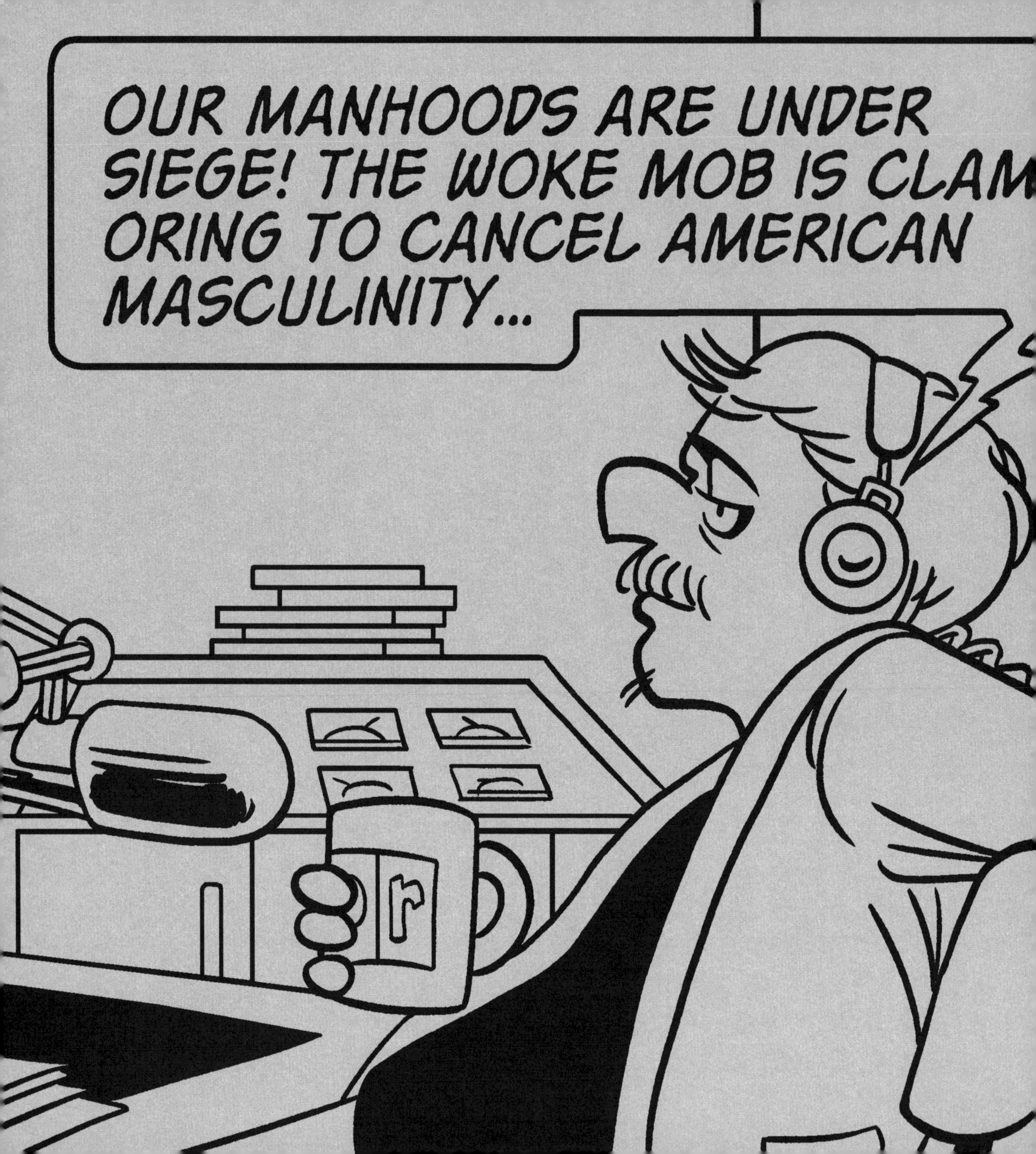
OUR MANHOODS ARE UNDER SIEGE! THE WOKE MOB IS CLAMORING TO CANCEL AMERICAN MASCULINITY...

PART 4

Cancel Culture

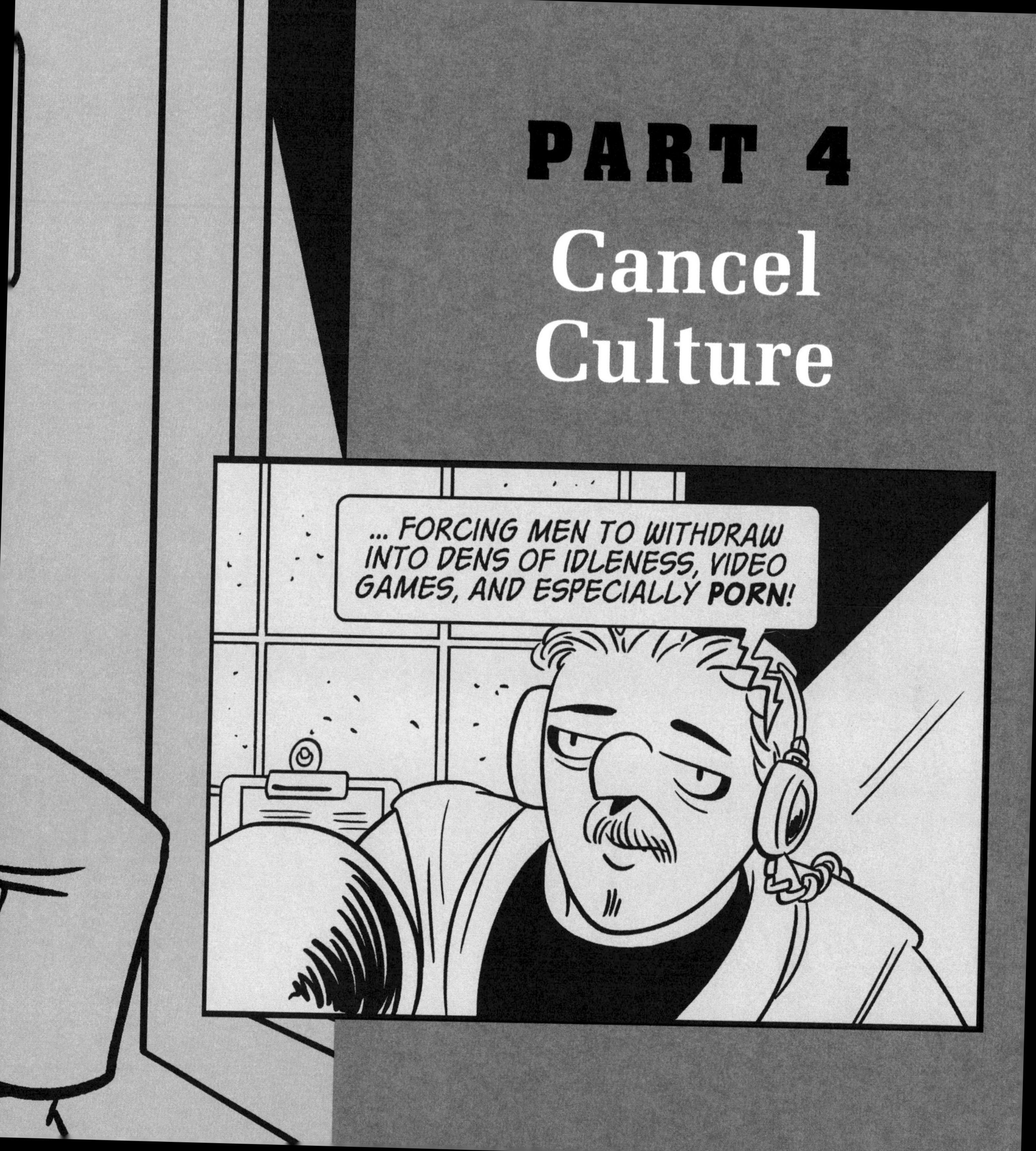

... FORCING MEN TO WITHDRAW INTO DENS OF IDLENESS, VIDEO GAMES, AND ESPECIALLY **PORN**!

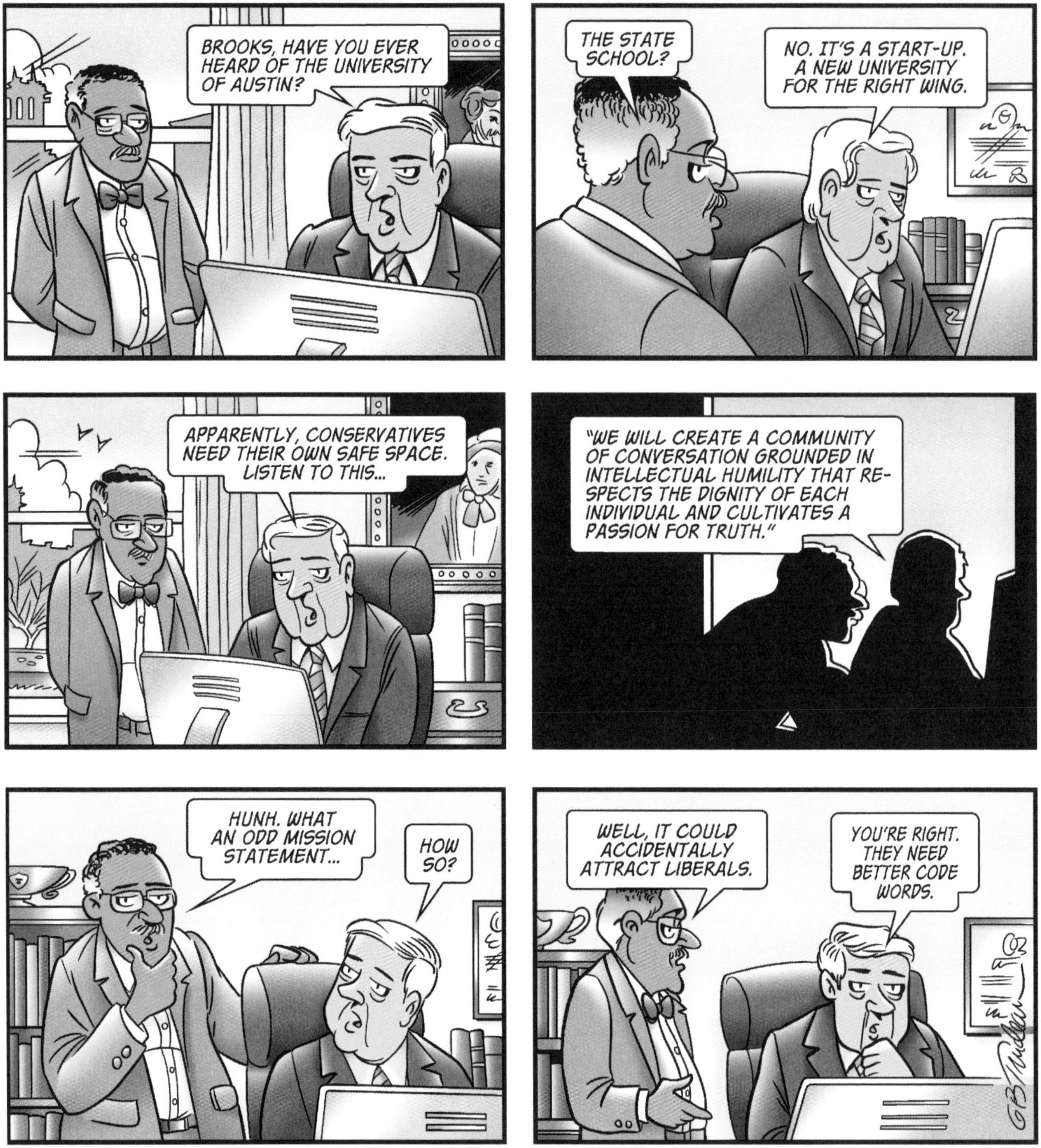
BROOKS, HAVE YOU EVER HEARD OF THE UNIVERSITY OF AUSTIN?
THE STATE SCHOOL?
NO. IT'S A START-UP. A NEW UNIVERSITY FOR THE RIGHT WING.
APPARENTLY, CONSERVATIVES NEED THEIR OWN SAFE SPACE. LISTEN TO THIS...
"WE WILL CREATE A COMMUNITY OF CONVERSATION GROUNDED IN INTELLECTUAL HUMILITY THAT RESPECTS THE DIGNITY OF EACH INDIVIDUAL AND CULTIVATES A PASSION FOR TRUTH."
HUNH. WHAT AN ODD MISSION STATEMENT...
HOW SO?
WELL, IT COULD ACCIDENTALLY ATTRACT LIBERALS.
YOU'RE RIGHT. THEY NEED BETTER CODE WORDS.
GBTrudeau

January 2, 2022

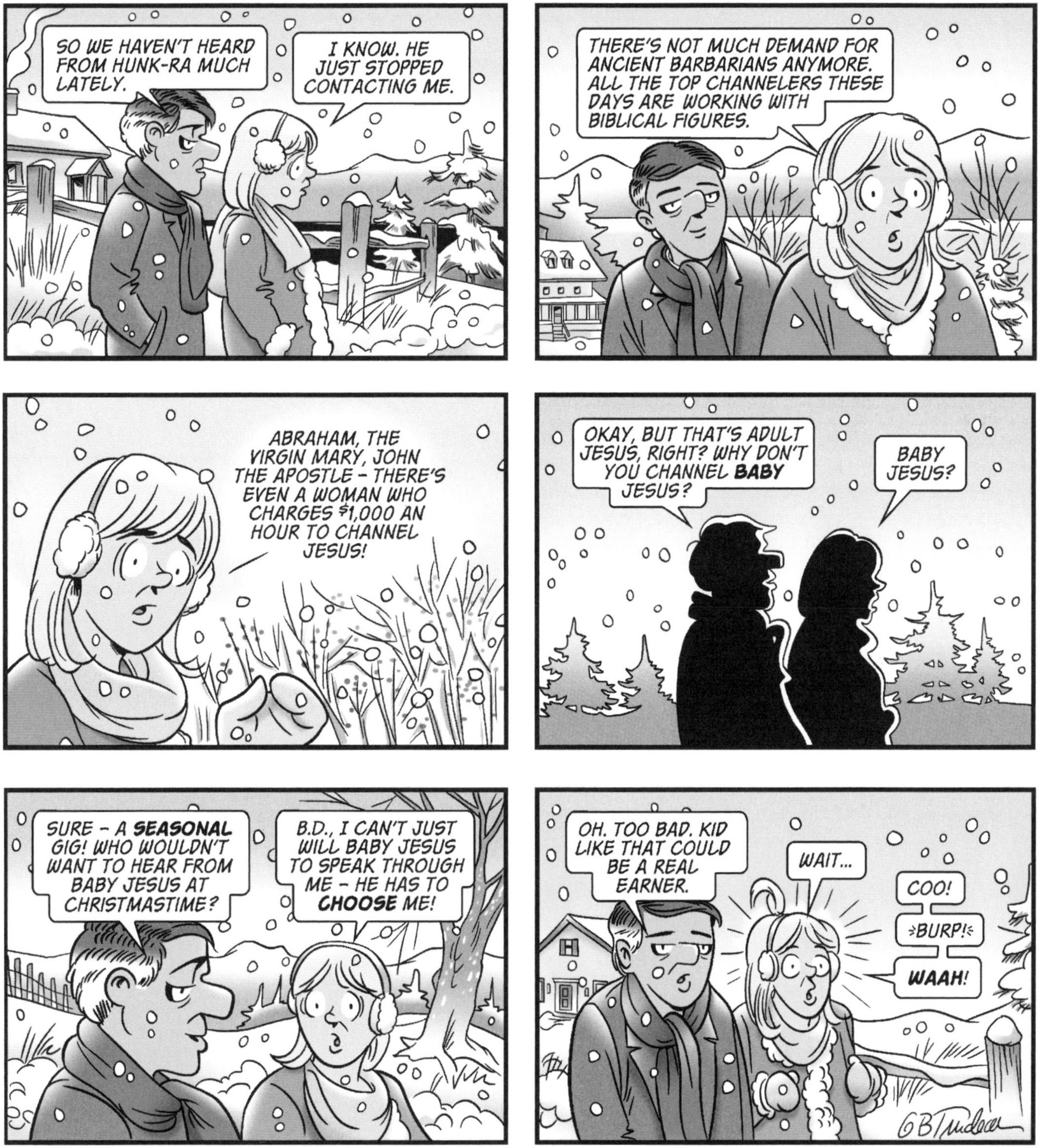

SO WE HAVEN'T HEARD FROM HUNK-RA MUCH LATELY.
I KNOW. HE JUST STOPPED CONTACTING ME.
THERE'S NOT MUCH DEMAND FOR ANCIENT BARBARIANS ANYMORE. ALL THE TOP CHANNELERS THESE DAYS ARE WORKING WITH BIBLICAL FIGURES.
ABRAHAM, THE VIRGIN MARY, JOHN THE APOSTLE – THERE'S EVEN A WOMAN WHO CHARGES $1,000 AN HOUR TO CHANNEL JESUS!
OKAY, BUT THAT'S ADULT JESUS, RIGHT? WHY DON'T YOU CHANNEL **BABY** JESUS?
BABY JESUS?
SURE – A **SEASONAL** GIG! WHO WOULDN'T WANT TO HEAR FROM BABY JESUS AT CHRISTMASTIME?
B.D., I CAN'T JUST WILL BABY JESUS TO SPEAK THROUGH ME – HE HAS TO **CHOOSE** ME!
OH. TOO BAD. KID LIKE THAT COULD BE A REAL EARNER.
WAIT...
COO!
BURP!
WAAH!
GBTrudeau

January 9, 2022

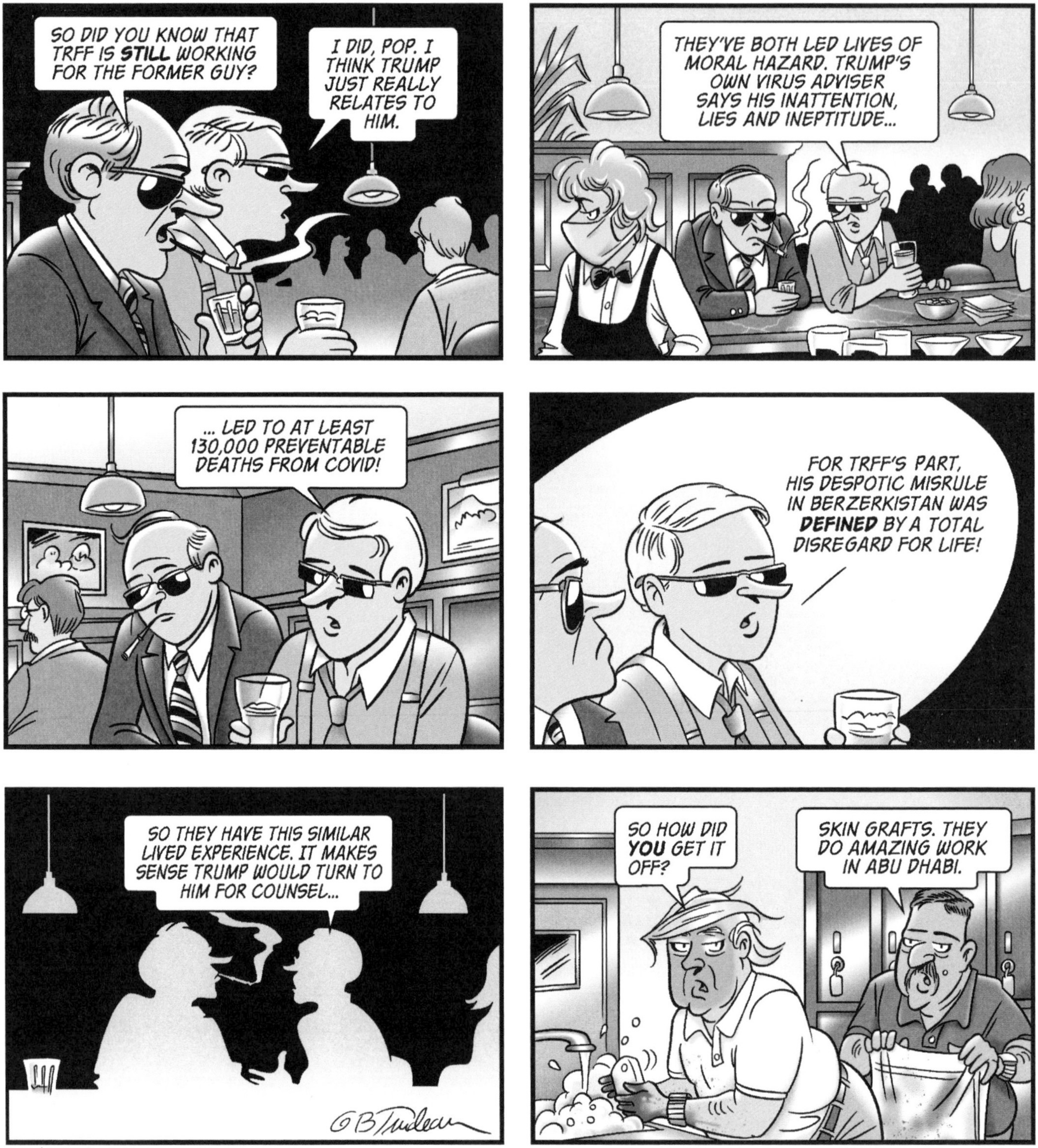
SO DID YOU KNOW THAT TRFF IS **STILL** WORKING FOR THE FORMER GUY?
I DID, POP. I THINK TRUMP JUST REALLY RELATES TO HIM.
THEY'VE BOTH LED LIVES OF MORAL HAZARD. TRUMP'S OWN VIRUS ADVISER SAYS HIS INATTENTION, LIES AND INEPTITUDE...
... LED TO AT LEAST 130,000 PREVENTABLE DEATHS FROM COVID!
FOR TRFF'S PART, HIS DESPOTIC MISRULE IN BERZERKISTAN WAS **DEFINED** BY A TOTAL DISREGARD FOR LIFE!
SO THEY HAVE THIS SIMILAR LIVED EXPERIENCE. IT MAKES SENSE TRUMP WOULD TURN TO HIM FOR COUNSEL...
SO HOW DID **YOU** GET IT OFF?
SKIN GRAFTS. THEY DO AMAZING WORK IN ABU DHABI.
© B Trudeau

January 16, 2022

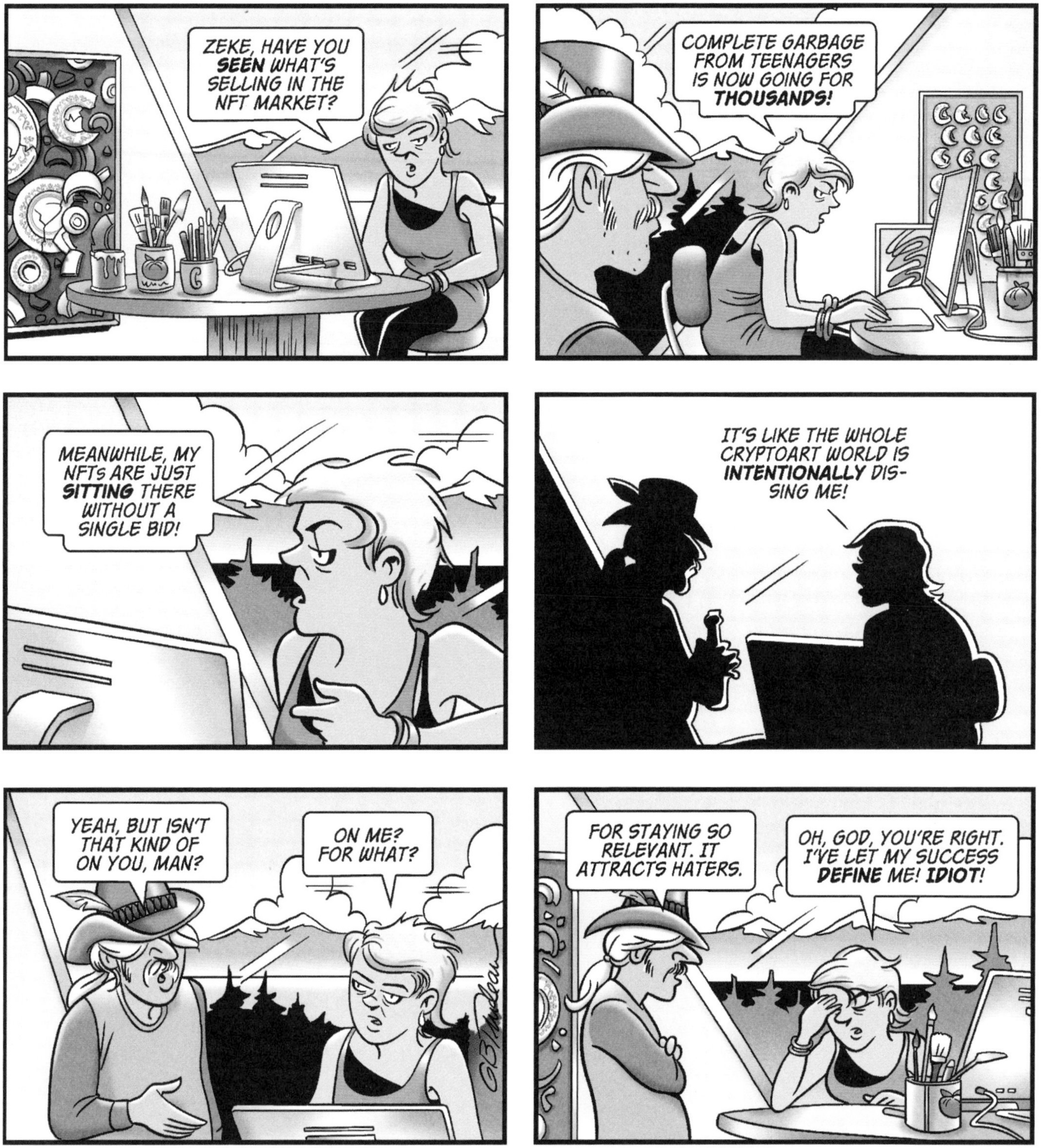
ZEKE, HAVE YOU **SEEN** WHAT'S SELLING IN THE NFT MARKET?
COMPLETE GARBAGE FROM TEENAGERS IS NOW GOING FOR **THOUSANDS!**
MEANWHILE, MY NFTs ARE JUST **SITTING** THERE WITHOUT A SINGLE BID!
IT'S LIKE THE WHOLE CRYPTOART WORLD IS **INTENTIONALLY** DIS-SING ME!
YEAH, BUT ISN'T THAT KIND OF ON YOU, MAN?
ON ME? FOR WHAT?
FOR STAYING SO RELEVANT. IT ATTRACTS HATERS.
OH, GOD, YOU'RE RIGHT. I'VE LET MY SUCCESS **DEFINE** ME! **IDIOT**!
GBTrudeau

January 23, 2022

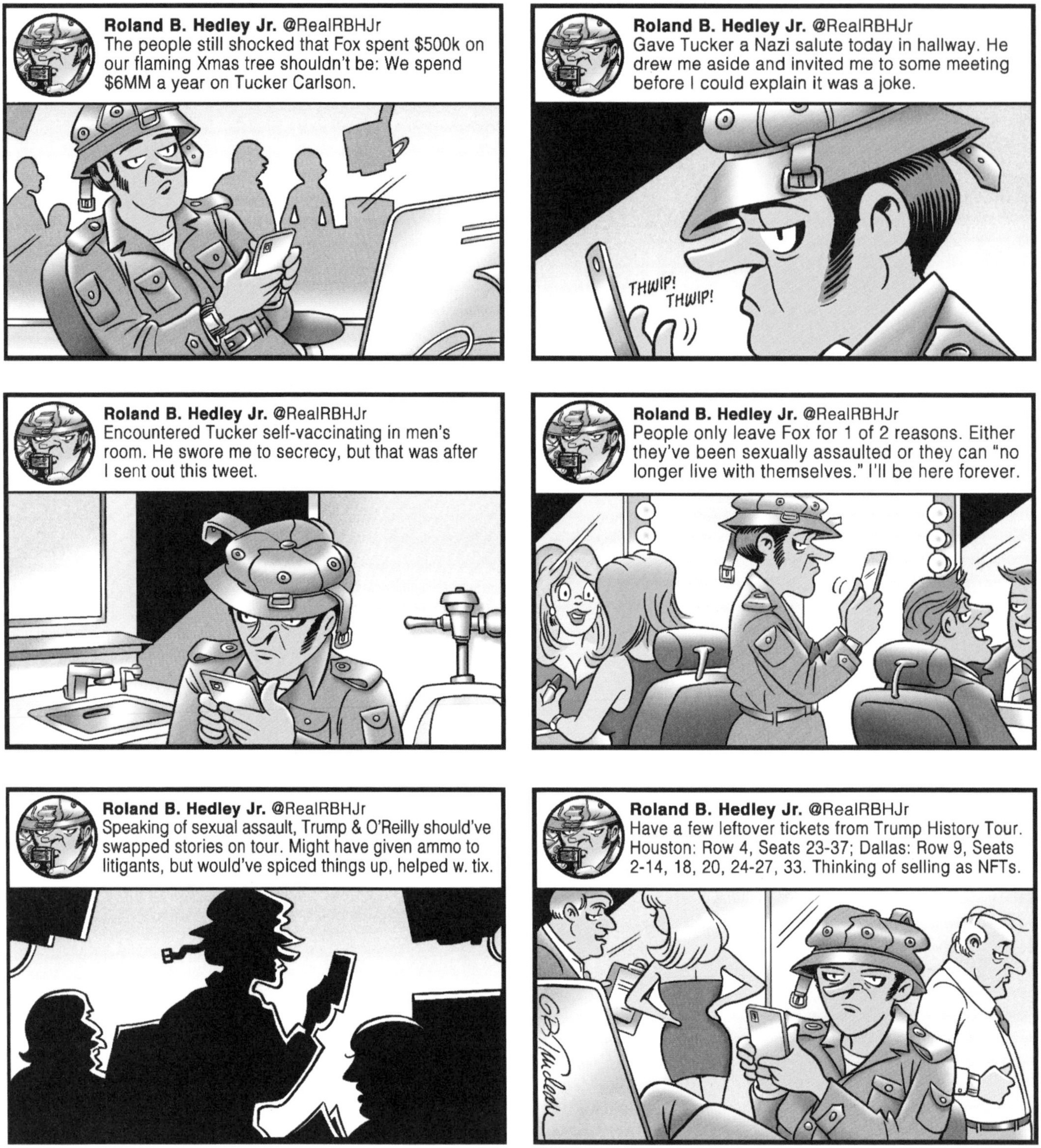
Roland B. Hedley Jr. @RealRBHJr
The people still shocked that Fox spent $500k on our flaming Xmas tree shouldn't be: We spend $6MM a year on Tucker Carlson.
Roland B. Hedley Jr. @RealRBHJr
Gave Tucker a Nazi salute today in hallway. He drew me aside and invited me to some meeting before I could explain it was a joke.
THWIP!
THWIP!
Roland B. Hedley Jr. @RealRBHJr
Encountered Tucker self-vaccinating in men's room. He swore me to secrecy, but that was after I sent out this tweet.
Roland B. Hedley Jr. @RealRBHJr
People only leave Fox for 1 of 2 reasons. Either they've been sexually assaulted or they can "no longer live with themselves." I'll be here forever.
Roland B. Hedley Jr. @RealRBHJr
Speaking of sexual assault, Trump & O'Reilly should've swapped stories on tour. Might have given ammo to litigants, but would've spiced things up, helped w. tix.
Roland B. Hedley Jr. @RealRBHJr
Have a few leftover tickets from Trump History Tour. Houston: Row 4, Seats 23-37; Dallas: Row 9, Seats 2-14, 18, 20, 24-27, 33. Thinking of selling as NFTs.

January 30, 2022

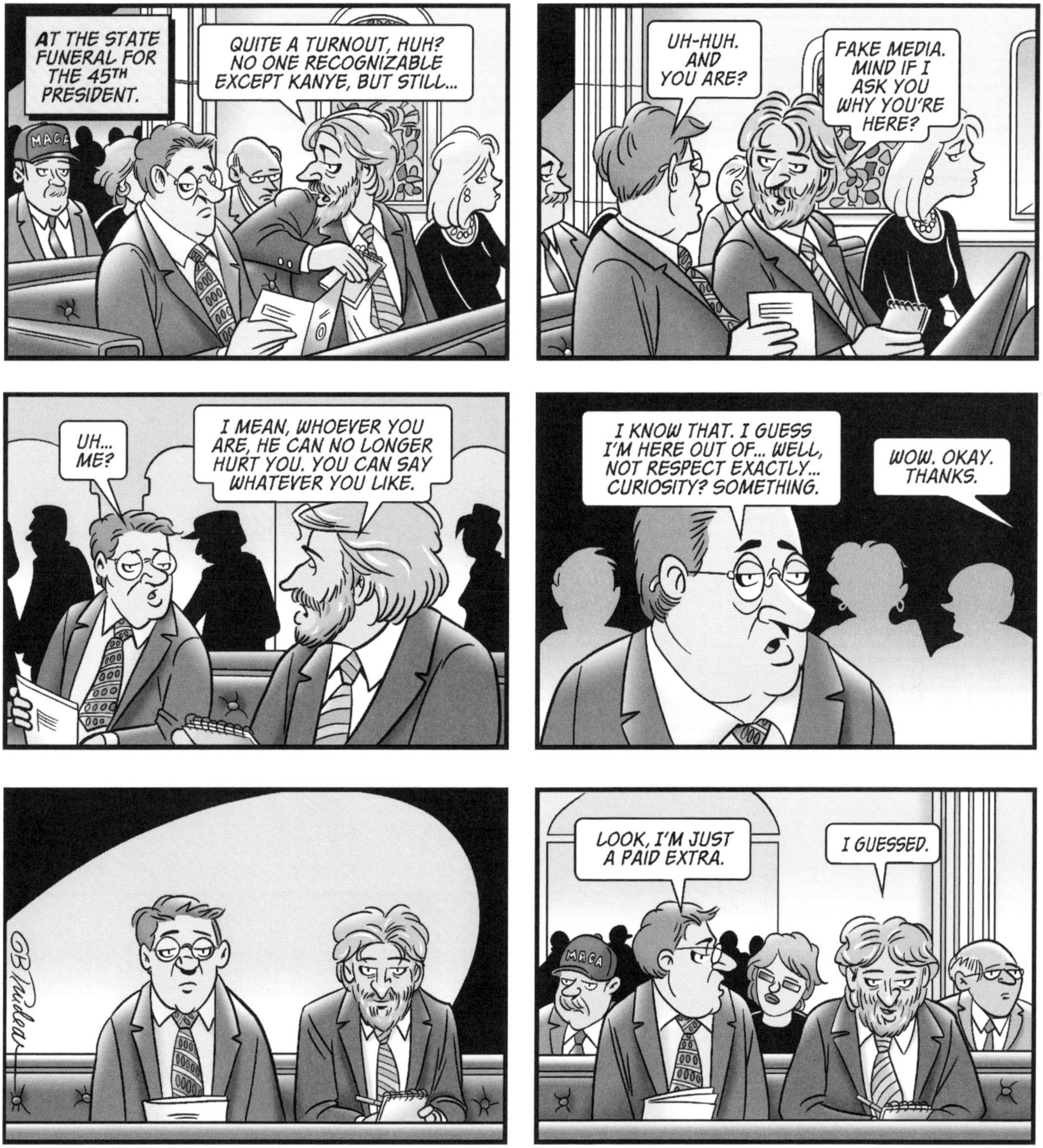

AT THE STATE FUNERAL FOR THE 45TH PRESIDENT.
QUITE A TURNOUT, HUH? NO ONE RECOGNIZABLE EXCEPT KANYE, BUT STILL...
MAGA
UH-HUH. AND YOU ARE?
FAKE MEDIA. MIND IF I ASK YOU WHY YOU'RE HERE?
UH... ME?
I MEAN, WHOEVER YOU ARE, HE CAN NO LONGER HURT YOU. YOU CAN SAY WHATEVER YOU LIKE.
I KNOW THAT. I GUESS I'M HERE OUT OF... WELL, NOT RESPECT EXACTLY... CURIOSITY? SOMETHING.
WOW. OKAY. THANKS.
GBTrudeau
LOOK, I'M JUST A PAID EXTRA.
I GUESSED.
MAGA

February 6, 2022

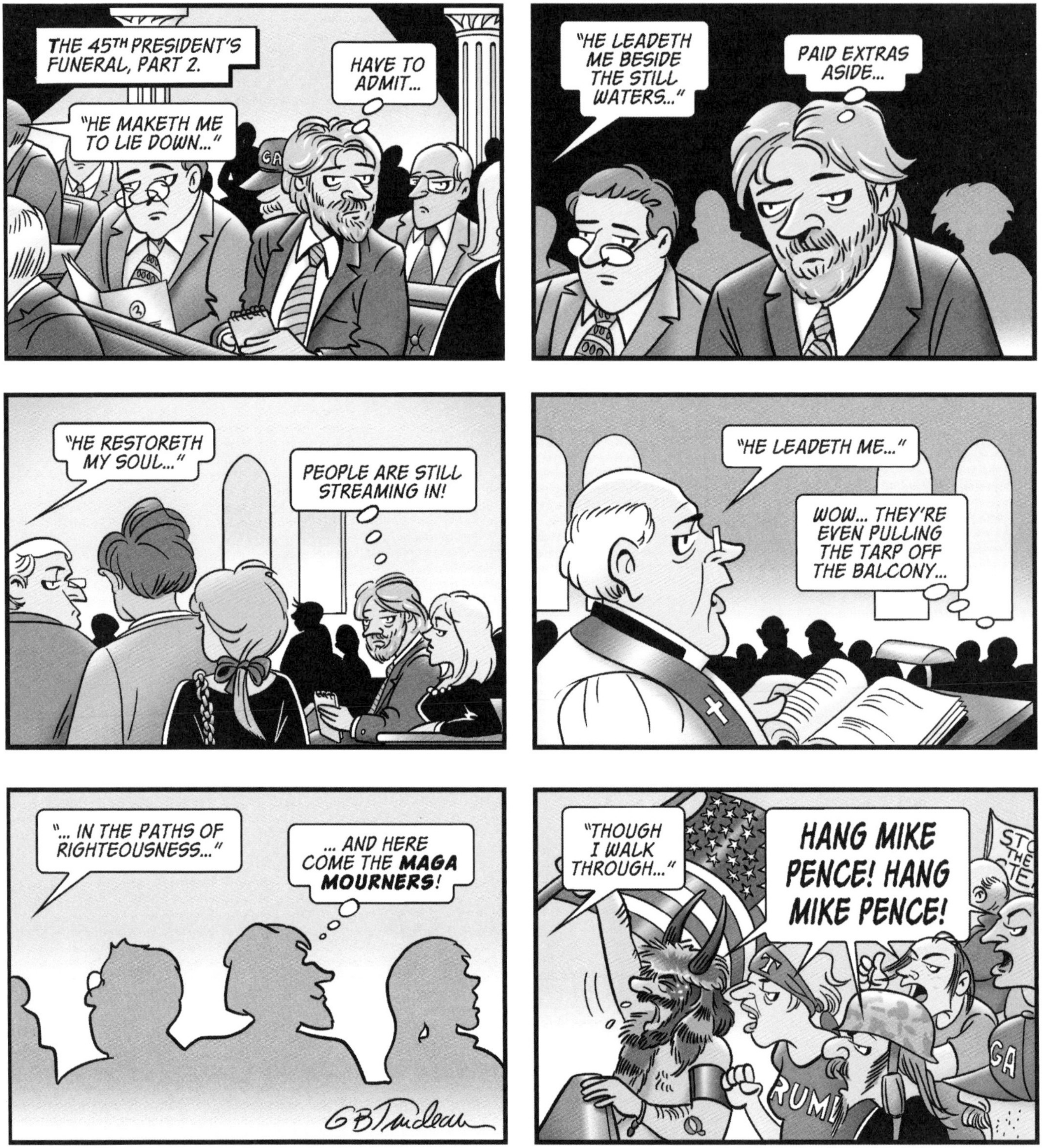
THE 45TH PRESIDENT'S FUNERAL, PART 2.
"HE MAKETH ME TO LIE DOWN..."
HAVE TO ADMIT...
"HE LEADETH ME BESIDE THE STILL WATERS..."
PAID EXTRAS ASIDE...
"HE RESTORETH MY SOUL..."
PEOPLE ARE STILL STREAMING IN!
"HE LEADETH ME..."
WOW... THEY'RE EVEN PULLING THE TARP OFF THE BALCONY...
"... IN THE PATHS OF RIGHTEOUSNESS..."
... AND HERE COME THE **MAGA MOURNERS**!
"THOUGH I WALK THROUGH..."
HANG MIKE PENCE! HANG MIKE PENCE!

February 13, 2022

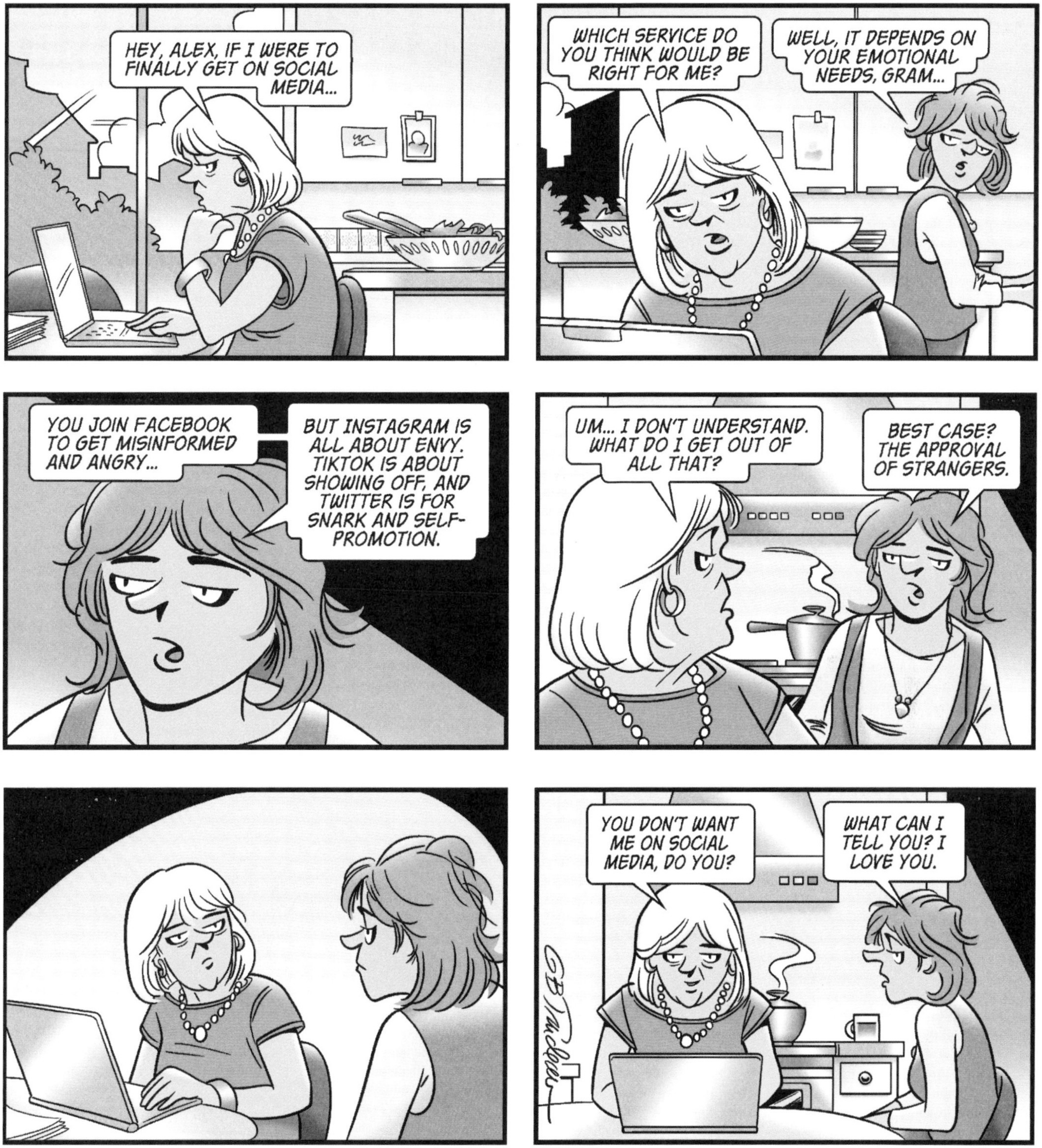
HEY, ALEX, IF I WERE TO FINALLY GET ON SOCIAL MEDIA...
WHICH SERVICE DO YOU THINK WOULD BE RIGHT FOR ME?
WELL, IT DEPENDS ON YOUR EMOTIONAL NEEDS, GRAM...
YOU JOIN FACEBOOK TO GET MISINFORMED AND ANGRY...
BUT INSTAGRAM IS ALL ABOUT ENVY. TIKTOK IS ABOUT SHOWING OFF, AND TWITTER IS FOR SNARK AND SELF-PROMOTION.
UM... I DON'T UNDERSTAND. WHAT DO I GET OUT OF ALL THAT?
BEST CASE? THE APPROVAL OF STRANGERS.
YOU DON'T WANT ME ON SOCIAL MEDIA, DO YOU?
WHAT CAN I TELL YOU? I LOVE YOU.

February 20, 2022

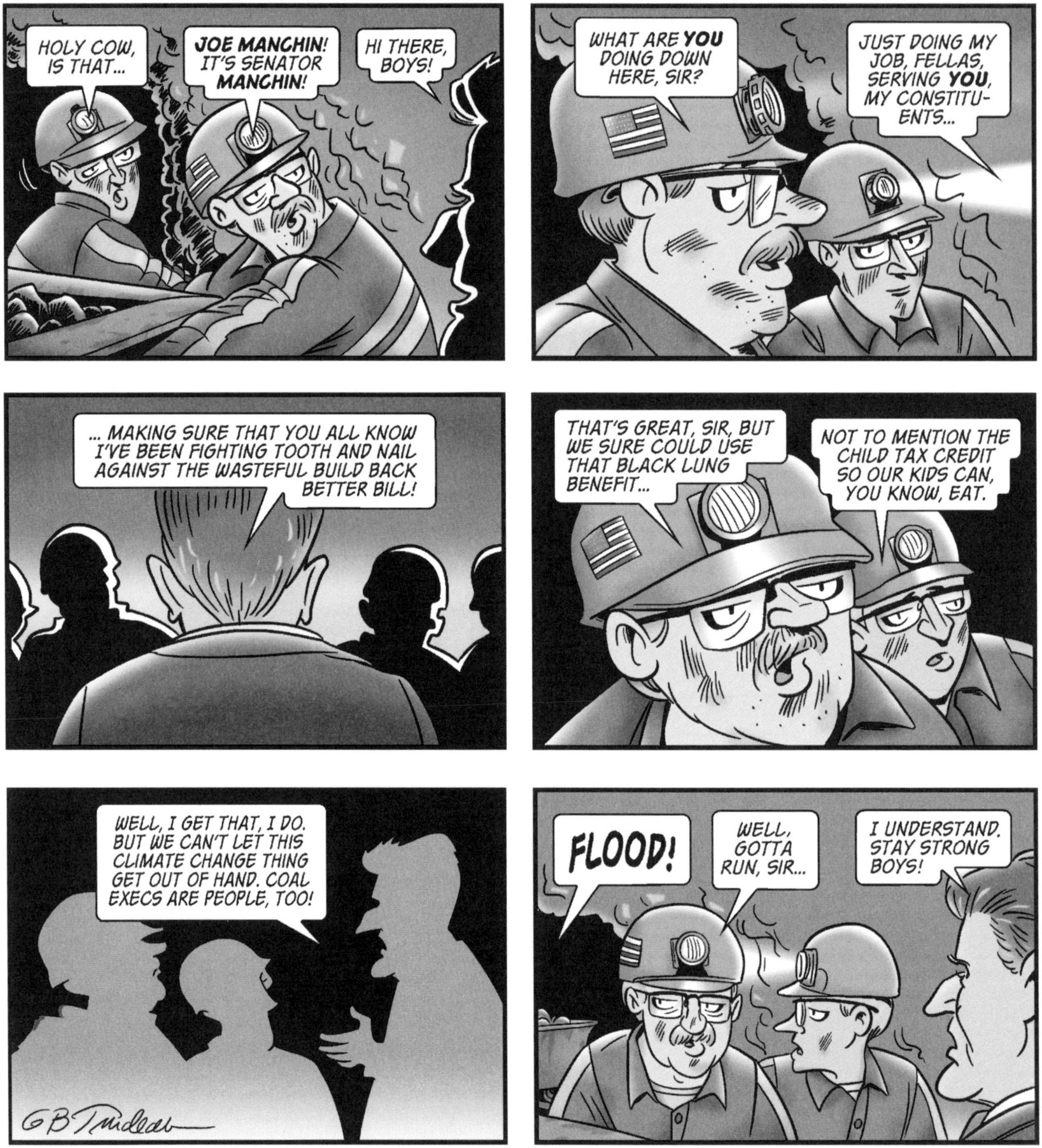
HOLY COW, IS THAT...
JOE MANCHIN! IT'S SENATOR MANCHIN!
HI THERE, BOYS!
WHAT ARE YOU DOING DOWN HERE, SIR?
JUST DOING MY JOB, FELLAS, SERVING YOU, MY CONSTITU-ENTS...
... MAKING SURE THAT YOU ALL KNOW I'VE BEEN FIGHTING TOOTH AND NAIL AGAINST THE WASTEFUL BUILD BACK BETTER BILL!
THAT'S GREAT, SIR, BUT WE SURE COULD USE THAT BLACK LUNG BENEFIT...
NOT TO MENTION THE CHILD TAX CREDIT SO OUR KIDS CAN, YOU KNOW, EAT.
WELL, I GET THAT, I DO. BUT WE CAN'T LET THIS CLIMATE CHANGE THING GET OUT OF HAND. COAL EXECS ARE PEOPLE, TOO!
FLOOD!
WELL, GOTTA RUN, SIR...
I UNDERSTAND. STAY STRONG BOYS!

February 27, 2022

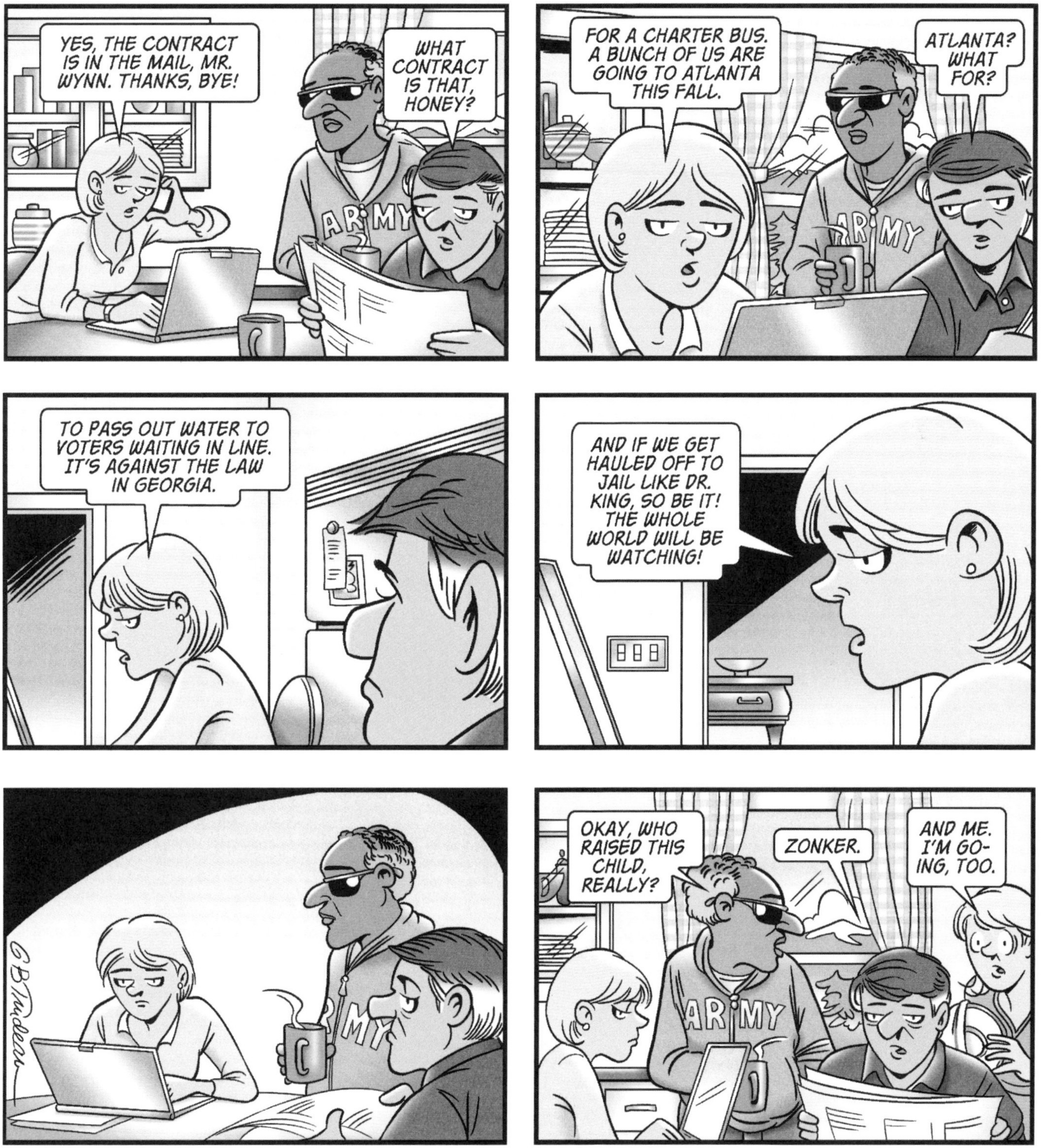
YES, THE CONTRACT IS IN THE MAIL, MR. WYNN. THANKS, BYE!
WHAT CONTRACT IS THAT, HONEY?
FOR A CHARTER BUS. A BUNCH OF US ARE GOING TO ATLANTA THIS FALL.
ATLANTA? WHAT FOR?
TO PASS OUT WATER TO VOTERS WAITING IN LINE. IT'S AGAINST THE LAW IN GEORGIA.
AND IF WE GET HAULED OFF TO JAIL LIKE DR. KING, SO BE IT! THE WHOLE WORLD WILL BE WATCHING!
OKAY, WHO RAISED THIS CHILD, REALLY?
ZONKER.
AND ME. I'M GO-ING, TOO.

March 6, 2022

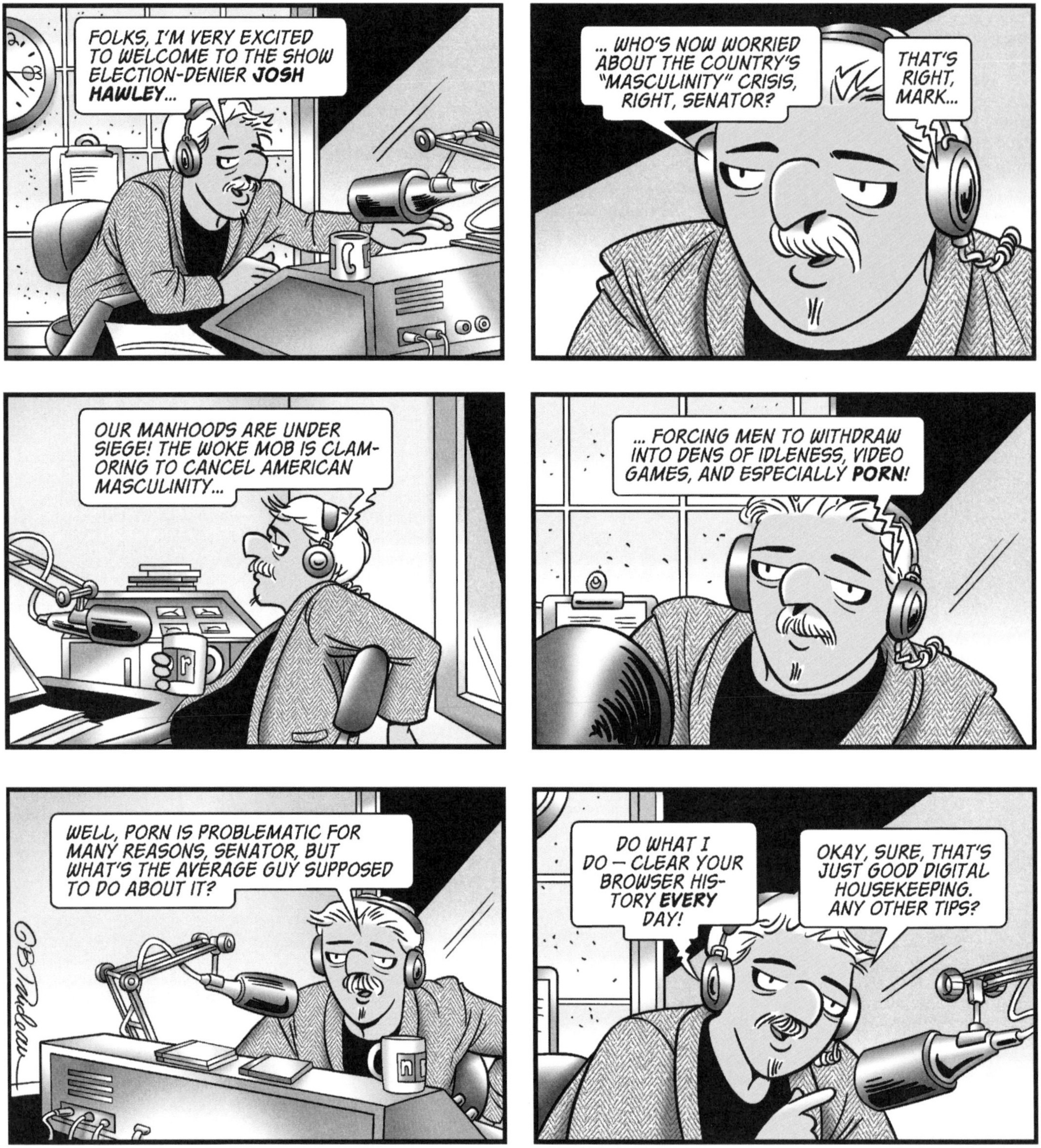
FOLKS, I'M VERY EXCITED TO WELCOME TO THE SHOW ELECTION-DENIER **JOSH HAWLEY**...
... WHO'S NOW WORRIED ABOUT THE COUNTRY'S "MASCULINITY" CRISIS, RIGHT, SENATOR?
THAT'S RIGHT, MARK...
OUR MANHOODS ARE UNDER SIEGE! THE WOKE MOB IS CLAMORING TO CANCEL AMERICAN MASCULINITY...
... FORCING MEN TO WITHDRAW INTO DENS OF IDLENESS, VIDEO GAMES, AND ESPECIALLY **PORN**!
WELL, PORN IS PROBLEMATIC FOR MANY REASONS, SENATOR, BUT WHAT'S THE AVERAGE GUY SUPPOSED TO DO ABOUT IT?
DO WHAT I DO — CLEAR YOUR BROWSER HISTORY **EVERY** DAY!
OKAY, SURE, THAT'S JUST GOOD DIGITAL HOUSEKEEPING. ANY OTHER TIPS?
GBTrudeau

March 13, 2022

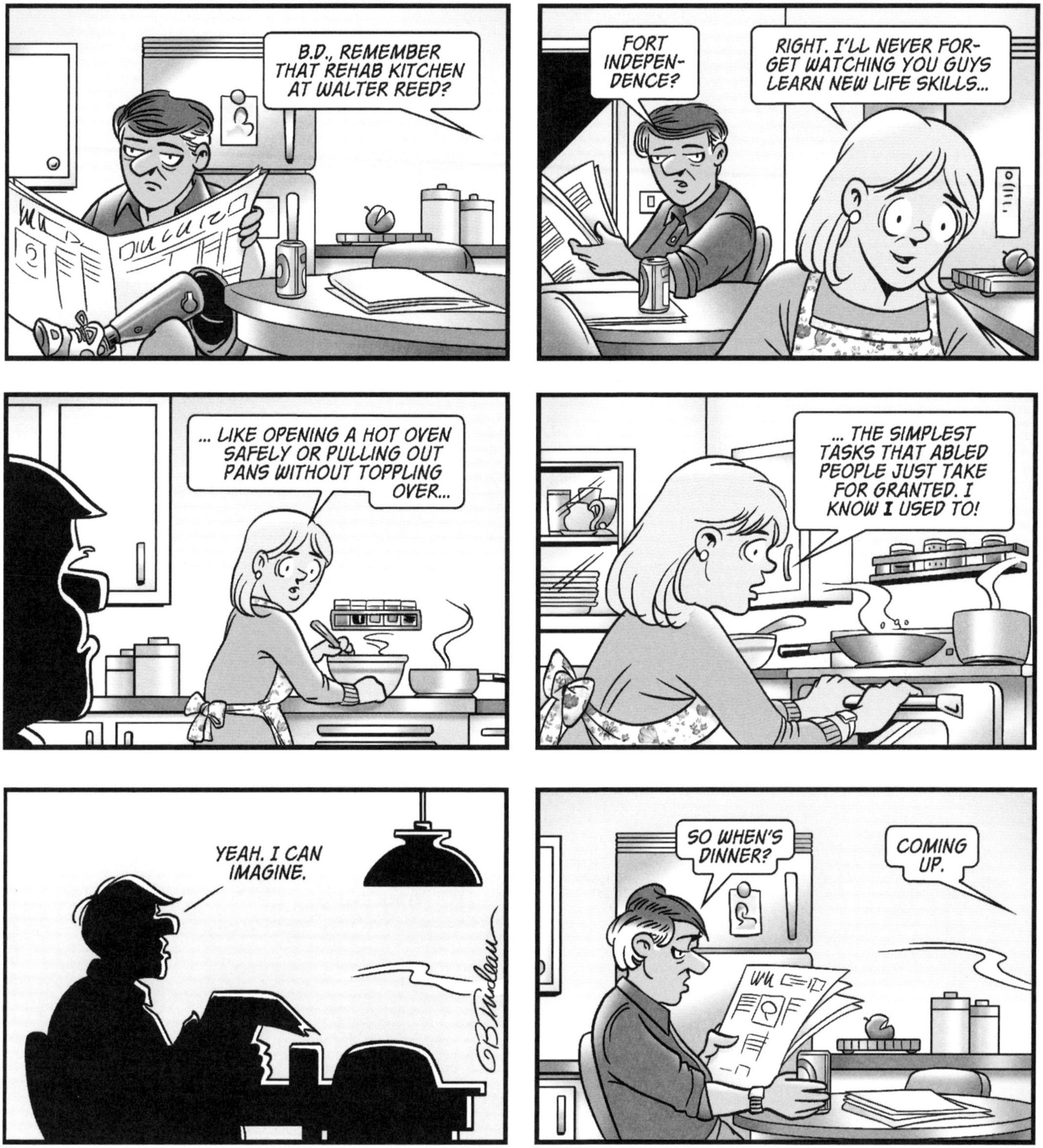
B.D., REMEMBER THAT REHAB KITCHEN AT WALTER REED?
FORT INDEPEN-DENCE?
RIGHT. I'LL NEVER FOR-GET WATCHING YOU GUYS LEARN NEW LIFE SKILLS...
... LIKE OPENING A HOT OVEN SAFELY OR PULLING OUT PANS WITHOUT TOPPLING OVER...
... THE SIMPLEST TASKS THAT ABLED PEOPLE JUST TAKE FOR GRANTED. I KNOW **I** USED TO!
YEAH. I CAN IMAGINE.
SO WHEN'S DINNER?
COMING UP.

March 20, 2022

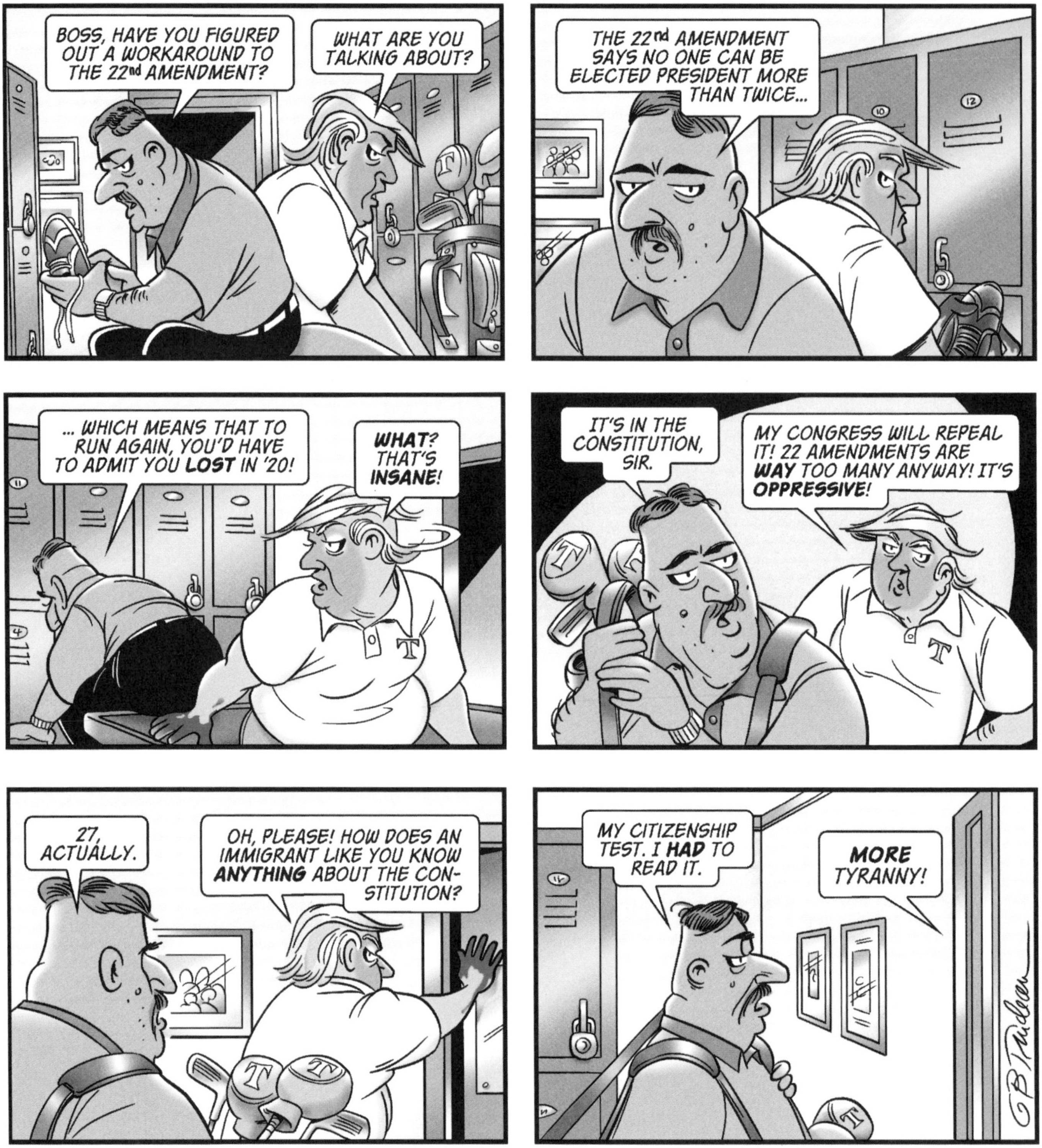
BOSS, HAVE YOU FIGURED OUT A WORKAROUND TO THE 22nd AMENDMENT?
WHAT ARE YOU TALKING ABOUT?
THE 22nd AMENDMENT SAYS NO ONE CAN BE ELECTED PRESIDENT MORE THAN TWICE...
... WHICH MEANS THAT TO RUN AGAIN, YOU'D HAVE TO ADMIT YOU LOST IN '20!
WHAT? THAT'S INSANE!
IT'S IN THE CONSTITUTION, SIR.
MY CONGRESS WILL REPEAL IT! 22 AMENDMENTS ARE WAY TOO MANY ANYWAY! IT'S OPPRESSIVE!
27, ACTUALLY.
OH, PLEASE! HOW DOES AN IMMIGRANT LIKE YOU KNOW ANYTHING ABOUT THE CONSTITUTION?
MY CITIZENSHIP TEST. I HAD TO READ IT.
MORE TYRANNY!
GB Trudeau

March 27, 2022

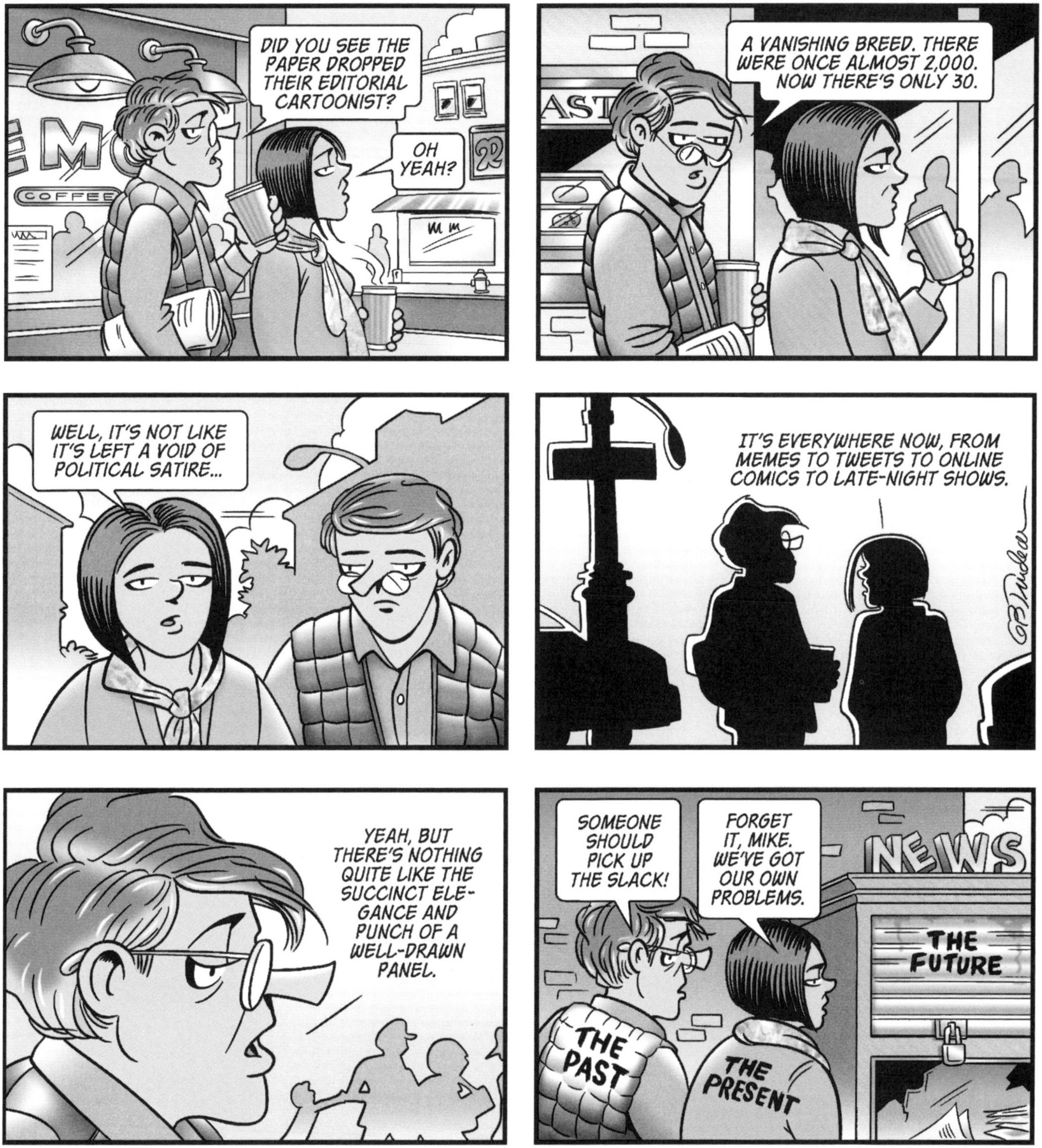
DID YOU SEE THE PAPER DROPPED THEIR EDITORIAL CARTOONIST?
OH YEAH?
A VANISHING BREED. THERE WERE ONCE ALMOST 2,000. NOW THERE'S ONLY 30.
WELL, IT'S NOT LIKE IT'S LEFT A VOID OF POLITICAL SATIRE...
IT'S EVERYWHERE NOW, FROM MEMES TO TWEETS TO ONLINE COMICS TO LATE-NIGHT SHOWS.
YEAH, BUT THERE'S NOTHING QUITE LIKE THE SUCCINCT ELE-GANCE AND PUNCH OF A WELL-DRAWN PANEL.
SOMEONE SHOULD PICK UP THE SLACK!
FORGET IT, MIKE. WE'VE GOT OUR OWN PROBLEMS.
NEWS
THE FUTURE
THE PAST
THE PRESENT

April 3, 2022

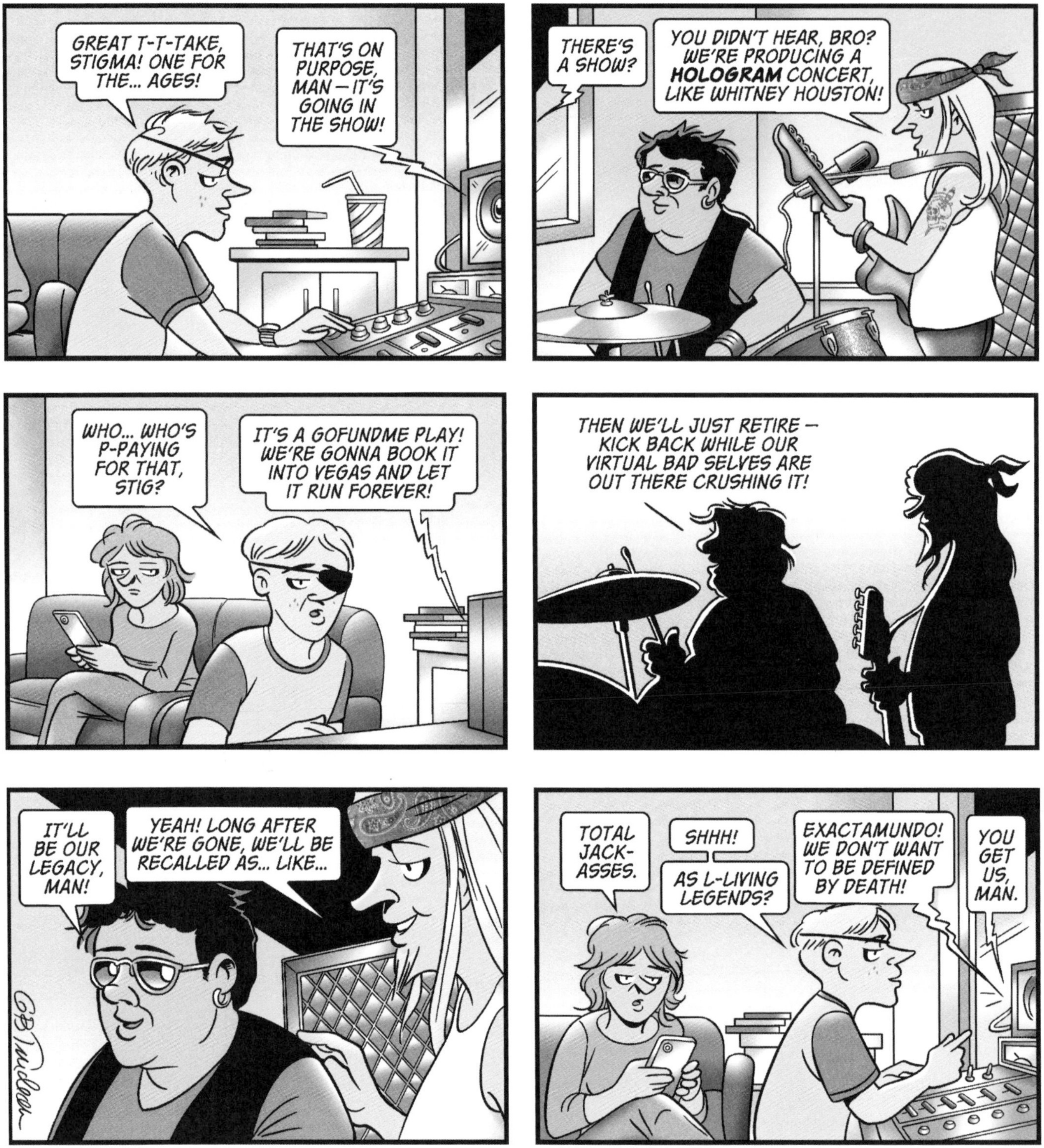

GREAT T-T-TAKE, STIGMA! ONE FOR THE... AGES!
THAT'S ON PURPOSE, MAN — IT'S GOING IN THE SHOW!
THERE'S A SHOW?
YOU DIDN'T HEAR, BRO? WE'RE PRODUCING A **HOLOGRAM** CONCERT, LIKE WHITNEY HOUSTON!
WHO... WHO'S P-PAYING FOR THAT, STIG?
IT'S A GOFUNDME PLAY! WE'RE GONNA BOOK IT INTO VEGAS AND LET IT RUN FOREVER!
THEN WE'LL JUST RETIRE — KICK BACK WHILE OUR VIRTUAL BAD SELVES ARE OUT THERE CRUSHING IT!
IT'LL BE OUR LEGACY, MAN!
YEAH! LONG AFTER WE'RE GONE, WE'LL BE RECALLED AS... LIKE...
TOTAL JACK-ASSES.
SHHH!
AS L-LIVING LEGENDS?
EXACTAMUNDO! WE DON'T WANT TO BE DEFINED BY DEATH!
YOU GET US, MAN.

April 10, 2022

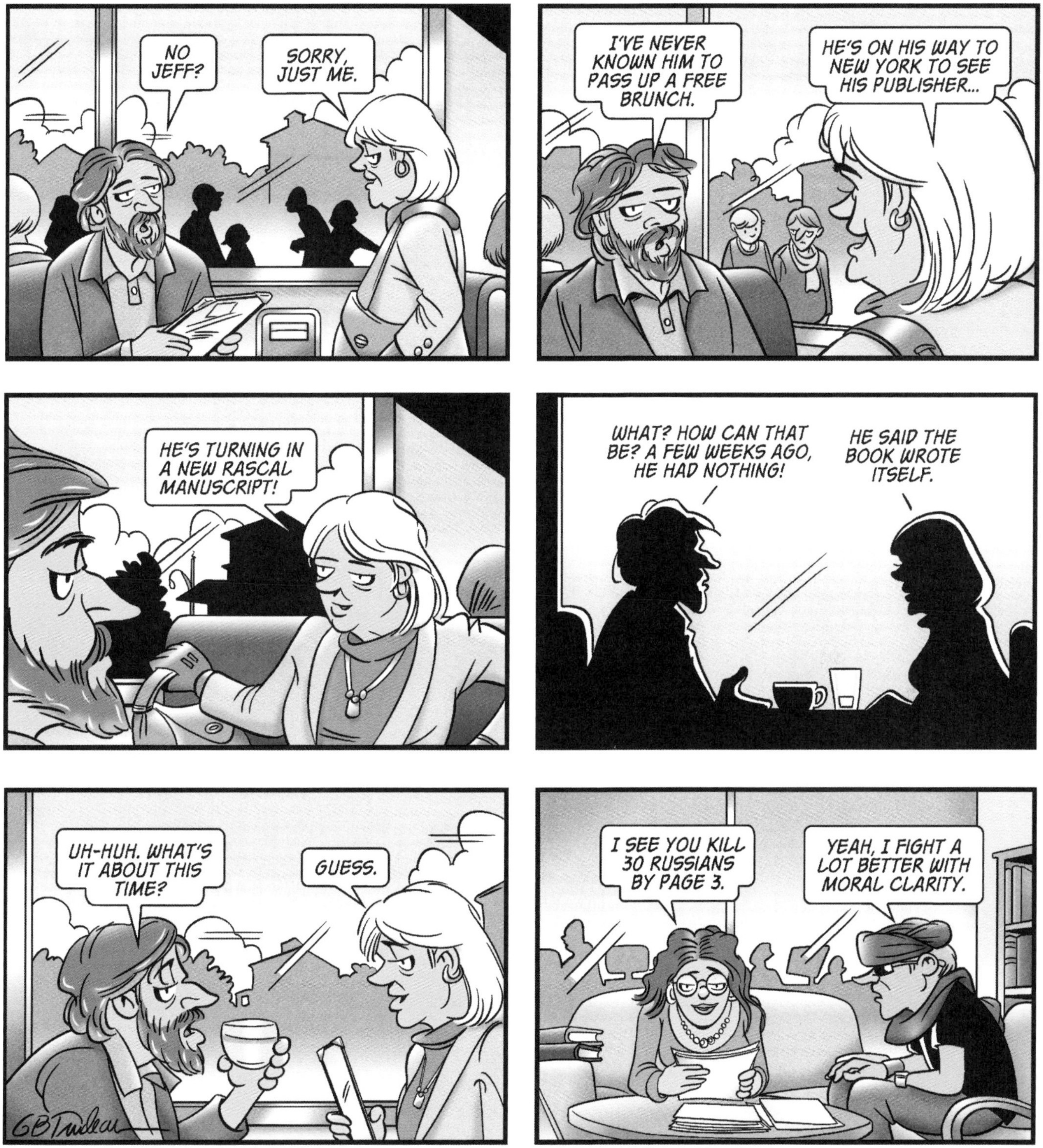
NO JEFF?
SORRY, JUST ME.
I'VE NEVER KNOWN HIM TO PASS UP A FREE BRUNCH.
HE'S ON HIS WAY TO NEW YORK TO SEE HIS PUBLISHER...
HE'S TURNING IN A NEW RASCAL MANUSCRIPT!
WHAT? HOW CAN THAT BE? A FEW WEEKS AGO, HE HAD NOTHING!
HE SAID THE BOOK WROTE ITSELF.
UH-HUH. WHAT'S IT ABOUT THIS TIME?
GUESS.
I SEE YOU KILL 30 RUSSIANS BY PAGE 3.
YEAH, I FIGHT A LOT BETTER WITH MORAL CLARITY.
GBTrudeau

April 17, 2022

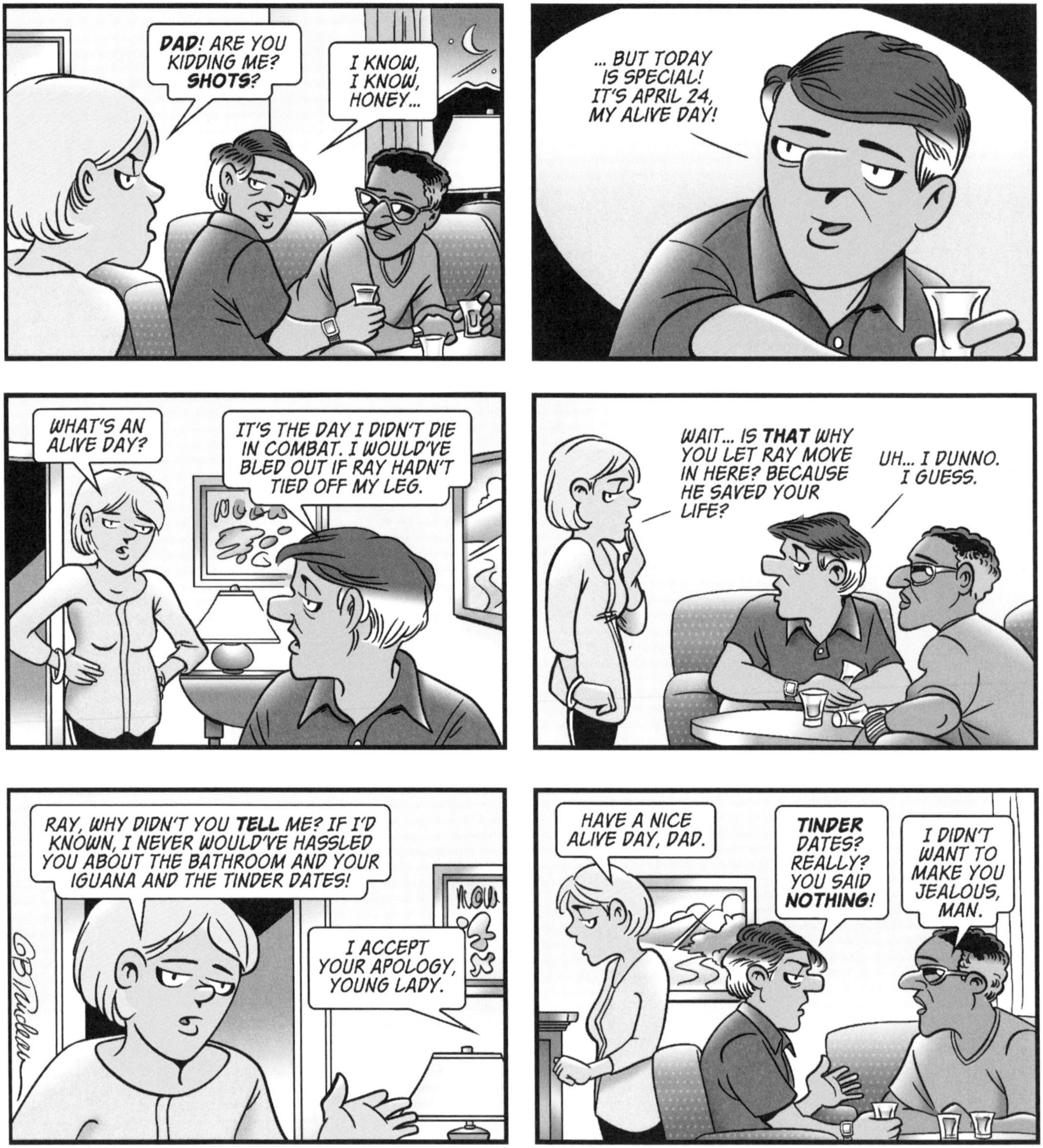
DAD! ARE YOU KIDDING ME? SHOTS?
I KNOW, I KNOW, HONEY...
... BUT TODAY IS SPECIAL! IT'S APRIL 24, MY ALIVE DAY!
WHAT'S AN ALIVE DAY?
IT'S THE DAY I DIDN'T DIE IN COMBAT. I WOULD'VE BLED OUT IF RAY HADN'T TIED OFF MY LEG.
WAIT... IS THAT WHY YOU LET RAY MOVE IN HERE? BECAUSE HE SAVED YOUR LIFE?
UH... I DUNNO. I GUESS.
RAY, WHY DIDN'T YOU TELL ME? IF I'D KNOWN, I NEVER WOULD'VE HASSLED YOU ABOUT THE BATHROOM AND YOUR IGUANA AND THE TINDER DATES!
I ACCEPT YOUR APOLOGY, YOUNG LADY.
HAVE A NICE ALIVE DAY, DAD.
TINDER DATES? REALLY? YOU SAID NOTHING!
I DIDN'T WANT TO MAKE YOU JEALOUS, MAN.

April 24, 2022

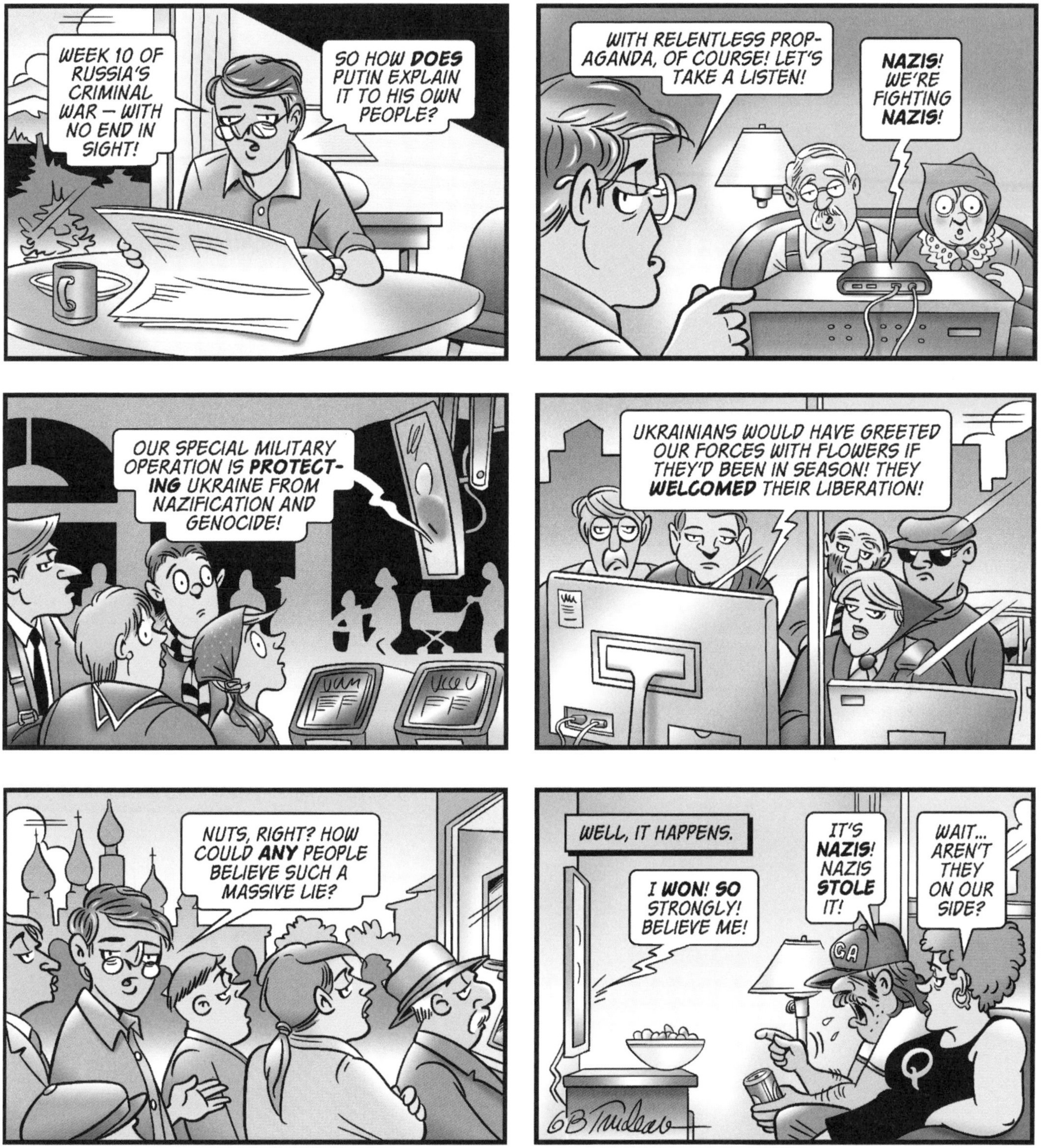
WEEK 10 OF RUSSIA'S CRIMINAL WAR — WITH NO END IN SIGHT!
SO HOW **DOES** PUTIN EXPLAIN IT TO HIS OWN PEOPLE?
WITH RELENTLESS PROP-AGANDA, OF COURSE! LET'S TAKE A LISTEN!
NAZIS! WE'RE FIGHTING **NAZIS**!
OUR SPECIAL MILITARY OPERATION IS **PROTECT-ING** UKRAINE FROM NAZIFICATION AND GENOCIDE!
UKRAINIANS WOULD HAVE GREETED OUR FORCES WITH FLOWERS IF THEY'D BEEN IN SEASON! THEY **WELCOMED** THEIR LIBERATION!
NUTS, RIGHT? HOW COULD **ANY** PEOPLE BELIEVE SUCH A MASSIVE LIE?
WELL, IT HAPPENS.
I **WON**! **SO** STRONGLY! BELIEVE ME!
IT'S **NAZIS**! NAZIS **STOLE** IT!
WAIT... AREN'T THEY ON OUR SIDE?
GA
GB Trudeau

May 1, 2022

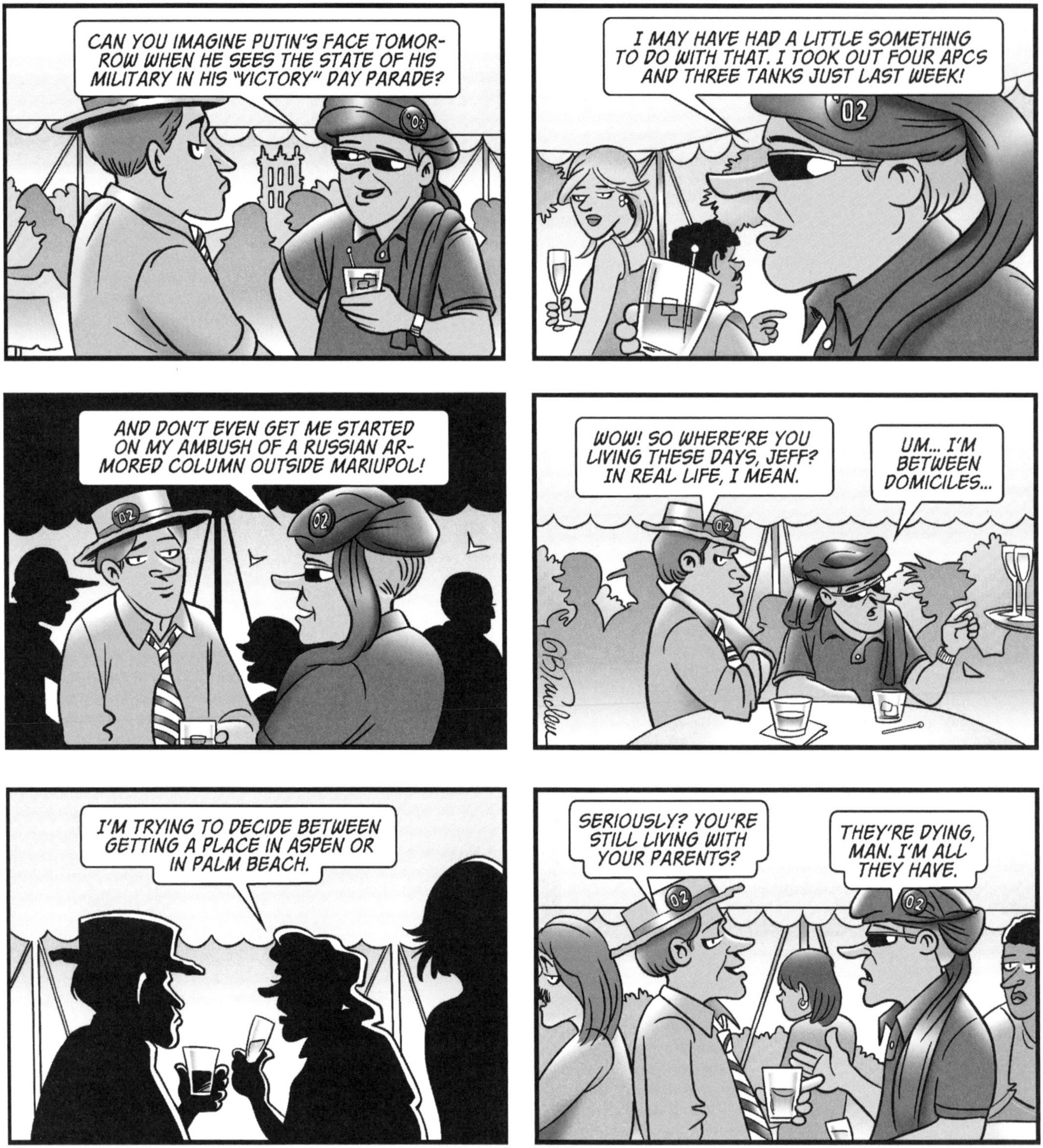
CAN YOU IMAGINE PUTIN'S FACE TOMORROW WHEN HE SEES THE STATE OF HIS MILITARY IN HIS "VICTORY" DAY PARADE?
'02
I MAY HAVE HAD A LITTLE SOMETHING TO DO WITH THAT. I TOOK OUT FOUR APCS AND THREE TANKS JUST LAST WEEK!
'02
AND DON'T EVEN GET ME STARTED ON MY AMBUSH OF A RUSSIAN ARMORED COLUMN OUTSIDE MARIUPOL!
'02
02
WOW! SO WHERE'RE YOU LIVING THESE DAYS, JEFF? IN REAL LIFE, I MEAN.
UM... I'M BETWEEN DOMICILES...
02
GBTrudeau
I'M TRYING TO DECIDE BETWEEN GETTING A PLACE IN ASPEN OR IN PALM BEACH.
SERIOUSLY? YOU'RE STILL LIVING WITH YOUR PARENTS?
THEY'RE DYING, MAN. I'M ALL THEY HAVE.
02
02

May 8, 2022

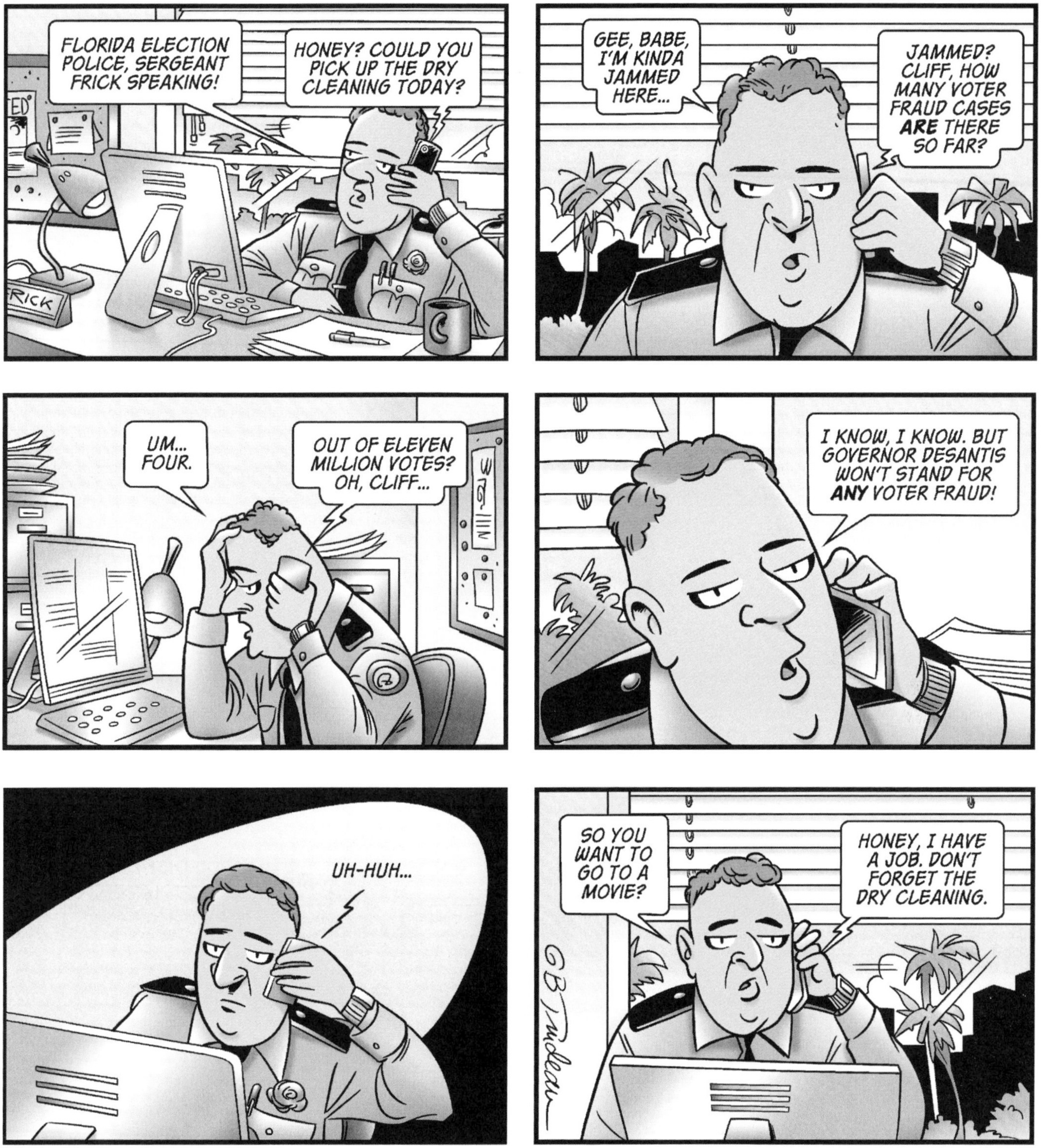
FLORIDA ELECTION POLICE, SERGEANT FRICK SPEAKING!
HONEY? COULD YOU PICK UP THE DRY CLEANING TODAY?
RICK
GEE, BABE, I'M KINDA JAMMED HERE...
JAMMED? CLIFF, HOW MANY VOTER FRAUD CASES **ARE** THERE SO FAR?
UM... FOUR.
OUT OF ELEVEN MILLION VOTES? OH, CLIFF...
I KNOW, I KNOW. BUT GOVERNOR DESANTIS WON'T STAND FOR **ANY** VOTER FRAUD!
UH-HUH...
SO YOU WANT TO GO TO A MOVIE?
HONEY, I HAVE A JOB. DON'T FORGET THE DRY CLEANING.
GB Trudeau

May 15, 2022

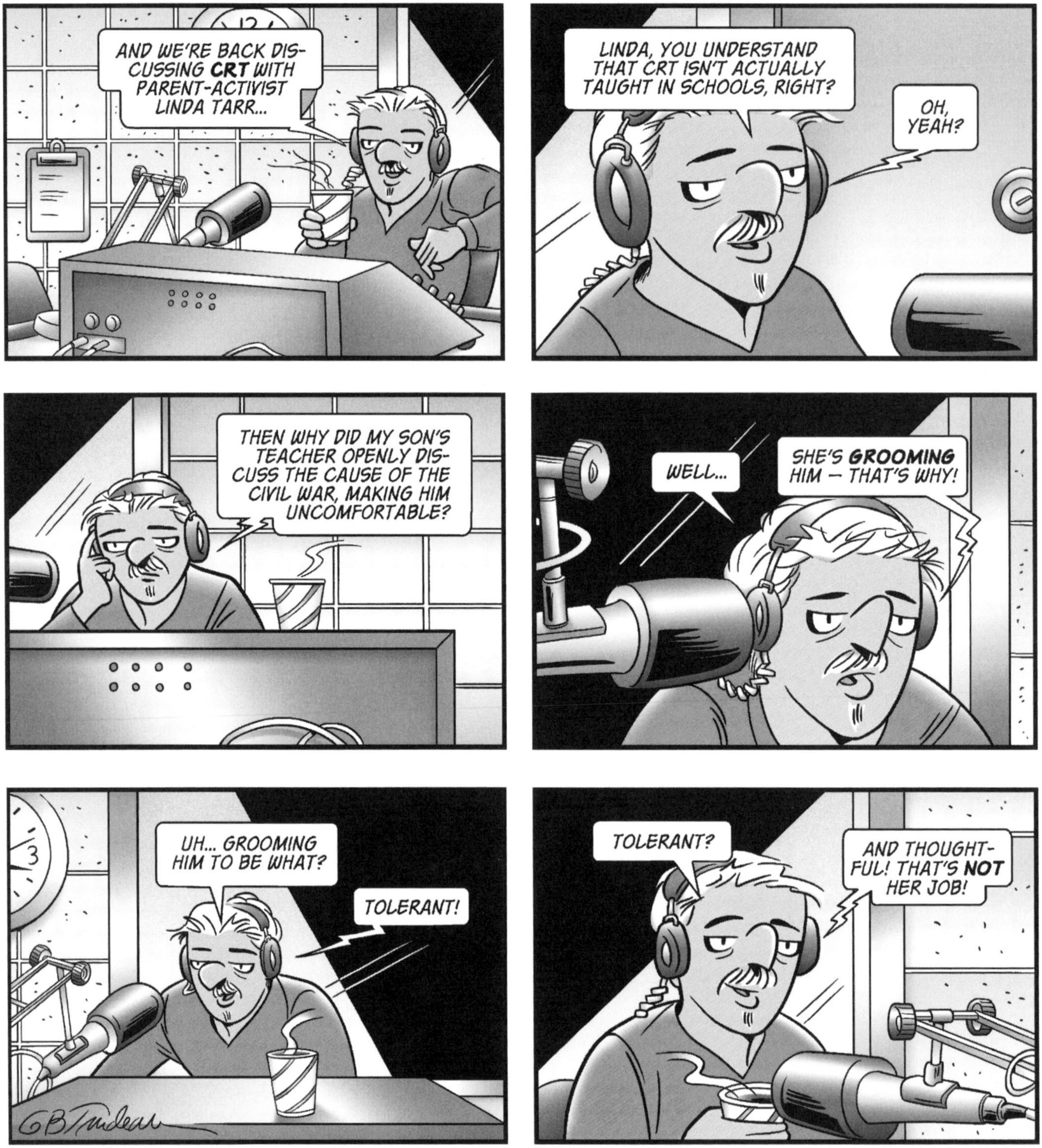
AND WE'RE BACK DISCUSSING CRT WITH PARENT-ACTIVIST LINDA TARR...
LINDA, YOU UNDERSTAND THAT CRT ISN'T ACTUALLY TAUGHT IN SCHOOLS, RIGHT?
OH, YEAH?
THEN WHY DID MY SON'S TEACHER OPENLY DISCUSS THE CAUSE OF THE CIVIL WAR, MAKING HIM UNCOMFORTABLE?
WELL...
SHE'S GROOMING HIM — THAT'S WHY!
UH... GROOMING HIM TO BE WHAT?
TOLERANT!
TOLERANT?
AND THOUGHTFUL! THAT'S NOT HER JOB!
GBTrudeau

May 22, 2022

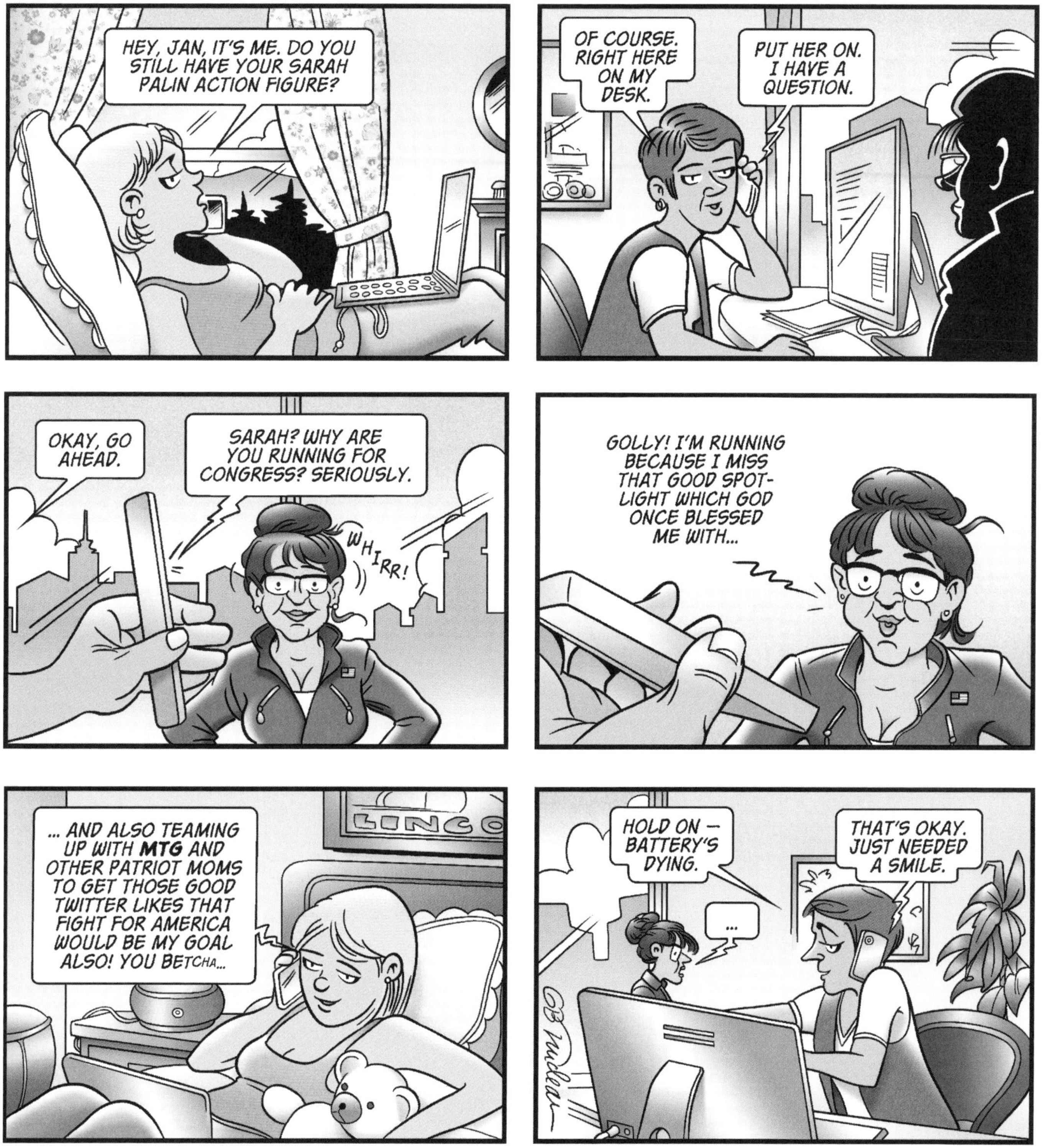
HEY, JAN, IT'S ME. DO YOU STILL HAVE YOUR SARAH PALIN ACTION FIGURE?
OF COURSE. RIGHT HERE ON MY DESK.
PUT HER ON. I HAVE A QUESTION.
OKAY, GO AHEAD.
SARAH? WHY ARE YOU RUNNING FOR CONGRESS? SERIOUSLY.
WHIRR!
GOLLY! I'M RUNNING BECAUSE I MISS THAT GOOD SPOT-LIGHT WHICH GOD ONCE BLESSED ME WITH...
... AND ALSO TEAMING UP WITH **MTG** AND OTHER PATRIOT MOMS TO GET THOSE GOOD TWITTER LIKES THAT FIGHT FOR AMERICA WOULD BE MY GOAL ALSO! YOU BETCHA...
LINCO
HOLD ON — BATTERY'S DYING.
...
THAT'S OKAY. JUST NEEDED A SMILE.
GB Trudeau

May 29, 2022

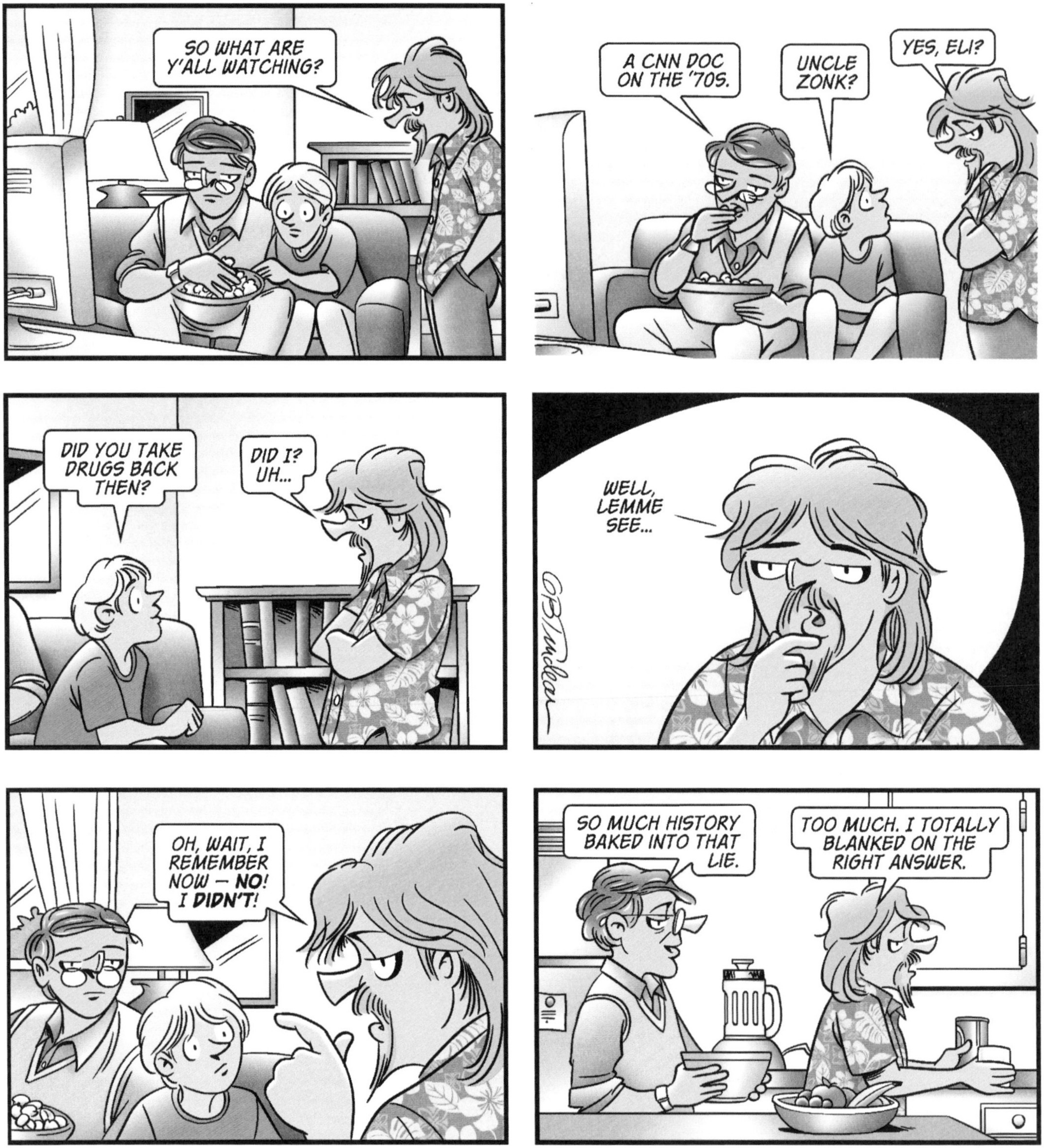
SO WHAT ARE Y'ALL WATCHING?
A CNN DOC ON THE '70S.
UNCLE ZONK?
YES, ELI?
DID YOU TAKE DRUGS BACK THEN?
DID I? UH...
WELL, LEMME SEE...
OH, WAIT, I REMEMBER NOW — **NO**! I **DIDN'T**!
SO MUCH HISTORY BAKED INTO THAT LIE.
TOO MUCH. I TOTALLY BLANKED ON THE RIGHT ANSWER.

June 12, 2022

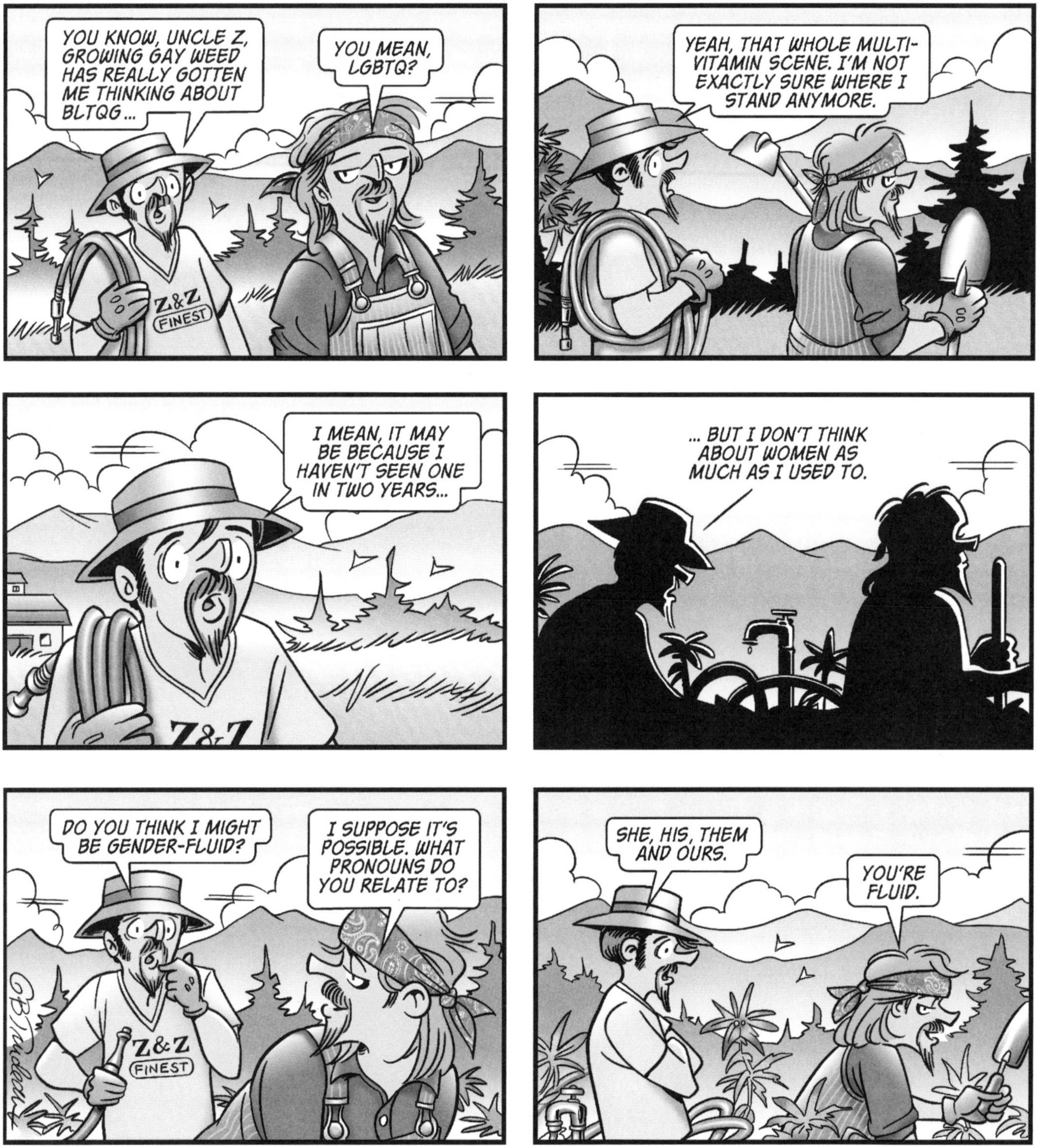
YOU KNOW, UNCLE Z, GROWING GAY WEED HAS REALLY GOTTEN ME THINKING ABOUT BLTQG...
YOU MEAN, LGBTQ?
Z&Z FINEST
YEAH, THAT WHOLE MULTI-VITAMIN SCENE. I'M NOT EXACTLY SURE WHERE I STAND ANYMORE.
I MEAN, IT MAY BE BECAUSE I HAVEN'T SEEN ONE IN TWO YEARS...
... BUT I DON'T THINK ABOUT WOMEN AS MUCH AS I USED TO.
DO YOU THINK I MIGHT BE GENDER-FLUID?
I SUPPOSE IT'S POSSIBLE. WHAT PRONOUNS DO YOU RELATE TO?
Z&Z FINEST
SHE, HIS, THEM AND OURS.
YOU'RE FLUID.

June 19, 2022

Nov. 15, 2020 — **Johnson v. Benson**, United States District Court for the Western District of Michigan: Voluntarily dismissed.

Nov. 16, 2020 — **Marchant v. Gloria**, Nevada District Court, Clark County: Dismissed.

Nov. 16, 2020 — **Integrity Project of Nevada v. Nevada**, Nevada District Court, Clark County: Dismissed.

Nov. 16, 2020 — **Becker v. Gloria**, Nevada District Court, Clark County: Dismissed without prejudice.

Nov. 17, 2020 — **Law v. Whitmer**, Nevada Supreme Court, Nevada District Court, Carson City: Dismissed with prejudice and affirmed on appeal.

Nov. 18, 2020 — **Becker v. Cannizzaro**, Nevada District Court, Clark County: Voluntarily dismissed.

Nov. 19, 2020 — **Rodimer v. Gloria**, Nevada District Court, Clark County: Dismissed.

Nov. 22, 2020 — **Bognet v. Boockvar**, U.S. District Court for the Western District of Pennsylvania: Dismissed.

Nov. 23, 2020 — **Wisconsin Voters Alliance v. Wisconsin Elections Comm'n**, Wisconsin Supreme Court: Dismissed.

Nov. 25, 2020 — **King v. Whitmer**, U.S. District Court for the Eastern District of Michigan: Dismissed.

Nov. 25, 2020 — **Kelly v. Pennsylvania**, Supreme Court of the United States, Supreme Court of Pennsylvania, Pennsylvania Commonwealth Court: Dismissed.

Nov. 25, 2020 — **Pearson v. Kemp**, U.S. District Court for the Northern District of Georgia: Dismissed.

Nov. 26, 2020 — **Johnson v. Benson**, Michigan Supreme Court, Lansing, Michigan: Dismissed.

Nov. 27, 2020 — **Mueller v. Jacobs**, Wisconsin Supreme Court: Dismissed.

Nov. 30, 2020 — **Ward v. Jackson**, Arizona Superior Court, Maricopa County: Dismissed.

Nov. 30, 2020 — **Boland v. Raffensperger**, Superior Court of Fulton County, Georgia: Dismissed.

Dec. 1, 2020 — **Feehan v. Wisconsin Elections Comm'n**, United States District Court for the Eastern District of Wisconsin: Dismissed.

Dec. 1, 2020 — **Trump v. Evers**, Wisconsin Supreme Court: Petition denied.

Dec. 2, 2020 — **Bowyer v. Ducey**, Arizona United States District Court, United States Court of Appeals for the Ninth Circuit: Dismissed.

Dec. 2, 2020 — **Trump v. Wisconsin Elections Comm'n**, United States District Court for the Eastern District of Wisconsin, United States Court of Appeals for the Seventh Circuit: Dismissed with prejudice. Dismissal upheld on appeal.

Dec. 4, 2020 — **Stevenson v. Ducey**, Arizona Superior Court, Maricopa County: Voluntarily dismissed.

Dec. 4, 2020 — **Trump v. Raffensperger**, Superior Court of Fulton County, Georgia, Supreme Court of Georgia: Voluntarily dismissed.

Dec. 7, 2020 — **Trump v. Biden**, Wisconsin Circuit Court, Milwaukee County: Ruled in favor of the respondents: Biden et al.

Dec. 20, 2020 — **Donald J. Trump for President, Inc. v. Boockvar**, US Supreme Court: Dismissed.

Dec. 23, 2020 — **Favorito, et. al. v. Fulton County, et al.**, Superior Court of Fulton County, Georgia: Active.

Dec. 31, 2020 — **Trump v. Kemp et al.**, United States District Court, Northern District of Georgia, Atlanta Division: Voluntarily dismissed.